THE SMART GUIDE TO

Hiking and Backpacking

BY BRIAN NORDSTROM

The Smart Guide To Hiking and Backpacking

Published by

Smart Guide Publications, Inc.
2517 Deer Chase Drive
Norman, OK 73071
www.smartguidepublications.com

For information, address: Smart Guide Publications, Inc. 2517 Deer Creek Drive, Norman, OK 73071

SMART GUIDE and Design are registered trademarks licensed to Smart Guide Publications, Inc.

International Standard Book Number: 978-1-937636-28-9

Library of Congress Catalog Card Number:
11 12 13 14 15   10 9 8 7 6 5 4 3 2 1

Printed in the United States of America

Cover design: Lorna Llewellyn
Copy Editor: Ruth Strother
Back cover design: Joel Friedlander, Eric Gelb, Deon Seifert
Back cover copy: Eric Gelb, Deon Seifert
Illustrations: James Balkovek
Production: Zoë Lonergan
Indexer: Cory Emberson
V.P./Business Manager: Cathy Barker

ACKNOWLEDGMENTS

In memory of my parents, Clayton and Marguerite Nordstrom, I would like to express my appreciation for their taking my brothers and me on so many wonderful camping trips when we were growing up. They took us to forty-six states and Canada; we camped at Yosemite, Mount Rainier, Yellowstone, Acadia, Great Smoky Mountains, Rocky Mountain, Grand Canyon, Mesa Verde, and Everglades National Parks, plus numerous state parks and recreational areas.

I would also like to express my gratitude to my children, Amy, Tim, Andy, and Bethany, for all the camping and backpacking trips they went on with me when they were growing up. Memories of the summers we camped at White Wolf at Yosemite, the camping trips throughout the United States and Canada, and the family backpacking trips at the Grand Canyon are very special to me.

I would also like to thank the publisher of Smart Guide Publications whose hard work made this book possible.

Brian Nordstrom

TABLE OF CONTENTS

Introduction

CHAPTER 1

Why Hike?

In This Chapter

➤ Benefits of hiking

➤ Backpacking: the next step

Why Do People Hike?

Why wouldn't a person want to go hiking? Hiking is walking, and walking is one of the most natural of human activities. It ranks right up there with eating and sleeping; walking is something most of us do every day of our lives already. A hike is just a long walk; a backpacking trip is just a long hike.

Nature Quote

"I love mountaintops and lovely places that you can get to only by hiking. I will hike until I can no longer walk!"

–Mae Holt, age 60

Why I Hike

I suppose the best way for me to explain why people hike is to explain why I hike. I've been hiking since I started walking. I was born in California, and my parents took me to Yosemite National Park about the time of my first birthday. I don't know if I was already walking; it's entirely possible my first steps were taken at Tuolumne Meadows, in Yosemite's high country.

I've been hiking ever since. I haven't kept track of all the trails I've been on in my lifetime, but the total distance must add up to thousands of miles. For the first forty years of my life, almost all my hikes were day hikes; I had done a little backpacking, but I didn't really get serious about it until my own children were old enough to backpack. Better late than never, I always say.

My family took lengthy vacations when I was growing up; we did a lot of hiking and camping during those years. My parents introduced me to the splendor of our national parks. Before my eighteenth birthday I had been to forty-seven states; three Canadian provinces; Yosemite, Grand Canyon, Rocky Mountain, Mesa Verde, Mount Rainier, Yellowstone, Mount Rushmore, Great Smoky Mountains, Acadia, Shenandoah, and Everglades National Parks; and numerous national historic sites and state parks.

When my own children were growing up, our family vacations took us to both coasts and to even more national parks than I had been to as a child. When my children were too little to hike on their own, I carried them in child packs. By their third birthdays, they were hiking on their own. By the time they graduated from high school, they had been to at least forty states and five Canadian provinces. I would like to believe they have fond memories of our camping, hiking, and sightseeing trips; I would also like to think that their not-so-pleasant memories of rain, mosquitoes, automobile breakdowns, and even taking shelter from a tornado have faded by now.

Hiking is my primary form of recreation. I participated in sports growing up, and to a lesser extent as an adult, but those days are past. Hiking is something I can do now. It's spontaneous; I can take a hike anytime I want. For over thirty years, I have lived in the highlands of northern Arizona at the edge of Prescott National Forest. I can literally step out my front door and take a hike.

Hiking is compatible with my other recreational pastimes—traveling, camping, photography, birding, and nature study. For day hikes at least, I don't need more gear than a day pack and a sturdy pair of hiking shoes. That leaves lots of room in my pack for my camera, telephoto lens, binoculars, and a field guide or two. Now that I'm a grandfather, hiking is a fun activity I can do with my grandchildren.

Personal Anecdote

When my twelve-year-old son and I returned home from our first Grand Canyon backpacking trip with his Scout troop, my fourteen-year-old daughter said, "Dad, I want to go." I got a permit for a three-day, two-night backpack trip to the bottom of the canyon. We didn't stay at Phantom Ranch, but we spent enough time there to realize what a special place it is. At the end of the hike, as my daughter stepped onto the rim, she turned to me and asked, "Can we go get a permit for next year?" We did, and we continued our father-daughter hikes until she graduated from college and got married. Special memories.

I am in reasonably good health; I'm sure that hiking keeps me that way. I don't have to take long hikes—even a few miles are better than none. There are a handful of times in my life when I've hiked 20 miles (32 kilometers) in a single day. That's hardly an outstanding achievement, but it's not trifling. Many times I've hiked 15 miles (24 km) in a day, both on day hikes and on backpacking trips. My usual distance is 8–10 miles (13–16 km). Carrying just a day pack, my pace is about 2.5 mph (4 kph). Carrying a full backpack, my downhill pace is about 2 mph (3 kph) and my uphill pace about 1–1.5 mph (1.6–2.4 kph). All of these paces are sufficient to provide cardiovascular benefits.

What does the future promise? Certainly more trails. In the past decade my travels have begun to take me abroad. I'm still several years away from retirement, but someday when I have more leisure time, my plan is to explore trails in the British Isles, the Alps, Scandinavia, and New Zealand. When I'm hiking the Grand Canyon, I often encounter people who are celebrating their eightieth birthdays by hiking the canyon. I plan to do the same.

Trails Take You Where the Road Doesn't

One of the benefits of hiking is that it takes you places your car doesn't. Right now I'm conjuring up images of wonderful places I've been to that I could only have gotten to on foot—the mountains around my home, the bottom of the Grand Canyon, the High Sierra camps at Yosemite, Dream Lake at Rocky Mountain National Park, Cascade Lake at Yellowstone, the Weminuche Wilderness in southwestern Colorado, McKittrick Canyon at Guadalupe National Park, even the depths of Carlsbad Cavern.

Whether your destination is 0.5 mile (0.8 km) from the nearest road or 20 miles (32 km), hiking takes you off the beaten path. I suppose in some cases a horse could, too, but I don't own a horse. In other cases a bicycle could, too. I own a mountain bike, and there are times

I pedal rather than walk. Most of the trails I hike, however, probably aren't conducive to bicycles. Even if the authorities permitted such a thing, I can't imagine sailing down the Bright Angel Trail at the Grand Canyon on a bicycle, pedaling up Mount Humphrey near Flagstaff, Arizona, or biking wilderness trails.

Here's to a Healthy You

Walking is good for your physical health. It's the one cardiovascular exercise that almost everybody can do. You don't even have to walk fast if you don't want to. Walking makes your heart and lungs work a little harder. Exercise decreases blood pressure, raises good cholesterol (the HDL kind), lowers triglycerides and bad cholesterol (the LDL kind), and promotes overall physical conditioning.

Walking on level ground burns about 110 calories a mile; walking uphill burns more. Walk 5 miles (8 km) and you've burned 550 calories. Do this two to three times a week, and you'll have a healthier heart. Hiking also exposes you to fresh air, sunshine, and exercise, all of which strengthen your immune system.

Trail Wisdom

A rule of thumb is that your hiking pace should allow you to carry on a normal conversation without getting winded. If you're too breathless to talk, slow down; you're walking too fast.

Burning those calories helps manage weight. Follow a regular walking regimen, and you'll probably shed a few pounds. You'll build muscle tissue at the same time.

The human body is meant for movement. Walking strengthens your ankles, knees, and hips, and moving your arms while walking benefits your elbows and shoulders. Regular exercise helps prevent injury to joints.

I don't have time to hike every day, and in the winter I usually leave work after dark. I work out on aerobic machines at a local gym three to four nights a week, but it's not the same as hiking. Aerobic machines provide the cardiovascular benefits, but treadmills and StairMasters are intended to be low impact, so working out on them doesn't strengthen joints. You need to spend time on a trail to do that. I have never suffered a sprained ankle;

I'm convinced it's because I spend enough time on the trail to keep my bones and joints in good condition.

An added benefit of having a gym membership is having a place to go to do upper-body workouts. Walking keeps the lower body in shape, but resistance training (weight lifting) is needed to strengthen arm, back, and shoulder muscles. If you're going to backpack, you need a strong upper body as well as a strong lower body.

Mental Health

Hiking promotes better mental health by relieving stress in at least two ways.

1. Being on the trail means you're away from work or school, which tend to be stressful environments.

2. Exercise releases hormones in our bodies called endorphins, which are a source of a natural high.

I often arrive at the end of the work week feeling run down; there's nothing like a 5- to 10-mile (8- to 16-km) hike on the weekend to pick me up. Most people sleep better after they've exercised.

We're meant to live in nature. Wildlife sightings, spectacular scenery, beautiful wildflowers make us connect with nature. That's better than anything on television.

Socrates said, "Know thyself." In today's rushed society where we're bombarded constantly with demands on our time; it's hard to find time for self-reflection. Time on the trail builds self-confidence and fosters self-discovery.

Hiking makes you self-reliant. You don't have a car or appliances on the trail. If problems occur—and they will occur—you have to solve them yourself. Learning to take care of yourself builds self-esteem.

The Ideal Family Activity

Hiking is an activity that family members can do together. It's a great way to get everyone away from the television. Children love being outdoors. They love wildlife; any outing is just that much more memorable for them if they see birds and animals. Throw in a lake or stream and the fun multiplies. Just remember to go at the child's pace. It really is okay to stop often and throw rocks in the water.

Take Grandma and Grandpa along; hiking is a multigenerational activity. I never knew three of my grandparents, so it's important to me to develop close relationships with my grandchildren. Spending time together outdoors is a great way to do that. I'd like to think that my love of nature is rubbing off on them. One of the best times with one of my grandsons was when just the two of us went on a nature walk together. We spent more time off the trail exploring some woods and a stream going through it than we spent on the trail.

Trail Wisdom

Invite one of your child's friends to come along when you go hiking. Being with someone the same age may be more fun for your child than just being out with Mom and Dad. There's an added benefit: it's easy for children to complain, "I'm tired," or "it's too far." It's a lot harder to do that if a friend is along; even children have to save face.

Hiking Is Educational

If you're observant about the world around you when you're hiking, you can learn a lot about nature. Being outside at all seasons teaches you the cycles that exist as nature progresses from winter to spring to summer to fall and back to winter again. If you live in an area with heavy winter snow, you can tune into changes that occur with the arrival of spring—what plants emerge first, what birds pass through on migration, when trees begin to leaf out.

Most people want to know the names of any animals they see when they're outdoors. Challenge yourself to also learn the names of the trees and wildflowers common to your area. If your community has a nature center, spend some time there. Go on a guided nature walk; enroll your children in classes that are offered.

Hiking Is a Low-Cost Activity

Golf is an extremely popular sport that also provides the benefits of exercise and sunshine. I have golfed a few times in my life. There are a couple of reasons I don't golf any more—one reason is golf is expensive.

One of the nice things about walking is that it doesn't cost anything. But there are some minimal costs to hiking depending on where you hike. There's the cost of driving to a trailhead, but that's probably less than the cost of eighteen holes of golf. There's the cost of a good pair of hiking shoes or boots, but golf shoes cost money, too. Some people wear sneakers for both activities, and that's all right. If you get into backpacking, there's the initial expense of a pack, sleeping bag, and tent, but if you play golf, a complete set of golf clubs is expensive.

Sometimes it pays to grow older. On my last birthday I qualified for the federal lifetime senior pass, which for a one-time cost of $10 gets me into all national parks, wildlife refuges, and recreational areas, and even gets me free parking where fees are charged in national forests.

Whatever your age, if you do a lot of your hiking where fees are charged, ask about annual passes, especially at your nearest national park. As a general rule, an annual pass costs less than paying individually for two visits. An added bonus is that an annual pass is not like a fishing or hunting license that's good just for a calendar year; if you buy it at Thanksgiving, it's only good for a month. A federal recreation pass is good for a year from the date of purchase.

A Metaphor for Life

You may have heard the saying life is a journey, not a destination. I feel the same way about hiking: hiking is a journey, not a destination. I often take hikes where I'm not really going anywhere in particular. I may have three to four hours available; I hike for an hour and a half to two hours, turn around and hike back to the trailhead. It doesn't matter that I didn't reach a specific destination; the journey was worth it.

You may also have heard the saying the worst day fishing beats the best day at the office. The same is true for hiking: the worst day hiking beats the best day at the office. Sometimes I start a hike knowing that a storm is approaching; I'm hoping to finish before the storm begins. Sometimes I make it back in time and sometimes I don't; if I get soaked, it still beats a day at the office.

There's also the saying no one on his deathbed ever wished he had spent more time at the office. The converse is true for hiking: I wouldn't be surprised if many hard-core hikers on their deathbed wished they'd spent more time on the trail!

You're Your Own Boss

Do you ever feel like you don't have much control over your daily life? Go take a hike. You're your own boss on the trail. Be spontaneous. Time permitting, I often explore side trails just to see where they lead. Again, time permitting, you may have the option of spending more time on a hike than you had planned because there is more to see and do than you had expected.

You can set your own goals when hiking. If you only want to hike 5 miles (8 km) a day, it's your choice. If you want to hike 20 miles (32 km) a day—and are capable of doing so—that's your choice, too.

Social Networks

Most people don't hike alone. They hike with spouses, significant others, their children, or friends. Conversations on the trail are real interactions; they sure beat Twitter or Facebook. Conversation doesn't need to be hurried; you have all day, so take your time to share your thoughts with your companions. Be a good listener, too.

Many communities have local hiking clubs; you can make new friends by joining a club and hiking with its members. You'll find that people who hike usually have similar interests. Groups that finish the day with dinner together often know where the best restaurants are.

Trail Wisdom

If you don't know anyone who hikes, contact your local parks and recreation department. If there's a hiking club in your community, parks and rec will know about it. If you have children who are Scouting age, contact a local troop and see what kinds of activities they have.

Why Backpack?

The number of backpackers in the world is probably a lot smaller than the total number of hikers. Lots of people enjoy day hiking but don't feel the need for extended hikes. That's fine. I'm sure over 90 percent of my lifetime hiking has been day hikes. I've been hiking ever since I started walking, but I didn't really get into backpacking seriously until I was forty years old.

My older son became a Boy Scout and joined a troop that went backpacking every month. Then my older daughter began hiking the canyon with me and other family members and friends. My younger son became a Scout, and soon he was backpacking. Finally, my younger daughter started coming on hikes when she was eleven years old. The kids are all grown up, married, and have children of their own, but I'm still backpacking.

There's an obvious advantage to multiday backpacking trips: you can get a lot farther into the wilderness when you're on the trail for several days than you can in only one day.

Over the years I had day hiked to three of Yosemite's High Sierra camps. It was a real treat a few years ago when my brother and I hiked a multiday loop of the camps. We stayed at the campgrounds adjoining the Sierra camps, not at the camps themselves. By spending several days on the trail, we hiked trails neither of us had been on before and went farther into the backcountry than ever before. I've been able to do the same at some other extremely scenic places around the United States.

Lots of people hike to the Colorado River at the bottom of the Grand Canyon and out in a day, even though the rangers strongly advise people not to. Today, even after more than twenty years' hiking to the bottom, camping one or more nights, and hiking back out, I've still never hiked to the river and back in one day. I suppose I'm physically capable of doing so, but I don't want to. The bottom of the Grand Canyon is such a special place that I don't want to turn right around and hike back out again; I really, really enjoy getting to spend time there.

What Others Have Said about Hiking

Backpacking can be an extremely gratifying and rewarding experience. Let me share with you what others have had to say about hiking.

In the words of traveler and author Paul Theroux:

"There is an intense but simple thrill in setting off in the morning on a mountain trail, knowing that everything you need is on your back. It is a confidence in having left the inessentials behind and of entering a world of natural beauty that has not been violated, where money has no value, and possessions are a dead weight. The person with the fewest possessions is the freest. Thoreau was right."

Naturalist and author John Muir had pithy ways of expressing the joy of backpacking:

> ➤ "Going to the woods is going home."
> ➤ "Going to the mountains is going home."
> ➤ "Between every two pines is a doorway to a new world."
> ➤ "In every walk with nature one receives far more than he seeks."

Richard Spray, an employee with the United States Forest Service, wrote:

"I have a basic belief that outdoor recreation in a natural environment is good for people and is good for society at large. Anything that will bring more people to outdoor recreation, I therefore consider a 'friend.'"

The late Supreme Court Justice and avid hiker William O. Douglas wrote:

"The thrill of tramping alone and unafraid through a wilderness of lakes, creeks, alpine meadows, and glaciers is not known to many… When man worships at the feet of avalanche lilies or discovers the delicacies of the pasque flowers or finds the fain perfume of phlox on rocky ridges, he will come to know the real glories of God's creations. When he feels the wind blowing through him on a high peak or sleeps under a closely matted white bark pine in an exposed basin, he is apt to find his relationship to the universe."

Jack Kerouac wrote, "Think what a great world revolution will take place when… [there are] millions of guys all over the world with rucksacks on their backs tramping around the back country."

These are inspiring words, aren't they? Don't you just want to hit the trail and not look back?

Conclusion

This book is filled with advice about hiking in general, with some sections intended specifically for backpackers. Part One describes how to prepare for a hike—what gear, clothing, and food you should carry. Part Two is about having a safe and satisfying experience on the trail. Part Three describes the regions of the United States and Canada, explaining the major features of large-scale ecosystems: mountains, forests, prairies, deserts, and tundra. Part Four is full of suggestions of trails to hike. Recommendations are given for every state and Canadian province.

I hope you have as much fun reading this book as I had writing it. I would love to hear about your adventures. Please feel free to contact the publisher of Smart Guides, who would be happy to pass your letters or e-mails on to me.

At the close of each episode of their 1950s western television show, Roy Rogers and Dale Evans would ride off on their buckboard singing "Happy trails to you." That's my wish for you—happy trails!

PART ONE

Preparing for the Trail

 # Buying Gear

---

In This Chapter

➤ Footwear

➤ Backpacks and sleeping bags

➤ Tents

➤ Cooking gear

An entire industry has been built around providing clothing for every type of outdoor activity imaginable, along with packs, sleeping bags and pads, tents, stoves, cookware, eating utensils, navigational aids, maps, freeze-dried food, and more. Even portable showers can be hauled in your pack.

When I first started hiking, there were far fewer choices. The outfitting industry hadn't even caught up yet with the number of women on the trail. Women had to buy backpacks and sleeping bags designed for men. Today, women can buy backpacks and sleeping bags that are fitted to a female torso.

Where to Shop

Before the Internet, consumers were pretty much limited to local suppliers. Hikers and campers were fortunate if they lived near the brick-and-mortar store of one of the major outfitters—Recreational Equipment Incorporated (REI) in Seattle, Washington; L. L. Bean in Freeport, Maine; Cabela's in Sidney, Nebraska; or The North Face in San Francisco, California. Mail order catalogs were also available from retailers such as Campmor or Sierra Designs, but even then the selection of gear was much less than it is today. Today's consumer can shop online from a large number of outfitters and are able to comparison shop. And the companies with brick-and-mortar stores have expanded to other states throughout the country.

There are so many outfitting companies to choose from that I am not presuming to list them all, let alone recommend one company over another. What I am recommending is that you find out what is available near you and pay a visit. Look over the gear, try on clothes, find out what appeals and does not appeal to you, and see what fits within your budget. Talk to salespeople. They can answer your questions; they can probably answer questions you haven't even thought to ask. If you don't find what you're looking for, or feel that gear or clothing are within your price range, then go online and see what's available.

Most of the gear in this chapter is necessary for overnight camping. Hiking boots are essential, however, whether you're going for a 5-mile (8-km) day hike or a three-month-long 1,000-mile (1,600-km) trek. We'll start with recommendations about hiking boots.

Trail Wisdom

Never buy hiking boots from someone who is not a hiker.

Footwear

Because hikers spend most of their time on their feet, a good pair of hiking boots is absolutely essential. There are many manufacturers of hiking boots and a variety of designs. The important thing is to find the pair of boots that is exactly right for you! I can't tell you what brand will be best for you. The only way to find the pair that is right for you is to go to a store that specializes in outdoor gear. When you go, be sure to take a pair of hiking socks with you to wear when you are trying on boots. If you don't have a good pair of hiking socks yet, ask the salesperson if you can borrow a pair. Stores usually have a supply of socks just for that purpose.

The first thing to look for is a salesperson who is wearing hiking boots. You are going to have questions about different kinds of boots and how they feel on the trail. A salesperson who is not a hiker is not going to be able to help you.

Choosing the Right Hiking Boots

Once you know you're in the right store, begin trying on every brand of boot in your size. Walk around the store. Take your time. Choosing the right boots is your most important decision. If the store has a short ramp to walk on, try walking up and down it a few times. If your toes are banging into the front of the boots when you walk downhill, the boots are too small for you. Try the next larger size. How comfortable are the arch supports and how snug are the heels? I can guarantee you that if your heels are sliding up and down in the boots, when you're on the trail you will develop whopping big blisters on your heels. You want boots to be snug in the heels and arches but still have plenty of room for your toes.

An important consideration with hiking boots is whether to buy low-top, mid-top, or high-top boots. Most hikers seem to prefer low-top; they have the feel of athletic shoes. I own both low-top and mid-top boots. The low-tops are my everyday boots for camping, birding, and light day hiking—outings when I'm not carrying a heavy backpack. The mid-tops are for my backpacking trips; their purpose is to provide ankle support.

I do most of my backpacking on trails that can be pretty rocky; I can't count how many times I've twisted my ankle on rocks or logs and felt that the support provided by my mid-tops saved me from a sprained ankle. I recommend them, but it's up to you. High-top hiking boots remind me of army boots. I know military personnel who say that army boots are extremely comfortable for hiking, but it's unusual to see high-top boots on trails.

Trail Wisdom

Each boot manufacturer uses a last, which is a piece of metal shaped like a foot, to make its boots. There's a different last for each size boot, and every manufacturer has lasts of slightly different shapes. If a boot that's your size feels uncomfortable, it probably means that your foot is not the same shape as the last used to make that boot. That's why it's so important to try on as many brands of boots as possible. You need to find boots that conform to the shape of your feet.

The Right Fit

Keep in mind that your feet swell during the day. If you go shopping first thing in the morning, boots you try on may feel loose. If you go in the evening, the same boots may feel tight. For that reason, it may be best to shop later in the day. It's better to buy boots that are a little loose part of the day than are so tight later on that they are uncomfortable to walk in.

My feet are a half-size different, which is not uncommon. Don't make the mistake of finding a boot that feels comfortable and assuming its mate fits, too. Try on both boots. If one boot feels snug, then go up one-half size. A boot that feels tight in the store feels uncomfortably tight after you've been hiking in it for a few miles.

I highly recommend insoles to protect the soles of your feet. Ask the salesperson to recommend insoles and ask if you can try them, inside the boots you are considering. If the boots feel just right without the insoles but too tight with the insoles, try on boots one size larger.

Hiking Socks and Liners

Before you buy the boots, also check out the different kinds of hiking socks the store carries. Do you see socks that look like they may be more comfortable than those you're currently wearing? If you do, then ask if you can try the boots on wearing the socks you think you like. I'm pretty confident that the salesperson sincerely wants you to find the optimum fit of boots, socks, and insoles, and sock liners if you think you want to use them.

Sock liners are usually thinner than hiking socks themselves. Some people choose silk or nylon because they feel silk and nylon are more comfortable than wool, cotton, or polyester to have next to the skin. It's an individual preference. Liners help wick moisture away from the skin and can help prevent blisters. The important consideration is if you're going to wear liners, then you have to allow for them when choosing boot size.

Ask the salesperson lots of questions. That's why he or she is there—to help customers find the gear that works best for them. After all, the store wants your repeat business. It's not going to get your repeat business if you end up being dissatisfied.

Cost of Hiking Boots

Prices of hiking boots vary considerably. I've found that I usually need to spend somewhere in the range of $120–$130 to get boots that will work for me. There are well-made hiking boots on the market that are much more expensive than that. Usually these are European made. I don't have to spend $250–$300, though, to get what works for me. If $120 frightens you, ask if the store expects to have any sales in the near future, but don't expect prices to come down too much.

Good insoles will probably run you $40 a pair. Socks usually run $10–$20 a pair. Expect to spend $10–$20 for a pair of sock liners. Remember, at a minimum, you should carry one clean pair of socks for each day you're on the trail; unless you plan to do laundry every night, buy the number of pairs you're going to need.

At the end of a long day on the trail, you may not want to wear your hiking boots in camp. I recommend buying a lightweight pair of moccasins or sandals; they'll give both your feet and your boots a chance to air out.

Backpacks and Sleeping Bags

After a good pair of hiking boots, the two most essential pieces of equipment for a backpacking trip are a backpack that fits properly and a lightweight sleeping bag that is rated for the nighttime temperatures anticipated on a particular outing.

I have put backpacks and sleeping bags in the same section because both have to fit your particular anatomy. Backpacks and sleeping bags come in various lengths to fit different torsos; different contours have been designed because different packs and sleeping bags fit men's and women's bodies differently. It is just as important to try on packs and bags in various sizes made by different manufacturers as it is when choosing the right pair of hiking boots.

Shopping for Backpacks

An important consideration with backpacks is whether to buy an external-frame or an internal-frame pack. Having an external frame means the pack attaches to the frame on the outside; having an internal frame means the frame is inside the pack. For decades external frames were the standard for backpacking. Internal frames were introduced for climbers who needed a pack that could squeeze into tight fissures in rock walls. The packs caught on with backpackers, however, and today you are likely to see a lot more internal-frame than external-frame packs on the trail.

In case you're wondering, I still use an external-frame pack. One of the reasons I've never changed is I like a pack I can prop against a tree or rock. With an internal-frame pack, you pretty much have to lay the pack on the ground. Another reason is that external-frame packs usually have more compartments, so I don't have to dig through the pack every time I need something. A third reason is that I'm not a gear hog; I don't have to own the very newest gear on the market.

It is important that you try on both kinds of packs and decide which style appeals to you. Backpacks are designed so that you should be carrying most of the weight on your hips, not on your shoulders. Before you make your purchase, it is extremely important for your salesperson to make any necessary adjustments to the frame to fit your torso.

If you buy an external-frame pack, be sure to also buy straps to attach your sleeping bag, pad, tent, and ground cloth. Otherwise you'll be carrying your sleeping bag and tent in your arms. I've actually seen people doing that, but it's pretty tiring to do so. The straps for sleeping bags should be 36–48 inches (90–120 cm) long, depending on how thick your bag is.

Shopping for Sleeping Bags

The main choice with sleeping bags is whether to go with down or synthetic filler. Down is lighter and usually warmer. The disadvantages of down are that it loses its insulating quality if it gets wet, and it's usually more expensive.

The advantage of synthetic material is that it retains its insulating quality even if it gets wet. The disadvantage of synthetic is that it's usually heavier. My recommendation is to buy a sleeping bag that weighs 5 pounds (2.3 kg) or less and is rated for temperatures of 15°F (9°C) or less.

Before you buy a sleeping bag, take off your shoes and crawl inside to make sure that the bag is the right length. You don't want a bag that is too long; that extra length of bag just fills with cold air at night. Be sure the bag is wide enough for you at your hips and shoulders. Bags are designed differently for men and women, so be sure you're trying the right one. I bought my current bag twenty years ago for $150. That seemed like a lot at the time, but I've certainly gotten my money's worth by now.

If you can't make up your mind, ask the salesperson if you can rent a backpack or sleeping bag. You can probably also rent a tent, if you wish. A rented sleeping bag comes with a liner for hygienic reasons. Renting equipment your first outing or two gives you the opportunity to get a better idea of what works or doesn't work for you.

Trail Wisdom

There's an old saying that you get what you pay for. This is especially true for hiking and camping gear. Don't be "penny wise and pound foolish." Buy the best quality you can afford. If you don't, you'll regret it on the trail. You don't have to buy the most expensive gear on the market, but if you want good gear that serves you well, be prepared to pay for it.

Sleeping Pad

Sooner or later, most backpackers purchase a sleeping pad. If you expect to sleep on hard or rocky ground, your body will appreciate the cushioning. An air mattress is all right, but it may be tedious if you have to inflate it yourself. It's more common for backpackers to carry self-inflating pads, which tend to be lightweight and roll up fairly compactly. A foam pad works, too, although it tends to be bulky.

Tents

There are many manufacturers of tents, with prices ranging from under $100 to over $300. I own two backpacking tents. One cost me $125 new, and the other is a used tent I picked up at a swap meet for $50. The used tent is roomier than the first one, so I use it for car camping, too.

Retailers probably have one or more tents set up in their stores so you can see what the tents actually look like. Most backpacking tents these days are dome tents. Dome tents come in different sizes and have different features.

Tent Size

One of the first considerations when selecting a tent is its size—how many people can sleep in it. Tents are rated as being for two, three, four, or more people. I always take those numbers with a grain of salt, however. Unless the occupants are fairly slender and don't mind sleeping shoulder-to-shoulder and hip-to-hip, I would suggest subtracting one from the number of people stated. A two-person tent is comfortable for one adult. A three-person tent is comfortable for two adults.

The next consideration is usually peak height. Peak height refers to how tall the tent is at the middle. If it's a dome tent, how high is the tent in the middle of the dome? Or, if it's a rectangular tent, how high is the center ridgeline? Most backpacking tents are less than 6 feet (1.8 m) high. In fact, many of them are less than 5 feet high; 4 feet 10 inches (1.5 meters) is an average height.

The tent I bought new is only about 3 feet (90 cm) high. Clearly, most adults cannot stand up to their full height in tents like these. Usually it isn't a problem. If all you're doing is sleeping in the tent, then it just means you can't stand up very well to dress or undress. Even if you're huddling in the tent waiting out a rain storm, it just means you have to sit or lie down the whole time.

Quality and Features

Next on your list of what to look for should be how well is the tent made. Do the seams look tight, or are they going to tear the first time a wind storm stretches them? How about zippers? Try the zippers on different models and compare how they feel. Some probably feel sturdier than others do. Since zippers are usually the first things to wear out on tents, it helps to have good zippers to begin with.

How much ventilation does the tent have? How well does the rain fly cover the tent? You don't want it to get stuffy during the night. Nor do you want rain to come in through the meshing. Again, compare different models.

Does the tent have a vestibule? A vestibule is a covered area in front of the door. Most tents are three-season tents, and are not designed for winter use. They are unlikely to have a vestibule. Four-season tents usually have vestibules. In stormy weather, it's safe to cook over a gas stove in the vestibule. It's also a place where you can leave your wet or dirty boots outside the tent itself. If you expect to encounter very much rain or snow on your treks, you might like to have a vestibule.

Weight Considerations

At this point on your shopping trip, you may already have narrowed your choice to only one model. On the other hand, if you like the features of two or more models pretty much equally, then it's time to consider weight.

Tents can range in weight from around 4 to 8 pounds (2 to 4 kg), or more. How much weight are you willing to carry? Quite honestly, since I do most of my backpacking in Arizona, I rarely carry a tent just to save weight. Most of the time the weather cooperates and I am fine without a tent.

If you're usually going to share the tent with one or more people, then you can split up the weight—one person carrying the tent, and the other person (or persons) carrying the poles and pegs. Just realize that if you're used to car camping, you haven't needed to worry about the weight before. Now you do. I would recommend choosing a tent that weighs less than 5 pounds (2.3 kg) unless you know you're going to have help carrying it or you're a big person and the extra weight won't bother you.

Freestanding Tents

You will discover that many backpacking tents are described as being freestanding. That means you don't have to stake them down; the configuration of poles suffices to hold up the tent. Having a tent that is freestanding is important if you have to pitch the tent on a rocky surface or another surface that is too hard to hold pegs.

Trail Wisdom

It would be interesting to know the statistics on how many backpackers have returned to their campsite on a windy day and found their tent missing. I've heard instances of tents blowing over cliff walls or into lakes or rivers. It's best to always stake a tent down!

Whether or not a tent is freestanding may or may not be true. If there's no wind, it's probably true. If you, or you and your companion, are in the tent asleep, your weight is probably sufficient to hold the tent down. The problem is if you are absent from the campsite and a strong wind begins to blow. In that case, there's a good chance the tent will blow away.

Price of Tents

There's an important consideration when buying a tent, and that's price. How much you're willing to pay is up to you. Fortunately—unlike hiking boots that wear out and need to be replaced—a tent that's well made to begin with may be the only one you'll ever need. Take good care of it and keep it clean. Remember that you get what you pay for. Invest in good-quality gear now and it should last you for many years.

Footprint or Ground Cloth

An optional footprint can be purchased for most backpacking tents. A footprint is a ground cloth that exactly fits the dimensions of the floor of a particular tent and keeps the tent cleaner. Footprints are expensive. Years ago I bought a roll of lightweight black plastic at the local hardware store. I've cut rectangles of plastic that fit the floors of my tents. Also, I've cut ground cloths for family members to use when we haven't carried tents.

A good ground cloth is somewhat longer than the sleeping bag and two to three times as wide. It helps keep you and your sleeping bag clean. In the event of rain, I roll up in my ground cloth cocoon-style; it's a lightweight alternative to a tent and does a remarkable job of keeping me warm and dry.

Warranties

An important consideration to remember when buying gear is that reputable manufacturers and dealers usually offer lifetime warranties on their gear. If you are ever dissatisfied for any reason, you can probably take it back for a full refund (or at least store credit). Shop from well-established dealers and buy quality gear to begin with.

A couple of years after I purchased a second-hand tent, the zipper stopped working properly. Usually the problem with nonworking zippers is not the zipper itself. The more likely problem is the zipper pull, which is inexpensive to replace. Whatever the problem was, I returned the tent to the manufacturer, the zipper was repaired, and the tent was shipped back to me for free. The company never asked for an original receipt or even if I was the original owner. The company honored its lifetime warranty without asking any questions.

Similarly, my sleeping bag is twenty years old. Its zipper also finally gave out. The bag has a lifetime warranty, so I returned it to the manufacturer, and the company replaced the zipper.

One of the seams in the bag's stuff sack had blown. I wasn't expecting it to, but the company also stitched the seam for me.

Both repairs were completely free. My only cost with either the tent or the sleeping bag was the shipping charge to send the tent or bag back to the company. Both companies paid the return shipping charges.

Cookware

You have to eat when you're on the trail. If you want hot food, an option could be to cook over a campfire. However, in some areas, fires are not allowed, and even if they are, firewood could be scarce. For most people having hot food to eat means having to pack a stove and fuel.

The choice of stove usually depends on what fuel you prefer to use. The two most common fuels are white gas and butane, or a propane/butane mixture.

White gas has several advantages:

➤ It burns hotter so less is used

➤ It is widely available

➤ It is easier to carry large enough quantities to last a week or more

The main disadvantage of white gas is that it is more hazardous to use, so it is sold in a heavier bottle than butane is sold in. That's more weight you have to carry.

A butane stove is sufficient for trips of one to five days. If you expect to take longer backpacking trips than that, white gas is better. Once you've chosen the fuel, that decision will probably dictate what stove you buy.

If you are planning on international travel, realize that white gas or butane may not be available in other countries. Airline restrictions usually prohibit carrying fuels onboard an airplane, so you have to buy fuel after you reach your destination. International travelers usually carry a stove that can use multiple fuels and buy whatever fuel is sold at their destination.

Trail Wisdom

Regardless of whether your destination is domestic or international, if you're flying anywhere, check with your airline about packing stoves in your checked baggage. It's possible that an airline may prohibit any kind of stove, so you will have to buy one at your destination.

Along with a stove you'll need at least one pot or pan plus utensils. For short trips, bringing a pot or pan from home may suffice, especially if all you're going to do is boil water. Otherwise, outfitters sell cook kits that are lightweight (they're usually made of aluminum) and that stack one pot inside another. A commercial cook kit can be expensive, but if you take care of it, you probably won't have to ever buy another one.

If I'm backpacking alone, or with only one or two other people, I find it's sufficient to carry a two-quart pot to cook in, and a one-quart coffee pot to boil water in. Since I can stuff them with other items in my pack, they don't take up much added room, and they're very lightweight.

As for utensils, many people carry a spoon and find it serves their needs. Outfitters sell plasticware that's durable enough to be washed and used repeatedly. Plasticware weighs less than the metal utensils you use at home, but it may not be necessary. It's your choice. What's more important is when planning your meals, think about how you will be preparing them. Will you need a spatula? If you're planning to cook pancakes, then you probably do; if you're cooking oatmeal, then probably not. The same is true for knives and forks. How many of them do you really need?

How Much Can You Carry?

 Packing for the trail has much in common with packing for a road trip, plane flight, or cruise. There are people who bring along everything except the kitchen sink, and there are people who bring almost nothing. Some people can fill a car with equipment for just an overnight or weekend trip. Some people arrive at the airport with two huge bags to check, and two more carry-ons. These people have a complete change of clothing for every day of their trip. The people who can fit everything they need for a month's trip into an overnight bag bring two pairs of underwear to last a month and plan to wash one pair every night. Most of us fall somewhere in between these two extremes.

The difference when packing for the trail is that on the trail you have to carry everything on your back. For most of us, that restriction imposes severe limitations on how much we are going to bring along. Unfortunately, much of the gear we bring is necessary whether we are camping one night or thirty. A backpack, tent, sleeping bag, sleeping pad, cooking gear, eating utensils, and first aid kit are necessary regardless of how many nights we plan to be on the trail.

How many pounds you can carry depends greatly on what kind of physical condition you are in. A general rule of thumb is that beginning hikers should pack no more than 25 percent of their weight. Therefore, a 140-pound (66-kg) person can carry about 35 pounds (16 kg), while a 200-pound (91 kg) person can carry 50 pounds (23 kg).

Naturally, there are individuals who are in such excellent physical condition that they can carry much more than 25 percent of their weight. I know a thirty-one-year-old professional backpacking guide who probably does not weigh more than 180 pounds (82 kg) and can carry a 100-pound pack (46 kg). He's probably the exception to the rule. After all, he backpacks all the time; it's how he makes his living.

Since the weight a person can carry is so variable, it is probably best to experiment before hitting the trail. Try a practice hike, carrying what you think you will need. If it seems too heavy, decide what can be left home. If you are hiking with a group, perhaps another member of the group can help with some of your load. Or, if you are the exceptionally physically fit member of the group, perhaps you can offer to help a beginning hiker with some of his load.

Speaking of group hiking, cooking gear and tents can be shared. In fact, a group of four to six hikers may need only one set of cooking utensils among them. Distributing the pieces among group members lightens everyone's load. Two people can usually share a tent; one person carries the tent itself, and his companion carries the poles and stakes. Or, one person carries the tent, the other person carries the rain fly, and the two of them divide the poles and stakes.

Dividing food among group members also helps. People who need to carry less can carry the meals for the first couple of days of the hike. People who can carry more can carry the meals intended for later in the hike.

There are other considerations. One is the season. Between late fall and early spring, it is reasonable to expect to have to carry more warm clothing on a hike. A summer hike usually requires lighter clothing. Changes of clothes are still important in the summer, though. After a day of sweating on the trail, it is always best to have a set of dry clothes to change into at the end of the day.

Another thing to consider is the availability of water. If water is available on at least a daily basis, then it is less necessary to carry a lot of water at a time. It is important, however, to be prepared to purify water. Filtration systems work well and are usually lightweight. Iodine tablets or drops work well, too.

If water sources are few and far between, then much more water has to be carried. A rule of thumb is 1 gallon (4 L) of water per person per day, although the amount varies tremendously with season and with the individual person. For some people—and especially in summer—2 gallons (8 L) of water per day may be necessary. Unfortunately, there is no way around the fact that water is heavy: 1 quart (1 L) of water weighs about 2 pounds (1 kg), 1 gallon (4 L) of water weighs about 8 pounds (4 kg). In a 40-pound (18-kg) pack, 1 gallon (4 L) of water makes up 20 percent of the weight. When taking that practice hike, be sure to include at least as much water as you expect to be carrying on the backpacking trip itself.

Flashlights, headlamps, and lanterns add weight to your pack but are handy to have. Flashlights that use C or D batteries tend to be heavy. I prefer lightweight flashlights that use AA or AAA batteries.

Many hikers use headlamps. The advantage of a headlamp is it frees up your hands, which is helpful when cooking after dark. A headlamp usually lights your way better than a flashlight.

Years ago, I bought a small lantern that uses the same fuel as my stove. It's lightweight, and I can set it on a rock or on the ground. Battery-powered lanterns are also available. Just remember to carry spare batteries and bulbs.

Conclusion

Do you have everything you need? Have you left at home everything you don't need? If you answered yes to both questions, go take a hike!

CHAPTER 3

Buying Food for the Trail

In This Chapter

➤ Menus

➤ Serving sizes

➤ Have everything you need

➤ Easy-to-prepare foods

There is an old saying that an army marches on its stomach. That is pretty much true of backpackers, too. Beyond the essentials of tent, backpack, sleeping bag, and changes of clothing, food is next in priority on most lists. It makes a huge difference if you are packing food just for yourself and maybe a companion, or if you are in charge of food for a group. On several occasions, I have taken on the responsibility of purchasing and packing food for a dozen or more hikers, and I can assure you it is not an easy task. Let us start with food for just one to four people.

Historical Quote

John Muir wrote of his urge to "throw a loaf of bread and a pound of tea in an old sack and jump over the back fence." That's probably less food than most of us would carry, but it shows that it's possible to travel light if you want to.

The Menu

If you are hiking with family members, you already know what their likes and dislikes are. Also, you are already aware of any food allergies. In fact, the foods you bring on a backpacking trip may not be too different from what the family is used to eating at home. Your main considerations are probably choosing nonperishable foods and keeping total weight manageable. If you are hiking with friends, however, you may be less aware of what their food preferences are. If you are hiking in a group that may include people you have never met before—or at least you do not know very well—then you are undoubtedly clueless about what they like or do not like to eat. The advice offered here is more for the situation where you are not particularly familiar with other people's food preferences.

Trail Wisdom

The first consideration when planning food for a backpacking trip is to be sure you are getting food that people are going to eat. There is no point in lugging food that no one eats.

Matching Trail Food to People's Usual Diets

Personally, I believe that food on the trail should not be extremely different from food eaten at home. This is especially true with children. A child who eats Fruit Loops for breakfast every day may turn up his nose at a package of instant oatmeal. Likewise, a dinner of freeze-dried lasagna on the trail may not compete with chicken nuggets and French fries at home. Even adults may turn up their noses at foods to which they are not accustomed.

Discuss food preferences with people ahead of time. Within the limits imposed by weight and lack of refrigeration, try to bring at least some foods that people are used to eating. If people do not eat, they will not have the energy to hike. That could be a serious problem with children. And, people get really cranky when they are hungry.

Incidentally, unless you are planning to eat granola three times a day, or mostly freeze-dried food, a five-day supply of food is probably about all a group can expect to carry. Even if weight is not really a problem, volume is. Food takes up room in the pack, and a pack can only hold so much.

If you are planning to be in the backcountry for a week or more, you may want to arrange locations where you can restock your food supplies and drop off garbage. If the trail is going to cross a road, you could arrange to have a car left nearby with a supply of food. Alternatively, perhaps someone can meet you when you are crossing the road, bring you more food, and take your garbage off your hands. It is also possible that the trail may pass near a town where you can stop for groceries. One way or the other, you probably need to make some kind of arrangements for restocking your food supplies.

Staying Healthy

Constipation and bloating can be problems for some people when hiking. The usual cause is dehydration. Be sure you plan to drink plenty of fluids when hiking. If you ordinarily tend not to drink a lot of plain water, carry flavored powders so that you feel encouraged to drink more. For weekend outings, apples, oranges, and bananas stay fresh and are a good source of fiber. For longer treks, bring dried fruit.

Developing a Menu

The best foods for the trail are nonperishable and high in carbohydrates. The exception to nonperishable foods is foods that can be frozen; they will thaw on the trail and be ready to cook the first night. In cool weather, perishable foods may keep longer than only one night, but in warm weather, stick with nonperishables.

Frequent snacks that replenish carbohydrates are often better than infrequent big meals. For a weekend outing, you don't need much protein; the important thing is to provide energy. Many hikers munch trail mix, which is a mixture of nuts, raisins, and dried fruits. Gorp is also a perennial favorite. If you want some protein in your diet, beef jerky is a good choice.

Start by contacting people. It is a good idea to poll nonfamily members ahead of time. Any coffee drinkers? If there are, be sure to pack some instant coffee. Any vegetarians in the group? Any vegans? Anybody who normally survives on double cheeseburgers and supersize orders of fries? Do people eat fruit? Not everyone does, you know. How do people feel about dried versus fresh fruit? What about food allergies? Snacks that contain peanuts are not going to be eaten by someone with an allergy to peanuts.

After you have a reasonable idea of people's likes and dislikes, begin developing a menu. How many breakfasts, lunches, and dinners will there be? Do not forget snacks along the trail, and bedtime snacks. Also, on an extended trip of more than three days, plan on people becoming hungrier and wanting more to eat than they did the first day or two.

If the individual preferences of your fellow hikers are too diverse, a one-meal-fits-all menu may not work. You may need to have choices for foods to accommodate different tastes. Just remember that all the food eventually ends up on people's backs. Too many choices could mean more weight than people can carry or more volume than packs can hold.

Trail Wisdom

Our bodies tend to carry a reserve of starch and fat that provides energy for at least twenty-four hours. On the first day or two of a hike, people draw on those reserves so they tend to eat less. Once those reserves have been depleted, however, people may become ravenous. More food needs to be carried for the third day onward than was needed for the first two days.

Food Has Weight and Volume

While pushing my shopping cart down the aisles of the supermarket, I compare similar products, prices, and—importantly—weight. Canned stew or chili may sound yummy when I'm putting the menu together, but canned goods are heavy. Since most of the weight is water, and hopefully water will be available at campsites, it makes more sense to purchase dry mixes or dehydrated foods.

Fresh fruit is heavy, too. You may be thinking that dried fruit (apricots, apples, bananas, etc.) make sense, but there can be a problem with dried fruit. For one thing, not everyone likes dried fruit. Someone who is used to slicing a banana over his granola is not going to be satisfied with dried bananas. Someone who really enjoys biting into an apple may not feel the same way about dried apple slices.

In cool weather, fresh fruit lasts several days. It may be that the taste and refreshment that accompanies eating the real thing trumps the disadvantage of weight. Check with the other backpackers in your group. See what they think.

Do not forget that food takes up space. I can remember times when we have arrived at our trailhead and have begun dividing the food among us. Sometimes the problem was not that there was too much weight; the problem was that people did not have enough room in their packs for all the food. It is easy when people are loading their packs at home to forget to allow enough space for the share of food they will be carrying. Try to give people a good estimate of how much room they need to reserve. Even with the best preparation, though, it is common to have to leave some of the food in the cars.

Think about how much trash the packages will generate. If you camp in an area where campfires are allowed, it is okay to burn cardboard boxes. Remember, though, that metal cans and plastic do not burn. And do not bury your trash! Animals will just dig it up. Anything that cannot be burned has to be packed out again.

Trail Wisdom

An important consideration when purchasing food is how much trash will be generated. It is definitely a no-no to bury trash in the backcountry. Food that can be packed in zippered bags is usually best. Remember the rule: pack it in–pack it out!

Preparing Meals on the Trail

Another important consideration is how difficult different choices of food are to prepare. At the end of a long day of hiking, do people feel like spending an hour cooking dinner, or do they want something that is fast, easy, and (hopefully) reasonably tasty? How difficult is a meal to prepare in the rain? How difficult is cooking if you do not get to your campsite until after dark? Even if you are feeling ambitious enough that you want to prepare some gourmet meals on the trail, you might also want to have a few meals that can be prepared quickly and easily just in case.

Some people pride themselves on their cooking abilities and like to show off in the backcountry. If a member or two of your group fits that description, then by all means plan some meals that take some skill to prepare, especially if those meals are likely to result in satisfied oohs and aahs while they are eaten.

If your group does not want to exert more effort than it takes to boil water, plan a menu accordingly. Maybe breakfasts and lunches that do not require cooking are best. Maybe instant oatmeal is the order of the day for breakfast. A lot of dinners require nothing more than bringing a pot of water to a boil and simmering a package of noodles and seasonings until the noodles are soft. Those kinds of dinners can be very tasty, satisfying, and—importantly—filling.

If you will be on the trail any length of time, variety is the spice of life. Nobody wants to eat the same thing day after day.

Meals that need to be prepared in the dark after a particularly long day of hiking should be quick to prepare and equally quick to clean up afterward. Otherwise, some people say they're too tired to eat, and they go to bed hungry.

Trail Wisdom

It doesn't hurt to practice at home fixing food you're planning to cool on the trail, especially if you're used to doing most of your cooking in a microwave oven. Practicing ahead of time lets you know what utensils you'll need and how much fuel a meal requires when it's cooked.

If you have planned a layover day or two, spending some time simmering a pot of beans may be just the thing. Maybe this is when people will be fishing, and you can hope to supplement the food you've brought from home with some fresh fish. I have often brought all of the ingredients to make tacos or burritos on a backpacking trip. Cheese, tomatoes, and lettuce keep well except in hot weather. Packages of taco and burrito seasonings and taco sauce are readily available.

I have brought dried pinto and black beans, soaked them overnight, and then simmered them for a couple of hours until they are fully cooked. That works if the group is carrying sufficient fuel. Otherwise, canned beans can be brought along, although they tend to be heavy and the cans have to be packed out as trash.

You may also be able to find dehydrated beans that plump up when cooked. Corn tortillas tend to be light, but flour tortillas can be pretty heavy. I've found, though, that Mexican dishes are popular on the trail, so people are usually willing to carry the extra weight.

Some People Don't Cook

I have backpacked with individuals who have gone to great lengths not to have to cook on the trail. One memorable hike occurred on a three-day trip from the South Rim of the Grand Canyon to the Colorado River at the bottom of the canyon and back again. The only food one man brought was a 1-gallon (4-L) zippered plastic bag of gorp, which is short for "gobs of raisins and peanuts," or "good old raisins and peanuts," depending upon whom you ask. For variety and taste, a package of M&Ms had been added.

We started down the trail mid-morning. He had gorp for lunch and gorp for dinner. So far, so good. The first day out, people are not really hungry anyway. The second day—gorp for breakfast and gorp for lunch again. Guess what? By dinner he was getting pretty hungry, was sick of eating gorp, and still had another day to go. That was the last time he ever did that!

Another time my hiking companion brought a large pizza for our one-night stay in the backcountry. Cold pizza for dinner and cold pizza again for breakfast actually was pretty good. I might not have wanted to bring pizza in mid-summer, though, but this hike was in November, so the pizza kept well. I am also not sure if I would have wanted more than two meals of pizza. A second night on the trail and I probably would have had a desire for something new.

Then there was the man who started our hike with a steak marinating in a zippered bag in his backpack. Since we would be camping in an area where campfires were allowed, he planned to cook his steak over a good, hot fire. Things went pretty well except that the bag leaked and everything in his pack except the steak became soaked with marinade. You can imagine what his pack smelled like! Fortunately, we camped that night in an area where the biggest animals we had to contend with were raccoons.

The lesson to be learned from these stories is that it is all right to have some meals—especially lunches on the trail—that do not require any preparation. However, most people find they prefer something a little more substantial for breakfasts and dinners. Just as most people do not eat the same food for many days in a row at home, most people do not want to eat the same for many days in a row on the trail either.

Trail Wisdom

There is a saying that variety is the spice of life. A varied menu is just as important on the trail as it is at home.

Serving Sizes

After I have prepared a menu, I run it by at least a couple of other members of the group. If the menu looks okay to everyone, I begin to calculate what quantity needs to be purchased. Have you ever read closely the nutrition labels on canned and packaged foods? A serving is 0.5 cup (118 ml) or 1 cup (236 ml) of food. After a full day hiking, how far is a cup of food going to go with most people? Probably not very far.

I have found that a good rule of thumb is that a package of dry food will serve half the number of people the label claims. The same is true of freeze-dried foods. Many packages containing two servings according to the label, will feed just one person after a day on the trail. Men and teenage boys definitely will eat two or more servings of anything placed in front of them. Women and teenage girls may eat only one serving the first day or two, but then their appetites will increase.

If a typical package of food is supposed to serve six people, assume it will serve only three, maybe four, depending on the ages and genders of the group. Pasta meals are usually good choices. They are lightweight, easy to prepare, filling, and very satisfying.

With menu and quantities of food to be purchased in hand, it is finally time to head for the supermarket.

Trail Wisdom

It always helps to have some extra food as a backup in case someone is still hungry. Who doesn't love mac 'n cheese? Mac 'n cheese is lightweight, doesn't take up much room, and is easy to prepare. Bring a few boxes along. They almost always get eaten.

Beverages on the Trail

The most important thing on the trail is that people stay well hydrated. Usually that means drinking plenty of water. Some people prefer flavored beverages like lemonade or Gatorade. By all means, bring whatever people will drink.

Warm beverages—hot cocoa, tea, or coffee—are usually appreciated at breakfast and dinner, especially in cool weather. It's important to keep people drinking and staying hydrated. No one should start the day's hike already dehydrated.

A word of caution about alcohol and caffeine: lots of people enjoy bringing a bottle of wine on the trail. Sharing a little wine around a campfire adds to the pleasure of the experience. So does a cup of hot coffee. Some people, of course, cannot get going in the morning without a cup or two of coffee. That's fine. Realize, though, that alcohol and caffeine are diuretics, which means they cause dehydration, not hydration. The consumption of alcoholic or caffeinated beverages should not be a major source of one's daily intake of fluids. Enjoy other drinks, but still drink plenty of water. Leave the caffeinated soft drinks at home.

Bear Canisters

A serious limitation on how much food can be carried occurs when you are going to be backpacking in bear country. The old days of bear-bagging your food over a tree limb may not work where you are going, and in some wilderness areas, bear-bagging may not be allowed. You may be required to purchase or rent a bear canister for your food.

A bear canister takes up a lot of space in a pack. If your group will be carrying bear canisters, you may be forced to restrict yourselves to freeze-dried, or at least dehydrated, foods. If you are going to be on the trail for only two or three days, this probably will not be a problem. For hikes of longer duration, you may be forced to restock your food supply at shorter intervals than you would otherwise.

Living off the Land

According to the 1959 edition of the Boy Scout Handbook, the one I used when I was a Scout, to become a First Class Scout I had to satisfy the following requirement: "Find at least four different edible wild greens, roots, buds, shoots, nuts, or fruits. Prepare and eat one of them selected by your leader." Suggested wild food items to look for—to paraphrase the book—included the following:

> ➤ Water cress and sheep sorrel: Eat raw

> ➤ Milkweed shoots: Cook and serve like asparagus

> ➤ Wild rice: Soak overnight, then boil in water

> ➤ Roots and tubers of Indian cucumber, arrowhead, cattail, hog peanut, Jerusalem artichoke, and chufa grass: Boil in water or roast in the coals of your campfire

> ➤ First-year roots of burdock: Best if dug up in the fall

Do you even know what most of those plants are? I certainly don't.

Fast-forward to the 1990 edition of the Boy Scout Handbook. That requirement is gone, and it still is from the current edition. Why? Because hundreds of thousands of eager Boy Scouts were munching up the meadows and hillsides like so many sheep in a pasture. As the number of Boy Scouts grew, if that requirement had been left in the handbook, a lot of native plants would have become extinct! Not to mention how many Scouts probably suffered in the meantime from food poisoning by eating the wrong plants.

The lesson to be learned from this story is do not try to live off the land (with a few exceptions). In national parks and monuments, it is illegal to dig up plants without a permit. And, really, would you be able to tell the difference between an edible plant and a poisonous one? The distinction is more difficult than it might seem. Some plants are edible during some seasons of the year and poisonous during other seasons. Parts of some plants are edible and other parts of the same plant are poisonous.

Would you pluck any old mushroom out of the ground and pop it in your mouth? I hope not. Just as distinguishing edible from toxic mushrooms takes an expert, distinguishing edible from toxic plants takes a lot of practice, if not the knowledge of an expert. Realize that you could get really sick, maybe even die, if you make a mistake.

Trail Wisdom

Do not try to live off the land. You are not Daniel Boone. You probably do not have the skills. Plus, spare the plants and animals. They're having a hard enough time surviving as it is.

Exceptions

I said there are a few exceptions to the prohibition of trying to live off the land. One exception is that picking and eating wild berries is usually fine as long as you know what it is you are eating. Fortunately, some foods, such as berries, do not taste good if they are not good for you. One bite and you are likely to spit them out. I love to find a blackberry patch in season. Wild strawberries, raspberries, huckleberries, gooseberries, and elderberries are all possibilities in the right locations and at right time of year.

The one concern with picking wild berries is if you are in bear country. Bears love wild berries, too. Before you plunge into a berry patch with a pot to fill, check first to see if Mr. or Mrs. Bruin is already there. If so, steer a wide berth. Intruding on a bear's territory is definitely an invitation for trouble.

Fishing is usually safe, too. As long as you have a state fishing license and are not in a place where fishing is specifically prohibited, catch and eat all the fish you want and the law allows. In fact, if you know you are going to be in an area where fish are abundant—and you have reasonably decent fishing skills—you might plan on fish for some of your meals. Supplementing the food you are carrying with fresh fish certainly adds variety to a menu, and—perhaps even more important—allows you to carry less food on your back.

Have a backup plan, though, if the fish are not biting. One summer I went on a week-long backpacking trip in the High Sierras of California with a group that did quite a bit of fishing.

People were very successful. The fish were small, but there were a lot of them and we ate well.

Another summer I went on a week-long backpacking trip with a large group in the mountains of southwestern Colorado. One of the men claimed we did not need to bring any food; we could eat fish three times a day. Several people spent a considerable amount of time fishing and what do you suppose was the result? You've got it. One fish was finally caught on our last night on the trail. I was in charge of the food for that trip. It was a good thing I had not planned on fish three times a day.

The lesson to be learned from these stories is that if you are backpacking in a state like Montana, and a river runs through it, the fishing is probably good and you can depend on fish for dinner. Otherwise, do not depend on fish. Catching a few fish makes a great addition to your meals, but be sure to have enough food with you if the fish aren't biting.

Another exception to my advice of not trying to live off the land is if you become lost or injured, and living off the land could mean the difference between life and death. Although you can easily go a couple of weeks or more without food, in cold weather you may need to eat to stoke your "internal fire" and stay warm. In a survival situation, it is likely that no one is going to fault you for digging up wild plants or skinning a squirrel or two. You can deal with the consequences later. Precautions about eating poisonous plants still apply. Be careful what you eat. Better yet, don't hike alone, or at least let someone know exactly where you are going and when you should be expected to return. That way help should arrive before matters get too out of hand.

Have Everything You Need

At home before your hike, begin laying out the food items according to meal. Start with day one. Put everything necessary for breakfast, lunch, and dinner into small piles. Do the same for day two and each subsequent day.

Determine which meals require cooking and how much cooking they require—just boiling a few cups of water or simmering in a pot for an hour. The number of meals that require cooking will determine how much fuel you need to bring. If you have just bought a brand-new backpacking stove, it is well worth your time to cook a couple of meals at home for practice—at least boil a couple pots of water. See how much fuel is used. That should tell you how much fuel your group needs to carry. White gas goes further than propane or butane. Stoves of different designs vary widely in how much fuel they use. If in doubt, plan to carry more fuel than you think you will need.

Trail Wisdom

Be sure to pack a measuring cup. Freeze-dried food in particular must be prepared according to the directions. If 1 cup (236 ml) of boiling water is required, be sure you are adding exactly 1 cup (236 ml). Too little water and the contents of the packet will not cook completely; too much water and your dinner will be soggy.

Once you lay out the food, carefully read the instructions on the packages to find out what ingredients are needed, such as powdered milk, butter, vegetable oil, or eggs, to make the food. In cool weather, fresh eggs or egg substitute should be okay for a couple of days. If in doubt, use powdered eggs. In warm weather, sticks of butter will melt. Carrying squeeze containers of butter usually works much better. Vegetable oil can be a problem. Be sure you carry it in a tightly sealed plastic bottle. For insurance, place the bottle inside a zippered bag. In fact, any liquid ingredients should be carried in sealed bags. It is a real nuisance if they spill inside your pack. For one thing, the odor is an open invitation to animals to find out what is making your pack smell so good.

Trail Wisdom

One of the problems with carrying liquids or perishable foods in your pack is their odor. Liquids can spill easily in a pack. Since odors attract animals, keep liquids and perishables to a minimum. The same goes for toiletries. Leave perfumes at home. The less fragrance, the better.

When you are sure you have everything you need for each meal, open each of the packages. Usually the different ingredients are in their own plastic bags inside the package. Put those bags into zippered bags and label them with the day and meal: Day One–Breakfast, Day One–Lunch, etc.

If you are going to divide food among several people, you might consider recording the weight of each bag on its label. That way, giving everyone equitable quantities of food to carry may be easier to determine.

Finally, cut out the cooking instructions and put them in the bag along with the food for that meal. Discarding the original packages cuts down on the amount of trash that you will have on the trail.

Food items that would tend to crumble in a pack can be packaged in plastic containers. This is especially true for bread, cookies, brownies, or other baked goods.

Tuna, chicken, and beef can be found in the canned goods section of your supermarket. Canned fish and meat does not spoil, but the cans do represent trash that has to be packed out. While canned meat is probably advisable for meals that occur several days into the hike, fresh meat can be purchased for at least the first night on the trail. All perishable food, of course, stays in the refrigerator or freezer until you are ready to leave home.

Make a list of perishable items that you have to remember to retrieve from the refrigerator or freezer before leaving home. It is probably best to plan to eat these foods early in the hike. In even mild weather, food such as beef or chicken should be kept frozen until you leave the trailhead. Meat can spend the first day thawing and should be ready to cook by the time you arrive at your first night's campsite.

Distributing Food

If everyone in your group can carry about the same amount of weight, then you can plan to distribute zippered bags so that each person is carrying at least one meal for each one or two days of the hike. Put people's names on the bags so everyone will know which bag is whose. If you have people of different sizes and abilities, it works best to assign meals for the first day or two to the smallest or least physically fit members of the group. That way they have to carry food for only one or two days. Let the larger and fitter members of the group carry the meals for days three and four, since that means they will have to carry the food longer. Most people are pretty understanding about this arrangement.

Easy-to-Prepare Foods

Walking the aisles of packaged and canned foods at your local supermarket should give you plenty of ideas for foods to take to the backcountry with you. Some meals are easier to prepare than others.

Most of the breakfast and lunch foods are packaged individually and are usually more expensive per person than foods that are packaged to feed a family. Dinners may serve two to six people and are usually easy to prepare. Examples of package weights and number of servings are listed below for dinners. Remember, though, the rule of thumb that a package will actually feed half the number of people it claims to feed. Most packaged foods, however, tend to be inexpensive.

Breakfast

Breakfast may be the easiest meal to make when backpacking. Here are some ideas:

➤ Granola bars

➤ Cold cereal

➤ Oatmeal

➤ Cream of Wheat

➤ Granola

➤ Hot cocoa

➤ Fruit drinks

➤ Tea and coffee

Lunch

By lunchtime, hikers have worked up an appetite and are eager for lunch to replenish their energy. Here are some lunch ideas:

➤ Granola bars (same as breakfast choices)

➤ Energy bars

➤ Peanut butter and jelly sandwiches

➤ Squeeze cheese and crackers

➤ Beef or turkey jerky

➤ Tuna salad and cracker packets

➤ Mixed nuts

➤ Chocolate bars

➤ Cookies and brownies

➤ Gatorade

➤ Lemonade

Dinners

Dinners are likely the most involved and complex meal to plan for and prepare while on a multiday hike. Here are some dinner ideas along with advice on portions:

➤ Packaged foods

➤ Couscous	6-oz (170-g) package	Serves 3 people
➤ Taboule	5 oz (142 g)	Serves 5
➤ Rice pilaf	6 oz (170-g)	Serves 3
➤ Red beans and rice	8 oz (227 g)	Serves 4
➤ Rice a Roni	4–6 oz (113–170 g)	Serves 2–3
➤ Macaroni and cheese	7 oz (198 g)	Serves 3
➤ Chicken-flavored fettuccini; add canned chicken	4.5 oz (128 g)	Serves 2
➤ Hamburger Helper; add hamburger	6.5 oz (184 g)	Serves 5
➤ Chicken Helper; add chicken	6.5 oz (184 g)	Serves 5
➤ Tuna Helper; add canned tuna	6.5 oz (184 g)	Serves 5
➤ Ramen noodle soups	3 oz (85 g)	Serves 2

➤ Canned goods

➤ Soups of all flavors

➤ Chili

➤ Spaghetti

➤ Ravioli

Conclusion

Most people have a more enjoyable time hiking and camping if meals are hearty and good tasting. Cooking on the trail can be fun, and eating meals together contributes to the camaraderie of the experience. Plan meals that people are going to enjoy. If you need to reduce the weight everyone is carrying, cut back on clothes—you can always wear a set of clothes an extra day or two—but don't cut back on food. You are out to enjoy yourself. Good meals are part of the enjoyment of backpacking.

CHAPTER 4

Packing for the Trail

In This Chapter

➤ Keep weight down

➤ Food is fuel

➤ Checklist

➤ Home again

You have been planning this trek for weeks, or maybe months. The big day is arriving! It is time to pack. Remember that you are going to be carrying everything—literally everything—on your back. While you are still at home is the time to do two things:

1. Be sure you have everything you will need

2. Keep the total weight within the range that you can carry

Some things are easy to remember. I keep my tent, backpack, sleeping bag, sleeping pad, ground cloth, cooking kit, and utensils together where I know I can find them easily. If you do not trust your memory, make a physical checklist of everything you will need. As you assemble your gear in one place, check off each item on the list.

Trail Wisdom

It may truly be said that a backpacker's best friends are duct tape and zippered bags. Duct tape will repair just about anything. Zippered bags will keep everything dry. Be sure to carry both with you.

Trail Wisdom

On your first backpacking trips, limit the total weight you are carrying on your back to 25 percent of your own weight.

Weigh Everything

If you do not own a bathroom scale but are on the threshold of entering into the wonderful world of backpacking, go out and buy a scale. The accepted rule is that, on your first treks anyway, you should not try to carry more than 25 percent of your weight on your back. If you find that you are in good condition and you can carry more, that's fine. But don't overdo it the first time out. I've seen people on the trail actually throw away tents (possibly rather expensive tents) they decided were too heavy for them. Let time and experience be your guide. If someday you decide that you can carry 50 percent of your weight, go for it.

Weigh everything. Start with the gear you must carry:

➤ Sleeping bag

➤ Tent (if you're expecting wet weather)

➤ Cooking utensils,

➤ Fuel

Let's consider a couple of examples:

1. You weigh 160 pounds (73 kg); 25 percent of your weight is 40 pounds (18 kg). Your sleeping bag weighs 3 pounds (1.5 kg), your tent 8 pounds (3.5 kg), your cooking and eating utensils and fuel another 4 pounds (2 kg), and your pack itself a few pounds.

You will need to carry water; don't forget about water! Water will probably be the heaviest item in your pack, about 2 pounds per quart (1 kg per liter). Let's say that water sources are situated far enough apart on your route that you should carry 1 gallon (4 L) at a time. That's about 8 pounds (3.5 kg). Let's say that leaves you about 14 pounds (6 kg) for everything else—food, clothing, sleeping pad, camera, paperback book, water filter, soap, toothbrush, toothpaste, toilet paper—everything.

Here's where judicious choices of food come in. I recommend scanning the supermarket shelves for as much dry packaged food as possible. It weighs a lot less than canned goods and is much cheaper than dehydrated meals. Depending on the time of year, clothing can be the next heaviest item, and probably the bulkiest. But, for a two- to three-night outing, you can probably fit in what you need and keep everything under 40 pounds (18 kg). Unless you're expecting inclement weather, this may be when you decide if you really need to pack a tent.

2. Suppose, though, you only weigh 140 pounds (64 kg); 25 percent of your weight is only 35 pounds (16 kg). That means when you get down to everything else on your list, you only have room for 9 pounds (4 kg). Food and clothing alone are going to be tough to keep under 9 pounds (4 kg), let alone the other items on the list.

Hopefully, you're getting the idea. Lay everything out in front of you, on a tarp for example. Picture how you expect to use each of the items. What do you really need? I can certainly tell you some of the things you definitely do not need. Nobody needs to carry a shovel (even a small folding shovel), an axe, or a saw. Leave those things at home.

With the equipment and supplies you really cannot go without, ask yourself what your lightest weight choices are. Substitute aluminum for steel. Substitute plastic for metal. Plan on one-pot meals. And, by all means, divide supplies among members of the group.

Personal Anecdote

Don't laugh. You'd be amazed at what some people bring on a backpacking trip. I've seen people lugging a huge ice chest on wheels down a trail. I've also seen guitar cases lashed to backpacks.

Trail Wisdom

Lay out all your food for the trip and make sure you have only what is necessary and sufficient for each meal and for snacks during the day. Leave the rest at home. There's no point in arriving home with uneaten food.

Food

If you eat a lot at home, chances are you'll want to eat a lot when backpacking. We've already covered menus in Chapter 3. When considering weight, remember that there are three important differences when eating on the trail:

1. There is no refrigeration

2. You have to carry it on your back

3. You don't have a microwave oven

Be sure to consider each of these issues when packing food and the fuel needed to cook it. Keep the weight as light as possible, but be sure you're not going to run out of food before you get home.

Miscellaneous

I'm not sure how people backpacked before the invention of zippered plastic bags—small ones for food, first aid supplies, and personal hygiene products; larger ones for clothing. Plastic bags keep items separate, clean, and—most important—dry.

Checklist of Gear for a Backpacking Trip

Make a checklist of everything you need, and double- and triple-check that you're remembering everything. The following list is assuming a long weekend backpacking trip—three days and two nights on the trail. You can leave out or add items according to the circumstances of your own hike.

➤ Hiking boots or sturdy shoes

➤ Backpack

➤ Sleeping bag

➤ Pocketknife

➤ Rain gear

➤ Clothing—the kind of clothes depends on season

➤ Water bottles

➤ Camp stove and fuel

➤ Matches

➤ Cooking pot or pan

➤ Flashlight or headlamp (or both)

➤ Extra batteries and bulb

➤ Cup or mug

➤ Snacks

➤ Eating utensils

➤ Sunscreen

➤ Biodegradable soap

➤ Toilet paper

➤ Toiletry items

➤ Feminine hygiene products

➤ Insect repellent (in season)

➤ Plastic trowel—for digging catholes (a pit for feces)

➤ Pack cover

➤ Trash bags

Following are items two or more people can share:

➤ Tent (optional in good weather)

➤ First aid kit

➤ Map and compass

➤ Stove and fuel

➤ Cooking gear and eating utensils

➤ About 20 feet (6 m) of rope (or more)

➤ Zippered plastic bags

➤ Ground cloth

➤ Water purification system

➤ Food

And here are optional items you may want to bring with you:

➤ Sleeping pad

➤ Hiking stick or poles

➤ Sunglasses

➤ Hat—one with a wide brim in sunny weather

➤ Camera

➤ Binoculars

➤ Notebook and pen or pencil

➤ Global positioning system

➤ Field guides

➤ Paperback book

➤ Fishing gear

When You Get Home

Your backpacking trip is not over just because you are home again. Spend a little time storing your gear correctly, and you'll be glad you did when you're ready for your next hike. If you just throw everything on a shelf, you will regret it the next time you have an outing planned. Proper care and storage of your gear are essential.

Sleeping Bags

It's very simple: wet fabrics mildew. The first rule when you get home is to dry your sleeping bag thoroughly.

Unzip your sleeping bag completely and spread it out where it can dry. If you encountered wet weather and muddy campsites on your hike, then laundering your sleeping bag is probably in order.

Dirty sleeping bags lose their loft and therefore much of their insulation. Besides, the longer the dirt has to dry and adhere to the bag, the harder it is later to clean the bag. It's best to wash your sleeping bag right away, before you even think about storing it. Don't put off caring for your sleeping bag properly. Clean and dry it now and it will be in good shape for your next outing.

There are different techniques for storing sleeping bags. Down bags are best hung from a ceiling. Otherwise, a down bag left in its stuff sack for long periods of time will lose much of its loft and insulating ability. If you don't have a good place to hang your sleeping bag, at least don't cram it into its stuff sack. A large, clean lawn trash bag will do. Just put the sleeping bag loosely into the trash bag.

Synthetic sleeping bags are also best stored loosely in large plastic bags, not in their stuff sacks. If you use your synthetic bag frequently, however, you will probably find that storing it in its stuff sack won't do any harm.

Tents

I once made the mistake of putting away a canvas tent for a couple of weeks not realizing it was damp. We had not had any rain on our camping trip, but we did camp for a couple of nights on the northern California coast, where we had heavy fog at night. From there we took a couple of weeks off from camping to visit relatives before going to Yosemite National Park to finish our vacation.

When we set up the tent at Yosemite, we found that it had badly mildewed. Had I just unpacked the tent at the first relatives' house and let the tent dry, it would not have mildewed. I learned my lesson: never store a tent in its storage bag until the tent is completely dry. Remember, too, that in addition to the fabric mildewing, metal zippers can rust.

Cookware and Eating Utensils

I think I do a pretty decent job of washing and sanitizing my pots, pans, plates, bowls, cups, and utensils while I'm on the trail. Even if you do the same, it doesn't hurt to wash them again when you get home. In particular, if breakfast was the last meal on the trail, you may have put everything away still wet.

All your cooking and eating gear is probably made of aluminum or plastic, so rust likely is not a problem, but it's best to make sure everything is clean and dry before storage. You definitely don't want bacteria or mold growing on your utensils because they were put away with food scraps still clinging to them.

First Aid Supplies

Did you use any of your first aid supplies? Replenish your first aid kit right away when you get home. If you don't, you'll probably forget about it later; when you need something on your next hike, you won't have it. Band-Aids and gauze pads don't remain sterile indefinitely. If what you have is getting old, replace it with fresh supplies.

Your Next Trip

Now is a good time to be thinking ahead to your next trip. Did you bring too much cooking equipment, too little, or just the right amount? While the meals on your hike are still fresh in your memory, it's a good time to make decisions for next time. If there were pots, pans, plates, bowls, cups, or utensils that you didn't use, then on a future trip of the same length you probably won't use them either. Separate out the nonessential gear and store in one place the items you know you'll want on the next trip. Conversely, if you wished you had had a different size pan, or an extra plate or bowl, then add it to your kit now so you'll have it next time.

Conclusion

Organizing and packing gear builds anticipation. Sometimes the planning can be almost as much fun as the trip itself. Pack enough of the right gear, food, and clothing, and your trip will be even more fun!

PART TWO

On the Trail

CHAPTER 5

 **Trail Etiquette**

In This Chapter

➤ People you meet on the trail

➤ People in your own group

This chapter is about the golden rule as it relates to backpacking: do unto others on the trail as you would have others do unto you. In other words, be considerate of other people and treat them the way you would like them to treat you. There are two aspects to trail etiquette:

1. How you interact with other people you encounter when hiking and camping

2. How you interact with other members of your own group

Encounters on the Trail

The assumption of this book is that you are a hiker. Your means of locomotion is your own two feet. That is not necessarily true, however, of everyone you meet on trails. Many trails, especially in urban areas, are intended for multiple uses. Equestrians (riders on horseback) may be on the trail, too. In some areas cyclists, particularly mountain bikers, may be sharing the trail. Since most trails are only a few feet wide, what should you do when you see horseback rider or a bicyclist coming toward you?

Horses on the Trail

I do not have a lot of experience with horses, but I have done a reasonable amount of trail riding in my life. At least I have learned how to groom and saddle a horse and how to get it to trot and canter. I have also learned to respect horses, both for the magnificent animals they are, and for their unpredictability. I have no problem sharing a trail with equestrians. They are enjoying nature in their own way just as I am; to each his own! Given that, there are some rules of etiquette that apply to the trail.

Trail Wisdom

Horses and their riders always have the right-of-way. Hikers and cyclists must yield to anyone on horseback.

Horses always have the right-of-way over hikers and cyclists. (For one thing, horses are a lot bigger than we are!) That is a big *always*, and one that is very important to pay attention to for the safety of the rider and of the hiker or cyclist.

Horses spook easily. A hiker, especially a hiker wearing a backpack, may look to a horse like a bear. At the very least, a horse may perceive any unknown person as a threat. You do not want to find yourself in the path of a panicky horse.

I learned a lesson the hard way—at least it was the hard way for the rider. I was hiking up a moderately steep incline. A horse that I had not heard coming down the hill, and did not see until the last moment, suddenly appeared about 30 to 40 feet (9 to 12 m) in front of me. The horse saw me and stopped abruptly. It stopped so quickly that its rider's momentum carried him over the horse's head, and he landed flat on his back.

A horse's head can be 7 or 8 feet (2 or 2.5 m) from the ground, so that is quite a distance to fall, not to mention the fact that the surface of the trail was hard and somewhat rocky. I thought for sure the rider had to have broken something. I ran forward asking him if he was all right. I was greatly relieved when he simply stood up, brushed himself off, and climbed back on his horse. I waited on the side of the trail for him to pass.

During the entire incident he never said a word to me. I don't know if he was too embarrassed to say anything, or if he blamed me for his tumble. It doesn't matter; I resolved then and there to try not to ever have a repeat of the incident, and so far there has not been one.

Fortunately, horses are often heard before they are seen. If I hear a horse approaching, or if I see a horse within a distance of about 50 yards (15 m), I step off the trail. If I can't step off immediately, then I try to do so within the next few yards or I back up a few yards. Most of the time I can do so; hiking along a cliff face is probably the main exception. In that case, I hug the wall of the cliff.

If the trail is on a hillside, I step off the trail on the downhill side so that I am lower than the horse. I am 5 feet 10 inches (1.5 m) tall and full-grown horses are taller than I am. If I were to step off the trail on the uphill side, it is possible that my head would be higher than the horse's head. A horse might perceive me as more of a threat than if I were standing below it.

Next I begin talking to the rider or riders so the horse hears my voice. If I sound like a human, then I am less likely to be mistaken for a bear. I try to speak in a relaxed, cheerful tone, again for the horse's comfort. My voice also alerts the rider to my presence.

Most riders know their animals. If riders know that their horses spook easily, they may already have their own plans for how to handle encounters with hikers or cyclists. Sometimes riders will stop, wait, and ask me to walk around. Other times, they thank me for having stepped off the trail and I wait for them to pass. We continue talking until we are past each other.

The most important thing is for the horse to know that I do not present a threat. If a horse is going in the same direction I am, then it is prudent just to wait and let it pass. As a general rule, horses walk faster than humans do, so it really doesn't make any sense to try to hustle ahead of one.

I try very hard not to stand directly behind a horse because the horse cannot see me, which may seem threatening to it, and because horses kick. If the horse perceives me as a threat, its first line of defense would be to give me a swift kick. I prefer to avoid that.

Trail Wisdom

When you encounter equestrians, speak to them in a soft, gentle voice to alert the horses to your presence and so the horses know you are not a wild animal.

In some wilderness areas it is possible that you may encounter a pack train of horses or mules. Chances are the animals belong to a commercial outfitter. Outfitters know their animals. The outfitter will probably tell you whether you should wait or go around the animals. It is prudent and courteous to follow his instructions.

Bicycles on the Trail

Cyclists must also surrender the right-of-way to equestrians. It is just as important for cyclists to get themselves and their bikes off the trail as it is for hikers to do so. In encounters between cyclists and hikers, however, cyclists have the right-of-way. It is much easier for hikers to halt and step off the trail than it is for cyclists to do so.

Going downhill, cyclists may have built up a bit of momentum and may have a hard time stopping safely. Since stopping quickly might be difficult for them, it's safest if you just step aside. Going uphill, most cyclists are probably moving pretty slowly, so it is possible they might prefer to stop and let hikers pass. Let the cyclist decide. At least bicycles don't spook, so there is probably no danger associated with who passes whom.

That brings up what is probably the main hazard associated with bikes on trails. Hikers usually walk at speeds of only 2 to 3 miles per hour (3 to 5 kph) depending on the terrain and how much weight they are carrying. Horses may walk at speeds of 4 to 6 mph (6 to 10 kph). A bicycle going downhill, however, may be traveling at speeds of 8 to 10 mph (13 to 16 kph) or more depending on the terrain and trail conditions. Encounters between cyclists and hikers or horses can occur so quickly that there isn't very much time to react.

It is the cyclist's responsibility to maintain control of his bike and to be aware of other people on the trail. Most cyclists are responsible, just as most drivers behave responsibly. Unfortunately, there are always the cyclists who are riding faster than conditions permit. I think the issue is that they may have just spent quite a bit of time struggling to ride uphill and are now trying to make up for lost time by going downhill as fast as they can.

Get to know which trails are likely to have cyclists on them, and try to stay alert. In the event of an encounter, the cyclist has the right-of-way and it is your responsibility to move to the side.

Other Hikers on the Trail

What about other hikers on the trail? Passing, or being passed, by other hikers is much more frequent than passing equestrians or cyclists. One rule that may not be well known among hikers is that on a slope, the hiker walking uphill has the right-of-way. It is the responsibility of downhill hikers to move to the side and let uphill hikers pass.

The reason for this is that it is much easier for someone who is walking downhill to get started again than it is for someone who is walking uphill. Downhill hikers need only lean forward and let gravity do the rest. Uphill hikers lose their momentum when they stop. They are working against gravity to start walking again. That requires just a little bit of extra effort on their part. The point is that if there is insufficient room on the trail for both hikers to keep walking, someone has to stop. I don't know who made the rule, but somebody once decided that the uphill hiker should have the right-of-way, and that is the practice.

Whenever I am hiking downhill and stop for people who are hiking uphill, they will often thank me. After all, hikers do tend to be courteous. I always say, "You're welcome; you have the right-of-way." That way if they didn't know about the rule, then hopefully the next time they are hiking downhill, they will know to yield the right-of-way to any uphill hikers they encounter. There is nothing wrong with educating people, and sometimes people even thank me for telling them about the right-of-way rule. On those occasions when I am hiking uphill and downhill hikers stop for me, I am also sure to thank them.

Unfortunately, things do not always work out the way they should when I am the one who is hiking uphill. Sometimes a lone hiker or a couple will stop for me, but if I encounter a group of several people, I guess they figure there is strength in numbers. Apparently they feel that it is harder for three or four people to stop than for just one person to stop. So, I just stop and wait for them. It is not a big enough issue to get upset about, and I just let it pass.

People in Your Own Group

The trail interactions I have described so far are brief and tend not to be serious. People pass you on the trail and you go your separate ways. People in your hiking group, however, are a different story. At a minimum, you are going to be with them on the trail for much of the day. If you're on a multiday backpacking trip, you will be with them on the trail for several days. In many situations, you will probably be hiking with family members or other close friends. On the other hand, if you are hiking with a club, a Scouting or other youth organization, or a professionally led group, you are likely to be spending time with people you have not hiked with before and who you may or may not know very well.

Group interactions on the trail are not terribly different from group interactions in Little League, service organizations, the workplace, places of worship, or other clubs to which we might belong. Some people are leaders; others are followers. Some people are impatient with everyone they meet; others have the patience of Job. Some people feel slighted by almost everything other people say or do; others are not ruffled in the slightest. As with any other situation, you need to be aware of the needs and limitations of your companions and to anticipate interactions that make everyone feel uncomfortable.

One of the first problems in hiking is that everyone likes to hike at his own pace. Some people hit the trail and act like they are in a race to get to the finish line. Other people just mosey along and figure they will get to the end of the trail when they get there. Hikers call this sauntering. Most people in a group will fall somewhere in between.

The best solution is to compromise and find a pace that gets your group where they are going but without being too fast for the slowest members. In practice that rarely works out. I have found that it is probably best to let the fast hikers, if they are adults, go at their own pace and just hope they don't take a wrong fork in the trail somewhere and get lost in the process.

Trail Wisdom

As much as possible, let people hike at their own pace. However, do not let the group get so strung out along the trail that there is the danger of someone getting lost.

In the age of cellular phones, I suppose it is possible that people can stay in communication with each other if they get lost on the trail. It has been my experience, however, that there is rarely cellular phone coverage in wilderness areas. Hiking through canyons or hilly terrain can easily put a person in a position where there is no direct line of sight to a cellular tower, so there is no reception. There is nothing wrong with carrying a phone on the trail. Just realize that it may not work when you most need it; do not fool yourself into thinking that your phone is going to save you if you get into a difficult situation.

I have often backpacked in groups where at least one person has never been backpacking before. I have backpacked with young people who have never slept outdoors before. People should be willing to look out for each other.

Unless someone else volunteers to bring up the rear, I usually take on that role, especially if I am hiking with young people. My rule in that situation is that no one is allowed to hike behind me. I do not want to run the risk that an inexperienced or slow hiker arrives alone at a fork in the trail, really does not know which fork to take, and chooses the wrong one.

Likewise, it is prudent to have an experienced hiker positioned at the front of the group with a similar rule—no one goes in front of the leader. My advice is that the leader should always wait at any fork in the trail until the rest of the group catches up. If one person is going to head off in the wrong direction, then it is best if everyone else at least goes the same way so the group doesn't get separated. Although it is true that at least one person in the group should be carrying a topographic map of the trail, it is also true that there are side trails that may not show up on the map, or there may not be any signage indicating which fork is the correct trail. It's best to stay together.

Sometimes nothing is more discouraging to slow hikers than to feel that the rest of the group has left them behind. Time after time, I have arrived at a rest stop with the slow hikers and found the fast hikers waiting for us. Instead of the fast hikers greeting the slow hikers with something friendly and encouraging, it is more likely that they will say something like, "It's about time you showed up; we've been waiting an hour for you." Then, just as the slow hikers drop their packs and sit down to take a break themselves, the people who have been waiting for them jump to their feet, throw their packs on, and race on ahead. The slow hikers have been left alone again.

Pretty soon the slow hikers stop feeling like they are part of the group. When people become too discouraged, their first backpacking trip may end up being their last backpacking trip. The slow hikers are doing nothing wrong, and certainly nothing that deserves derision or criticism. Give them a break; be encouraging.

Trail Wisdom

Presumably, you hike because you enjoy hiking. Your enthusiasm should be infectious. Help people who are new to hiking or backpacking have a good time. Don't be the reason their first backpacking trip is also their last backpacking trip.

Be patient with others. If it really looks like someone is struggling, you might even offer to help carry something for them. After many years of hiking, I have become convinced that whether or not someone makes it through a hike is mostly psychological. Just knowing that their companions care and are willing to help can make a world of difference.

At the Campsite

It is amazing what kind of friction can develop between people at the end of a day of hiking. I have seen people get into arguments over who gets the best sleeping spot. There are people who zealously guard their personal space; lay out your sleeping spot too close to them and you have invaded their space. The moral of the story is watch where other people are setting up camp, and be sensitive to their sense of privacy.

In some groups, everyone brings their own food and does their own cooking. In other groups, someone is chosen to plan meals for the whole group and package the food. In this scenario, if most people in the group are looking forward to beef stew at the end of the day, it is probably better not to have a vegetarian in charge of the menu. Hopefully, the group agrees upon the menu before food is purchased, but if that is not the case, watch out. Someone is bound to complain.

Trail Wisdom

Even if the weather turns out to be perfect, even if the trail conditions are ideal, and even if everyone remembered to bring everything that was needed for the hike, a backpacking trip can still be a disaster if people don't get along. Be extra sensitive to other people's feelings and needs. If tensions seem to be developing, then by all means talk to each other. Not communicating isn't going to solve any problems.

When is the group expecting to break camp in the morning and hit the trail again? I have hiked with people who feel that everyone should be on the trail no later than sunrise, and I have hiked with people who are perfectly happy to start their day at 9 or 10 a.m. Again, people may need to compromise. It is probably a good idea the night before to discuss the matter. If tomorrow's destination is only five or six hours away, a very early start probably isn't necessary. But if the next camp site is eight to ten hours away, it is not unreasonable to expect people to get an early start.

I think a good rule of thumb is that it is desirable to reach the next camp site before sunset, unless the group consists of very experienced hikers who all carry headlamps and are accustomed to night hiking. Getting everyone to camp before sunset helps assure everyone makes it, there is still sufficient daylight to set up camp, and preparations can get started for the evening meal. Being able to stop before sunset is especially important in winter when temperatures can drop dramatically after dark. It is probably less of an issue in the summer, but in the summer sunset is much later anyway.

One time I was on a three-day, two-night backpacking trip with the Boy Scouts. The scoutmaster and I stayed at the rear of the group helping along a boy who was new to scouting and who had never been backpacking before. As the day progressed, we knew we were falling behind the rest of the group. The new Scout became very discouraged by not being able to keep up with the others. I think he assumed the other Scouts were miles ahead of us. Fortunately, the other Scouts had adults with them, so we weren't worried about them.

Finally, the sun began to set. Not knowing how far away we were from the rest of the troop, the scoutmaster and I decided that the three of us would stop for the night and camp rather than hike in the dark. It turned out to be a very enjoyable evening. It was certainly a lot quieter to camp with only one teenage boy than with a dozen. The next morning, we discovered that we had stopped only a mile short of the rest of the troop. When the new Scout discovered he really had not been very far behind the rest of the troop, he felt encouraged enough that he had no trouble keeping up with them the remaining two days of the hike. Sometimes, just a little encouragement like that is all it takes for people who are new to hiking to discover abilities they didn't know they have and to have a good time.

Trail Wisdom

Try to set your group's pace so that everyone arrives at the designated campsite before dark. That way everyone can set up camp and at least get the evening meal started while they can still see what they're doing.

Other Groups at Campsites

Unless you are backpacking in a truly remote wilderness area, chances are that more than one group may be sharing a camping area for the night. This is true not just along popular routes such as the Appalachian Trail in the eastern United States or the High Sierra camps at Yosemite National Park. Certain lakes, meadows, or streams may be popular destinations in any given area, and it is just natural that more than one group at a time may be camping at them.

Noise is one of the major issues when multiple groups are camping at the same site. Some people like to party all night, while others who are camping nearby may want to hit the sack shortly after sunset so they can get an early start in the morning. Out of respect to other people, it is simply courteous to keep the noise down, and not just after sunset—pretty much all the time.

Trail Wisdom

Leave electronics at home. When hiking and camping, tune into the sounds of nature, not to an iPod.

Most people go into the wilderness partly for the peace and quiet the wilderness affords. They want to be able to hear birds singing and brooks babbling, not country and western music from someone else's portable CD player. Whether there is a place in the wilderness for electronics is a subject of debate, but courtesy dictates that nobody should have to listen to another person's music. At least wear earphones. Certainly after dark, the volume of all conversations and other noise should be kept to an absolute minimum.

Huts

Another issue that groups might encounter is sharing huts or shelters, such as the ones located along the Appalachian Trail. Nobody should hog a hut. If more than one group is present, then everyone needs to cooperate and give everyone some space. This is especially important in wet weather. It is poor trail manners for one group to take up all the floor space in a shelter, leaving others out in the rain. Learn to share. Who knows? You just might meet someone really interesting.

Conclusion

Rules of the trail may not be matters of life and death like they are on a highway, but they are still important. Treat others the way you want to be treated by following these rules:

> ➤ Hikers and bicyclists always yield the right-of-way to equestrians.

> ➤ Hikers always yield the right-of-way to cyclists.

> ➤ Let people hike at their own pace, but don't let anyone become separated from the rest of the group and risk the possibility of becoming lost.

> ➤ Keep the volume of conversations low.

> ➤ Leave electronics at home or wear earphones.

> ➤ Respect the privacy of others.

 Low-Impact Hiking

---

In This Chapter

➤ Leave no trace

➤ Campsites

➤ Sanitation

➤ Coastal areas

This chapter is about outdoor ethics—how we treat the natural environment. Several national programs have been developed to teach outdoor enthusiasts how to conduct themselves in the outdoors. All these programs have similar goals—preservation of the natural environment for the enjoyment of generations to come.

Tread Lightly in the Wilderness

Tread Lightly! is a public program designed to educate people about minimizing their impact on wilderness areas. TREAD is used by the program's leaders as an acronym for the following principles:

➤ Travel only where permitted.

➤ Respect the rights of others.

➤ Educate yourself.

➤ Avoid disturbing streams, meadows, wildlife areas, and other fragile environments.

➤ Drive and travel responsibly.

Let's look at each of these principles.

Trail Wisdom

Respect private property. If you must cross private property, ask the owner's permission before you do so.

Travel Only Where Permitted

Respect No Trespassing signs. Private property is just that—private; you shouldn't be on it. If private property adjoins public lands, there should be a means of bypassing the private property.

Stay on the trail. The vegetation on either side of a trail often is more fragile than it looks. Hiking compacts soil so that water is more likely to cause erosion than to be absorbed, which would cause problems if you hiked off-trail. You would likely trample flowers and other plants.

In deserts, soil is a living community of fragile microorganisms. Once disturbed, desert soils can take a century to recover. Off-trail, you're more likely to kick loose rocks and disturb the soil and organisms under the rocks.

If nothing else, trampled landscapes don't look natural anymore. You're in the wilderness to encounter nature. Keep it as pristine as possible. Let the next hikers who come along see nature in its beauty, not soil and plants that have been trampled by your thoughtlessness.

Wildlife knows where trails are. Animals may even use the trails, especially at night. Unlike people, animals generally do most of their feeding and sleeping away from trails. Wandering off established trails means you're more likely to stumble into their territory. I enjoy wildlife encounters as much as the next person, but not if it causes stress to the animals. Stumbling into a denning area where there may be young animals is just as stressful to them as it would be to you if someone stumbled into your home.

Trail Wisdom

Stay on the trail. Enjoy wildlife from a distance. If you must step off the trail, try to do so in rocky areas, where you will cause the least disturbance.

On slopes, it is especially important that you do not cut across switchbacks. Doing so contributes to increased soil erosion and deterioration of the trail. I can't begin to think of how many times I've witnessed other hikers taking shortcuts on switchbacks. Every time they have kicked loose rocks and soil and caused damage to the slope downhill from the trail.

Cutting across switchbacks can be dangerous. By definition, switchbacks follow the gentlest gradient of the landscape. By cutting across a switchback you are going up or down a slope at a steeper gradient. It's easy to slip and fall when going down a steep slope, especially if the soil is loose or you're off balance because of a heavy backpack.

Respect the Rights of Others

If you have pets with you, keep them under control. Under no circumstance should a pet be allowed to chase wildlife, nor should a pet pose a threat to other hikers. You or your pet should not be the cause of someone else's outing becoming an unpleasant one.

Trail Wisdom

Don't cut across switchbacks. It is probably impossible to cut across a switchback without doing damage. Switchbacks are there for a purpose. Stay on the trail and encourage others to do the same.

Speak softly. In other words, no loud talking or yelling. This is particularly important if you're camping close to other groups. Other people shouldn't be able to hear your voice.

I have mixed feelings about bringing electronics into wilderness areas. Personally, I feel that people should be communing with nature and not listening to rap, classic rock, or whatever other genre of music strikes their fancy. But, if you must listen to music on your hikes, wear earphones, and keep the volume at a level only you can hear.

I'm sure you're familiar with the expression pack it in, pack it out. The obvious reason for that is not to be littering the wilderness. Another reason relates to respecting other people. You don't want to see other people's litter, so you shouldn't leave litter either. It doesn't matter whether or not something is biodegradable. Chances are it isn't going to completely decompose before the next hiker comes along.

Trail Wisdom

If you come across litter on the trail, pick it up! It is not someone else's responsibility to pick up litter. It's your responsibility. It doesn't hurt to carry a plastic grocery bag in your pocket to put trash in.

You may also be familiar with the saying leave an area cleaner than you found it. Leaving a campsite exactly the way you found it may not be enough. If the previous occupants left a mess at the campsite, clean it up. One of the biggest problems is caused by campers who try to burn aluminum or steel cans, plastic, and other nonburnable trash. They end up just leaving the charred remains in the fire ring. If you find a previously used fire ring in that condition, clean it up. Put all that trash into a bag and pack it out.

Educate Yourself

Familiarize yourself ahead of time with the area in which you will be hiking. Maps are almost always available. Purchase one. Study it in advance, and carry it with you. Let someone else know where you are going. Also carry a compass and/or a GPS. Be sure you know how to use them.

You can find a lot of information on the web. Check for permit requirements, restrictions, weather alerts, and any trail closures that might affect your trip. There may be limitations on group size or where people can camp. In wilderness areas, for example, camping may be prohibited within a certain distance to a road. You need to know where you are and are not allowed to camp. Always assume that camping on private property is prohibited unless you have permission from the property owner.

Respect your own limitations. You may be comfortable hiking 15 miles (24 km) in a single day on level ground carrying only your lunch and water. But can you hike the same distance in a single day carrying a 45-pound (20. 5-kg) pack and traversing rough and possibly hilly terrain? Study the map in advance and have a good idea of how far you can go in a day and how far it is to where you want to camp. If necessary, take two days to reach a particular destination.

t
Trail Wisdom

Remember the saying burn only what is dead and down. Do not cut live trees. Don't break branches off trees, even if they look dead. Use for firewood only what's already lying on the ground.

Avoid Sensitive Areas

Sensitive areas include lakeshores, seashores, streams, meadows, marshes, swamps, deserts, and tundra. Stay on established trails. Avoid disturbing vegetation any more than is absolutely necessary. Never cut down or dig up live trees or plants. Pitch tents on rocky or gravelly areas, not in meadows or other vegetated areas. Set up camp well away from streams, lakes, and ponds. Try incredibly hard not to contaminate natural water supplies in any way.

Do not disturb archaeological or historic sites. People always like to take home souvenirs. (I know I do!) However, are you aware that removing any materials, including rocks, from national parks is prohibited by law? You might think that taking a rock with you can't possibly do any harm, but suppose all of the hundreds of millions of visitors to our national parks each took home a rock. I think you get the idea. Leave the rocks alone. If you pick up a rock to admire, put it back the way you found it.

Trail Wisdom

Federal law states, "Collection of, unauthorized removal, possession of, and sale or commercial use of rocks, minerals, and paleontological specimens, for either recreational or educational purposes, is generally prohibited in all units of the National Park System (36 C.F.R. § 2.1(a))." If you see rocks or fossils for sale in park gift shops, those specimens were gathered outside the park.

You might feel tempted to remove a prehistoric artifact out of fear that if you don't, someone else will steal or damage it. Even that is not a good idea. Much of the value of an artifact is the context in which it is found. Removing a pot, bowl, or spearhead from its original location could make it valueless to an archaeologist, who would much rather be able to examine such items *in situ*, in other words, in place. If you think an artifact could be important, report its precise location to forest or park authorities when you leave. If you carry a GPS unit with you, record the exact latitude and longitude of the site so that someone else can be sure to find it again.

Trail Wisdom

Picking wildflowers in national parks is strictly prohibited. The saying, "Take only pictures, leave only footprints" definitely applies.

Leave most manufactured objects the way you find them. A rule in the backcountry is if you encounter a gate that's closed, close it after you; if the gate was open when you found it, leave it open. Don't deface any human dwellings. Archaeologists prize pictographs and petroglyphs that were made by prehistoric peoples, but if you make them, they are nothing more than graffiti.

Here are some rules for visitors to follow at sites of archaeological significance (adapted from National Park Service guidelines):

➤ Keep your feet off the furniture; do not walk on walls or artifacts.

➤ Don't eat in the living rooms: crumbs of food attract rodents, which may then build nests in the site.

➤ No slumber parties; don't sleep inside the site.

➤ Don't touch the paintings; oils from your skin can corrode the drawings.

➤ Don't pee in the parlor; no explanation necessary.

➤ Don't go in if you're not invited; some sites are sacred to Native Americans.

➤ Don't rearrange the furniture; leave everything the way you found it.

➤ Tell a ranger if you see anything wrong; report signs of any infractions of the rules.

Hiking Vocab

Do you know the difference between a pictograph and a petroglyph? A pictograph is a painting on a rock surface. A petroglyph is a picture carved or etched into a rock surface.

Drive Responsibly

Wilderness areas have their own restrictions. Any motorized vehicles are prohibited—so no all-terrain vehicles (ATVs), dune buggies, motorcycles, etc. On roads through national parks, national forests, and state parklands, observe speed limits. Watch for wildlife crossing the roads. If you're in a car and encounter wildlife at night, turn off your headlights; animals that are blinded by light tend to freeze in place. I think it's a good idea if I see a turtle crossing a road to pick it up and carry it to the other side. Doing so does the turtle no harm, and it may prevent it from being run over by a car or truck.

Hike Responsibly

Food scraps do not burn completely, especially meat. This is why planning ahead is advisable. I pack as much of my food as possible in plastic bags. Even though I can't burn the bags, at least they are lightweight and don't take up much room in my pack. On those outings when I do carry canned food—usually canned meat or fish—at least I can remove both ends of the cans and crush them to minimize their volume.

Don't try to burn your toilet paper, even if fires are permitted. For one thing, you're likely to be using the paper in a brushy area away from your campsite. It's too easy for a fire to get out of hand; wildfires have been started by people trying to burn their toilet paper. For another, your companions may find your burning your used toilet paper in the communal campfire a bit gross. If I'm only on the trail for a few days, I pack out my used toilet paper in a large plastic bag. For longer treks, if the terrain permits it, toilet paper can be buried but needs to be deep enough that animals aren't likely to try to dig it up again.

Trail Wisdom

Pack as much of your food as possible in plastic bags. Then reuse the bags to carry out your trash.

Leave No Trace

Leave No Trace is a program similar to Tread Lightly! designed to educate people who plan to travel in wilderness areas. The principles of Leave No Trace are the following:

➤ Plan ahead and prepare.

➤ Camp and travel on durable surfaces.

➤ Dispose of waste properly.

➤ Pack it in–Pack it out.

➤ Leave what you find.

➤ Minimize use and impact of fires.

➤ Respect wildlife.

➤ Be considerate of other visitors.

Some of the principles of Tread Lightly! and Leave No Trace are the same but stated a little differently. It doesn't matter which group formulated a principle. They are all good principles and should be followed.

Fragile Environments

Any type of groundcover tends to be fragile. Desert soils may be covered with a thin layer of cryptobiotic crust, an essential part of the ecosystem that contains thin layers of bacteria, algae, fungi, lichens, and mosses. The cryptobiotic crust serves to retain moisture, stabilize sand, and fix nitrogen (make atmospheric nitrogen available to plants). Disturbed desert soils may take a century to heal. It is especially important in deserts to stay on the trail. When camping, look for rocky or sandy surfaces without vegetation.

Nature Note

Soil is teeming with living organisms—from bacteria, fungi, and algae to insects, earthworms, and small mammals and reptiles. The soil is their home. Try very hard not to disturb it.

Meadows are sensitive to disturbances for at least two reasons:

1. Walking across meadows compacts the soil. Compacted soil does not drain well. Water is likely to run off the soil rather than penetrate to the roots of plants. Runoff also increases soil erosion, which means less soil in the meadows and more soil clouding streams and lakes. Bits of soil clog the gills of fish and amphibians living in aquatic environments, adversely affecting their health. Silt covers eggs of aquatic organisms, diminishing reproductive success.

2. Walking across meadows crushes wildflowers. Since one of the pleasures of hiking is experiencing wildflower displays, hikers should want to protect the flowers as much as possible. If a trail already exists that cuts through a meadow, then feel free to use it, but stay on the trail. If no trail exists, and the meadow can be skirted, then hike around the meadow. If hiking around a meadow is not possible, then the members of a hiking party should spread out so at least any stretch of soil gets stepped on by only one person.

Land above the tree line is particularly fragile. Alpine tundra has a very short growing season and any plants that are stepped on may be damaged enough that they are unable to reproduce that season.

Never build campfires above the tree line. For one thing, firewood is in short supply. For another, alpine soils are easily sterilized. If you really want a campfire, then descend below the tree line and camp at a lower elevation. Otherwise, if you're camping above the tree line, then observe the rule of no fires.

Most people may never have the experience of hiking or camping in regions of Arctic tundra, but the same rules that apply to Arctic tundra also apply to alpine tundra. Fragile soils must be protected and campfires should not be built. You may not have thought about it before, but Arctic tundra is also above tree line, even though it's at, or near, sea level, in contrast to alpine tundra, which is at high elevations. Arctic tundra doesn't have trees either, just grasses and low shrubs.

Choosing Campsites

You are unlikely to be camping in areas where no one has ever camped before. Look for sites that others have used, especially where there are already fire rings. Here is some common campsite etiquette to keep in mind:

➤ Always try to camp on bare ground.

➤ Avoid camping in meadows or other grassy areas.

➤ Try not to trample vegetation.

➤ Fire rings are unnecessary, but if you want them, don't build new ones if fire rings are present already. If there were no fire rings before you arrived, disassemble your ring before you leave.

➤ Leave no trace you were there.

➤ Try not to disrupt the natural environment.

➤ Camp a reasonable distance from water sources and game trails.

➤ Don't wash dishes or use soap in streams or lakes. Dish water should be sprinkled over as wide an area as possible.

It's best to camp on relatively hard ground. When I was a Boy Scout earning the Camping merit badge, one of the requirements was to prepare a ground bed from fresh pine boughs. We don't do that anymore. Use a sleeping pad.

Campsites are like prime real estate: location, location, location. The edges of dry meadows, if out of the wind, are often good campsite choices. Avoid low, wet areas, which are likely to be home to mosquitoes anyway. It's best to camp on higher, drier ground. Slightly higher ground may also be warmer because cold air descends at night.

Trail Wisdom

Don't trench around tents. Trenching was done in the old days before tents had floors. Today's tents all come with stitched-in floors, so trenching isn't necessary.

Campfires

Most people love a good campfire in the backcountry. Campfires add a certain ambiance to the camping experience. Be practical about them, however. You don't need a roaring bonfire. If you can't get closer than 3 to 5 feet (1 to 1.5 m) to your fire, your fire is probably too big.

Remember to only use wood that is dead and down. That means don't cut live branches from trees. It also means don't break dead branches off trees. Use only branches that are already dead and lying on the ground. Also, wood that is more than about 6 inches (15 cm) in diameter is probably too large; wood the thickness of your forearm burns very well, so don't start hauling dead logs to your fire ring. The small stuff is fine for cooking and perfectly adequate to provide warmth and toast marshmallows.

Trail Wisdom

Bonfires are unnecessary in the backcountry. Build small fires. Try not to scorch rocks with your fires. Fire-scarred rocks are unsightly for the next campers.

Esthetics is not the only issue with campfires. Safety is also an important issue. The best location for a campfire is an area of bare soil that is devoid of vegetation. Soil is better than rocks because fires scorch and blacken rocks. Smooth an area at least 6 feet (2 m) in diameter and scrape it clear of any organic matter (also known as duff). In forests, that means you should remove any of the decayed or decaying vegetation—pine needles, leaves, twigs, etc.—that is covering the soil. Have a container of water handy in case a fire needs to be doused quickly. A container of dirt is also a good idea, since dirt can smother a fire.

On a Boy Scout outing my older son and I were on, the troop learned the importance of clearing away all vegetation in a rather dramatic fashion. We were on a winter campout and had a roaring fire going to provide warmth against the cold night. The ground around the fire pit looked like it had been adequately cleared of any organic matter. We were sitting in a ring around the fire when suddenly a flame burst up right at the feet of one of the Scouts. The fire had crept under the duff and traveled about 15 feet (4.5 meters) without any indication it was there. When the flames did break through the surface, they took everyone by surprise. Fortunately, no one was injured and the flames were quickly extinguished.

Under other circumstances there could have been a different outcome. Wildfires have started this way. Had we retired for the night earlier, it's entirely possible that we could have been woken up in the middle of a conflagration. So, a word of wisdom—be sure to scrape away the organic matter until you are absolutely certain that you have reached bare dirt.

When you're ready to leave an area, be sure to let the fire burn down to coals. Douse the coals with liberal amounts of water. Using a stick, stir the coals/water thoroughly. Remember that where there's smoke, there's fire. Place your hand on the ashes; they should be cold to the touch. If there were multiple fire rings when you arrived at the site, dismantle all rings except one.

Trail Wisdom

Fires must be completely extinguished. Any ashes or unburned wood must be cold to the touch. Do not leave the campsite until you know for a fact that your fire is completely out. If you leave and your ashes start a wildfire, you can be held financially liable for any damage the fire does. A common practice is to place a stick in the ground in the middle of the ashes. If a wildfire occurs afterward in the vicinity of your campsite, investigators can tell that your campfire was not the source of the wildfire.

Reusing existing campsites and fire rings helps minimize the total disturbance to the area. Camping well away from the trail ensures that anyone who is hiking through the area doesn't have to hike through your campsite; hikers shouldn't even be aware that anyone has been camping there.

Sanitation

If there's an outhouse, use it—no matter how gross it may smell. Do not dispose of trash in outhouses. Many outhouses are now composting, which means they decompose the waste. When fully composted, the waste has the consistency of fine topsoil, does not contain any disease pathogens, and can safely be spread on the ground as fertilizer.

Ideally, all human waste should be packed out of the wilderness. In fact, some wilderness areas require it. You should check on the regulations ahead of time so you'll be prepared with a supply of plastic bags. Otherwise, burying waste in a cathole 6–10 inches (15–25 cm) deep is fine. The microorganisms that are capable of decomposing fecal material live in topsoil. If you dig a hole that's too deep, you'll reach subsoil material, which tends to be relatively sterile. You can tell the difference between the two because topsoil tends to be fairly dark due to the organic matter in it. Subsoil is light because of the lack of organic matter.

After burying your waste in the topsoil, fill the hole back in completely. Be sure that you're at least 100 feet (30 m) from any lakes, streams, or springs, and also well away from any trail or campsite. To discourage animals from digging up your waste, you can position a large rock over the hole.

Trail Wisdom

Human fecal matter can spread disease—to you, other hikers, and wildlife. Try to bury your waste in such a way that other people are unlikely to come across it and animals can't dig it up.

The Smear Method

A few years back, the gospel on disposal of human feces in desert areas was to use the smear method. Then-current wisdom was that desert soils lack the bacteria and fungi necessary to break down feces, so digging catholes was discouraged. Instead, campers were encouraged to smear their feces on the tops of flat rocks. The hot desert sun was supposed to desiccate and sterilize the feces. Once the feces were completely dry, the wind would just blow them away.

I haven't seen that method advocated lately. Apparently, groups were leaving camping areas in such a disgusting condition that camping there was unpalatable for the next group. Also, before the feces had finished drying, they were an invitation to animals that would become contaminated by them and would spread the feces around even more. Catholes are still preferable.

Soap

Here's a rule of thumb: all soap is at least partially biodegradable, but no soap is completely biodegradable. Even if you use brands of soap that claim they're biodegradable, they're still foreign to the natural environment and should be used sparingly. Soap alters the pH value (acidity) of water. Use soap that doesn't have phosphate because phosphorus promotes algal blooms.

Carry water at least 200 feet (60 m) from natural sources, and wash yourself and your dishes using as little soap as possible. Wastewater is best sprinkled over sandy soil. At least try to avoid pouring soapy water directly on any vegetation.

Wildlife

Humans are the top predator in most environments. Almost any interaction with humans stresses wildlife. Watch animals and photograph them from a distance. Don't let children or dogs chase them. And, above all else, never feed wildlife! For one thing, human food is unhealthy. For another, feeding animals teaches them that humans are a source of food, so they learn to seek out humans and to even beg for food. If that's not enough, animals bite and can transmit diseases, including bubonic plague. I think Bambi and Chip 'n Dale are cute, too, but don't feed them.

Trail Wisdom

Don't feed the wildlife—either deliberately or by leaving food where animals can get it. In national parks, feeding wildlife is illegal and you could be fined. If you see someone feeding wildlife, especially dangerous animals like bears, you should report them.

Coastal Areas

The single most distinctive feature of a coastal area is the tides. If you are unfamiliar with a tidal area you are in, you probably don't know how high the water gets at high tide. You have to stay aware of what's happening around you. If you are hiking along a coastline, be careful not to become stranded when the tide comes in.

Oceans are large enough that some of the rules about freshwater ecosystems don't apply to them. Generally speaking, it's best to do all cooking in the intertidal zone. Wastewater can be dumped into the sand in the beach's intertidal zone. Any waste or debris will be washed away when the tide comes in. Be careful about camping low enough on a beach that the tide could come in during the night and swamp your campsite.

Hiking Vocab

The intertidal zone is that portion of a beach that marks the limits between high and low tides.

Sand dunes are unique features. Don't camp on dunes, and try not to hike on them more than necessary. Dune vegetation is fragile and easily disturbed. Try not to harm it.

If driftwood is abundant, it's okay to burn it. Build fires in the intertidal zone. Let the tides clean the beach of ashes and unburned wood.

Trail Wisdom

When camping on ocean beaches, do your cooking and cleaning in the intertidal zone. The tide will wash the beach clean.

This one may seem kind of strange, but as a general rule, it's all right to urinate directly into the water. People on fishing boats do it all the time. Oceans provide a huge dilution factor. However, do not urinate into tide pools since numerous living organisms are present there.

Beaches and estuaries can be breeding grounds for numerous species of wildlife. Do not disturb nesting seabirds. You could cause the parents to abandon their nests, dooming their young. The nests of terns (which look like small gulls) often are just depressions in the sand. Watch out for them, and give any nests you see a wide berth.

On sections of the Atlantic beaches, nesting sites of endangered piping plovers are protected. On sections of Pacific beaches, similar sites of snowy plovers and least terns are protected. Watch out for areas that are off-limits, and give them a wide berth.

Collecting and consuming shellfish may or may not be legal. Observe any posted regulations about collecting shellfish. In well-used areas, signs are almost certain to be present. In more remote areas, you should check with local authorities. Be aware that toxins in the water may make the consumption of shellfish unhealthy. Likewise, the consumption of shellfish may be safe certain times of the year and prohibited for health reasons at other times.

Conclusion

All the rules in this chapter are simply common sense. Obey them and your outing will be healthier and more enjoyable. Above all else, remember the following:

> ➤ Respect the rights and property of others; don't trespass on private property.

> ➤ Enjoy wildlife from a distance; do not disturb or feed wild animals; do not let your pets harass wildlife.

> ➤ Protect fragile environments.

> ➤ Pack it in–pack it out.

> ➤ Take only pictures; leave only footprints.

CHAPTER 7

 **Finding Your Way**

> ## In This Chapter
>
> ➤ Using map and compass
> ➤ The sun and stars
> ➤ GPS

Most hikers stay on established, well-marked trails. If your hike is a loop, chances are good that you will eventually return to the trailhead. If your hike is an out-and-back trip on the same trail, your chances of getting lost are slim. Even then, it doesn't hurt to have some basic orienteering skills. Just keeping track of which way is north and which direction is the way back to the trailhead should keep you from getting lost. Being able to find your way is fun; thousands of recreationists engage in orienteering activities just for the fun of it.

> **Hiking Vocab**
>
> Orienteering refers to the process of finding your position or location on a map or with respect to points on a compass.

Reading Trail and Topographic Maps

An important orienteering skill is being able to read a map. Doing so requires an understanding of latitudes and longitudes for several reasons:

➤ Positions on topographic maps are marked with lines of latitude and longitude.

➤ GPS units display your location in terms of latitude and longitude.

➤ Differences in latitude, longitude—and elevation—are important factors that determine a region's general climate and what kind of environment to expect along a trail.

Becoming proficient with map and compass adds to the enjoyment of a hike. I often carry a topographic map with me, but not because I necessarily need it for navigation. Prominent features are indicated on the map; I like to know what peak I'm passing or the name of a lake or river at which I'm camping. If there are a number of lakes or peaks in an area and I'm planning to camp at a particular one, being able to pinpoint my destination on a map assures me I'm actually camping where I think I am.

Being able to orient yourself by judging the direction of the sun during the day, or the direction of the North Star at night, can also be fun. Being in the wilderness away from city lights may be the best opportunity most urban dwellers have of actually seeing the night sky and learning to recognize constellations. Knowing where you are and in what direction you are headed builds confidence, and being confident about your skills contributes to the enjoyment of being outdoors.

Personal Anecdote

One time I was at Boy Scout camp in northern Arizona with one of my sons. A troop was visiting from Baltimore. All the boys from Baltimore stood in the meadow each night in awe; they had never seen the Milky Way before and were having fun learning to identify major constellations and bright stars. Find a location remote from city lights and you can have the same experience.

The advent of the GPS in recent years has added a whole new dimension to the field of orienteering. A GPS either has internal maps or needs to be used in conjunction with a map.

For hikes on well-traveled trails, general maps that are handed out at visitor centers or come with guidebooks are usually sufficient. They at least give a general impression of the route the trail takes, its length, and some of the natural features you can expect to encounter along the way. However, if you are going into the backcountry, hiking on trails less frequently traveled, or venturing into terrain unfamiliar to you, topographic maps are superior.

Trail Maps and Guides

Most established trails in the United States and Canada have been mapped, whether the trails are 5 or 1,000 miles (8 or 1,600 km) long. National parks, monuments, forests, and recreation areas; state parks and recreation areas; and city and county parks very likely provide maps of their trails. I am calling these trail maps because they give a general impression of the trail, distances, and landmarks, but without the detail topographic maps provide. Parks and recreation areas may also have guidebooks that provide general information about trails, such as the following:

> ➤ Length of the trail either one-way or round-trip

> ➤ Estimated time required to hike the trail

> ➤ General description of difficulty

> ➤ Directions for reaching the trailhead

> ➤ Descriptions of natural features (lakes, rivers, mountains), wildlife, and other points of interest

> ➤ Options, such as hiking the trail as a loop, or connecting to other trails.

Day hikes typically range in length from 2 to 10 miles (3 to 16 km). If you're planning a multiday hike, the number of days the hike will take you to finish is usually based on the assumption that you're walking 8 to 10 miles (13 to 16 km) a day. You should know what your own limits are. If 10 miles (16 km) is your limit for a day, it is probably unwise to attempt a 15-mile (24-km) loop.

There are several good estimates of hiking time. On trails with little or no elevation change, a reasonable pace is thirty to forty-five minutes a mile (twenty to thirty minutes a kilometer). Guide books describe these hikes as easy.

On trails with moderate to substantial changes in elevation, a reasonable pace is about 1 mph (1.6 kph). Guide books describe those hikes as moderately strenuous to strenuous.

Your perception of the level of difficulty of a hike varies with your age, experience, and state of physical fitness. What should be factored into estimates of hiking speeds or lengths of time to complete trails is what else you like to do on the trail besides hike.

I have known people who do nothing but hike; they walk from one end of a trail to the other as though they're in a race. On the other hand, there are those of us who like to stop to smell the lupines. When I am actually moving, I probably maintain a pace of 2 to 3 mph (3 to 5 kph). However, I may also stop frequently to identify plants along the trail, watch wildlife, take photographs, enjoy the scenery, or eat lunch. Under those conditions a 10-mile (16-km) hike can take five to six hours, or more, not the four hours a 2 to 3 mph (3 to 5 kph) pace would suggest.

Keep your own interests and energy level in mind. If your destination for the day is a trout stream where you plan to try out a new fly you've just tied, don't also plan to put in a lot of hours hiking. Allow yourself enough time to do the other activities you enjoy in addition to hiking.

Trail Wisdom

Why you hike, the pace at which you hike, and what you enjoy doing are very personal. If you hike alone, then you are in complete control of your day. However, if you hike with other people, be sure that your interests and preferences are compatible with theirs.

How Topographic Maps Are Marked

Trail Wisdom

In the United States, topographic maps are produced by the United States Geological Survey (USGS). Distances are marked in feet or miles.

Mapmakers place a large imaginary grid over Earth's surface, which represent lines of latitude and longitude. Lines of latitude circle parallel to Earth's equator. The equator is an imaginary line that runs around Earth exactly halfway between the North and South Poles. The equator is labeled as 0° (0°). The North Pole is at latitude 90° north (90° N, also written N 90°) and the South Pole is at latitude 90° south (90° S, or S 90°). Each degree of latitude corresponds to roughly 69 miles (111 km) of distance on Earth's surface.

Lines of longitude (meridians) are imaginary lines perpendicular to the equator and running from the North Pole to the South Pole. (All lines of longitude converge at the poles.) Going all the way around Earth are 360° of longitude, beginning at a longitude of 0°—called the prime meridian—which passes through Greenwich, England. Going west from England (through North America), you go through 180° of longitude to get halfway around the world. That would put you in the Pacific Ocean. Going east from England (through Europe and Asia), you go through 180° of longitude to get halfway around the world in the other direction. Where longitude 180°W meets longitude 180°E is the international date line.

Nature Note

Earth is not a perfect sphere; it is close to a sphere, but not exactly so. Because of Earth's rotation, it bulges slightly at the equator, giving Earth a shape called an oblate spheroid. Instead of Earth's circumference being the same regardless of how it's measured, the circumference is exactly 24,901.55 miles (40,075.16 km) around the equator and slightly less— 24,859.82 miles (40,008.00 km)— around a circle that passes through the poles.

Distances between lines of longitude are greater at Earth's equator than they are closer to the poles because lines of longitude all intersect at the North and South Poles. At the equator, 1° of longitude corresponds to a distance of 69 miles (111 km). That distance shrinks as the poles are approached. For example, at latitude 40°, 1° of longitude corresponds to a distance of about 53 miles (85 km).

Since there are 360° of longitude going completely around Earth, 1° corresponds to 69 miles at the equator. Since there are sixty minutes in 1°, dividing 69 by 60 gives exactly 1.15 miles (1.85 km) as the distance corresponding to one minute of longitude. A distance of 1.15 miles is called a nautical mile.

Hiking Vocab

The nautical mile has been used by mariners for centuries, and they and aviators still use it. What Americans call a distance of 1 mile—5,280 feet (1,609 m)—more correctly should be called 1 statute mile. The unit of speed called the knot is short for "nautical mile per hour."

The purpose of topographic maps is to describe the terrain accurately, including all natural and constructed features, and all elevation changes. It is pretty hard to get lost if you have a topographic map and compass and know how to use them.

Reading Latitudes and Longitudes on a Map

Both latitude and longitude are expressed using a system of degrees, minutes, and seconds. It's a system similar to units of time. Just as 1 hour equals 60 minutes (60'), and 1 minute equals 60 seconds (60"), 1° equals 60 minutes and 1 minute equals 60 seconds. A reading of 35°, 40 minutes, and 23 seconds is written 35°40'23".

A location on a map is designated by its latitude and longitude. For example, if you were camping at Moraine Park in Rocky Mountain National Park, Colorado, you would be at approximately latitude N 40°21' and longitude W 105°36'. Since 1 second (1") is a distance of only about 100 feet (30.5 m), the number of seconds of latitude or longitude would depend exactly upon where you were standing.

On the other hand, if you were camping at Tuolumne Meadows in Yosemite National Park, California, you would be at latitude N 37°52 and longitude W 119°22'. A good rule of thumb is that latitudes in the lower forty-eight states range from about N 25° in south Texas to about N 45° in northern Minnesota. (Latitude N 45° is halfway from the equator to the North Pole.) Longitudes in the continental United States range from about W 67° on the East Coast to about W 125° on the West Coast. The hundredth meridian passes through the middle of the central states and Canadian provinces.

The Arctic Circle is located at latitude N 66°33'34". Latitudes along the coast of the Arctic Ocean in Alaska and Canada are about N 70°. A midlatitude location in Canada is the town of Banff, Alberta, in the Canadian Rockies, which is located at N 51°10' and W 115°34'.

Nature Note

An interesting observation can be made about the world's time zones. The distance around Earth at the equator is a little more than 24,000 miles (38,600 km), and there are twenty-four time zones. That means the boundaries between time zones at the equator are spaced about 1,000 miles (1,600 km) apart because 24,000 divided by 24 equals 1,000.

Estimating Distances on a Map

Lines of latitude are parallel to each other. Since distances between parallel lines are always the same, regardless of how far you are north (or south) of the equator, 1 minute of latitude always equals 1.15 statute miles (1.85 km).

On the other hand, since lines of longitude get closer together as you head north (or south in the southern hemisphere), 1 minute of longitude only equals 1.15 statute miles (1.85 km) if you're standing at the equator. As you head north or south from the equator, 1 minute of longitude equals a shorter and shorter distance; the distance equals 0 at the poles.

You can approximate what the distances are between lines of longitude. If you are familiar with a little trigonometry, the exact relationship is that at latitude n degrees north, 1 minute of longitude varies as the cosine of n. Don't worry about being able to do that calculation since you're not likely to be carrying a calculator with you anyway. Just to give you an idea of what the results look like, though, I've done the math for you. The results are shown in table 7.1.

Table 7.1: Distances that Correspond to 1 Minute of Longitude at Various Latitudes

Latitude	1 minute of longitude =
0°	1.15 statute miles (1.85 km)
30°	1.00 miles (1.50 km)
35°	0.94 miles (1.51 km)
40°	0.88 miles (1.41 km)
45°	0.81 miles (1.30 km)
50°	0.74 miles (1.19 km)

You may be wondering what all this has to do with reading topographic maps. The answer is that topographic maps are laid out in quadrangles. Older maps are referred to as having 15-minute-series quadrangles, and newer maps usually as having 7.5-minute-series quadrangles. Quadrangles are just four-sided figures. Because of the curvature of Earth, the maps aren't exactly squares or rectangles, but they're close.

Consider 7.5-minute maps; they cover a smaller area, so they have more detail. We can write 7.5 minutes as 7'30". Suppose the lower right corner of the map identifies a location corresponding to N 37°37'00" W 119°30'00". Moving left on the map means moving west, so the lower left corner will be at N 37°37'00" W 119°37'30". Since you are moving along a line of constant latitude, the latitude doesn't change, but the longitude increases by exactly 7'30".

Likewise, moving from the bottom (south) edge of the map northward, the top edge of the map will mark a line of latitude 37°44'30", exactly 7'30" farther north.

What north-south and east-west distances does the map cover? We know a change in latitude of 7.5 minutes corresponds to a distance running north to south of about 8.63 miles (13.88 km), which you can determine by multiplying 7.5 minutes by 1.15 miles in a minute). Looking at Table 7.1, we see that at a line of latitude close to 35°, a change in longitude of 7.5 minutes corresponds to a distance running east to west of about 7.0 miles (11.3 km), which you can determine by multiplying 7.5 minutes by 0.94 miles in a minute). Therefore, the map covers an area that is 8.63 miles (13.88 km) from the top of the map to the bottom and 7.0 miles (11.26 km) from left to right. That's close to a square, but not exactly one.

Maps usually have a distance scale on them. On a 7.5-minute map, the scale is 1 inch (2.54 cm) on the map equals 24,000 inches (60,960 cm) on the ground. Then we can determine that 24,000 inches equals 2,000 feet (609.60 m), or 0.38 miles (0.61 km). Therefore, 1 inch on the map equals 0.38 miles.

Reading Elevations on a Map

Topographic, or topo, maps do more than just show positions horizontally. Any map does that. What makes topo maps especially useful to hikers is they also show elevation. Topo maps use a system of contour lines. Each contour line represents a specific elevation above sea level. On a 7.5-minute map, adjacent lines represent a change of elevation of 40 feet (12.2 m). Contour lines are 80 feet (24.4 m) apart on a 15-minute map. That distance of 40 or 80 feet is called the contour interval.

Trail Wisdom

It may take a little practice getting used to relating contour lines on topographic maps to the landscape at your feet. The map is necessarily only two-dimensional, while the landscape is three-dimensional. It helps to study topographic maps in the field to get used to seeing cliffs where lines are roughly parallel and bunched closely together and hills where lines are shown in roughly concentric circles.

Imagine contour lines that are spaced very far apart—the elevation is changing slowly; the terrain is relatively flat. On the other hand, lines that are spaced closely together indicate that elevation is changing rapidly, which means there are hills or valleys.

Contour lines on a map never touch each other. To do so would be a contradiction; it would imply that one location on the map is at two different elevations, which is impossible. If lines appear to touch (or almost touch), it means that the elevation is changing extremely rapidly. Very likely the map is indicating the presence of a cliff.

Contour lines that form small enclosed loops indicate tops of hills or bottoms of depressions. Summits of mountains, or points of highest terrain, may be indicated with an x and their elevation given.

Contour lines that are multiples of 200 feet (61 m)—e.g., 1,200, 1,400, or 1,600 feet—are called index contour lines. These lines are shown on the map as slightly thicker than intermediate contour lines and have their elevation written on them. There are four unnumbered intermediate contour lines between any two index contour lines. For example, if the major lines (the ones with numbers on them) are 1,400 and 1,600 feet, then the four lines between them will be 40 feet apart in elevation—1,440, 1,480, 1,520, and 1,560 feet, respectively.

If a line on a map marking a trail runs parallel to, or almost parallel to, a contour line, it means the trail is relatively flat; the trail is going neither uphill nor downhill. If a trail line crosses contour lines, it means the trail is going either uphill or downhill, depending on whether the numbers indicating elevation are increasing or decreasing. The more contour lines the trail crosses per inch on the map, the steeper the trail.

Color and Symbols on Topographic Maps

If a topo map is in color, it is coded according to the following conventions:

➤ Green: Broad types of vegetation—grasslands, meadows, forests, chaparral, and other scrubland

➤ Brown lines: Contour lines that represent changes in elevation—mountains, hills, valleys, or cliffs

➤ Blue: Water—lakes, ponds, rivers, streams, swamps, marshes, wells, and springs

➤ Black: Artificial features—buildings, water tanks, mining sites, bridges, major roads or highways, etc.

➤ Red: Secondary roads

Reading a Compass

Compasses have been around since ancient times. In the earliest days of oceanic exploration, sailors didn't have maps. They learned to navigate using the stars and the sun, but they also carried compasses. The first compass was just a magnetized needle that floated in a cup of water. Those early explorers would be impressed with modern compasses (and GPS units!).

Compass Directions

Let's begin with the four cardinal directions: north, east, south, and west. The arrow on a compass always points to magnetic north, which is not in exactly the same direction as true north (the direction of the North Pole).

Imagine holding a compass horizontally and turning the compass so that the arrow and the point marked N (or 0°) line up. If you face in that direction, you are looking north. East is to your right, south behind you, and west to your left.

There are 360° in a circle, and the compass is numbered in degrees in a clockwise direction. Divide 360 by the four cardinal directions and you get that north corresponds to a compass reading of 0°, east to 90°, south to 180°, and west to 270°. To get the four ordinal, or intercardinal, directions, add 45° to each of those numbers. The result is that northeast (NE) is 45º, southeast (SE) is 135°, southwest (SW) is 225°, and northwest (NW) is 315°.

It is common to refer to easterly readings between 0° and 180° as, for example, 15° east or 35° east. To refer to westerly directions, we can number the degrees in a counterclockwise direction, and refer to westerly directions as ,for example, 15° west or 35° west.

Declination

I mentioned that true north and magnetic north may not be in exactly the same direction. It depends upon where you are located. The magnetic north pole is located south of the geographic North Pole east of Ellesmere Island in northern Canada. If you happen to be in the Great Lakes, northeastern United States, or eastern Canada and the needle on your compass points to the magnetic north pole, it is pointing very close to the geographic North Pole also. However, if you are located in the Great Plains, Rocky Mountains, Pacific coast, or western Canada, the needle on your compass will point toward the magnetic pole, but not as close toward the geographic North Pole.

Nature Note

The magnetic north pole does not stay fixed in position. Because of shifting rock layers inside Earth, the magnetic north pole is moving at a speed of about 35 mph (56 kph) toward Russia.

You can see this for yourself by doing this exercise on a night when the North Star is visible. The farther west you are, the greater the deviation you should notice between the direction of the North Star and the direction the needle on the compass is pointing. The angle of declination will also depend upon how far your position is north or south of the equator.

The difference between the direction of true north and magnetic north is called the angle of declination, or just declination. The angle of declination is marked on topographic maps. In California, for example, that angle is about 15°. In New Mexico, it's about 10°. Declination continues to decrease as you move in an easterly direction. By the time you get to the Mississippi River, declination can be ignored. Most people probably ignore it anyway because they don't even know about it.

The importance of declination when using both a compass and a topographic map is that the map should be rotated by an angle equal to the declination marked on the map; the arrow on the compass and the arrow on the map pointing toward magnetic north should line up with each other.

Using Map and Compass Together

Suppose your trail is taking you through meadows and valleys and you know that your ultimate destination is a lake that has a reputation for its prize rainbow trout. Mid-morning you are beginning to wonder where you are and how much farther it is to the lake. This is where orienteering skills come into play—using map and compass to find out where you are and whether you are actually going in the right direction!

Triangulation

A time-honored method of using map and compass to determine location is called triangulation. Let me explain the technique of triangulation by using an example.

Lay your topo map flat on the ground. Using your compass, orient the map so that the top of the map is pointing north, correcting for declination. Look around you. Find two hills or other landmarks that are shown on your map.

Suppose Crawford's Peak is on the map and the peak itself is visible from your current location. You orient your compass and determine that Crawford's Peak lies at a bearing of E 73°. Pretend someone were standing on Crawford's Peak and getting a bearing on your location. That person would say you are exactly opposite (180°) your bearing of 73°. The sum of 73 and 180 is 253. Starting at Crawford's Peak on your map, use a pencil to draw a straight line pointing at a direction of E 253° (or W 107°) from the peak. If your compass has a plastic base, you can use the base as a straightedge. Otherwise, the edge of a book or even the side of a very straight stick will do.

Now look for a second natural feature that is shown on your map. If you are facing Crawford's Peak, you will get the best results if the second feature is roughly either to your right or to your left at a 90° angle to Crawford's Peak. Suppose Mount Garfield is also on the map, and you determine that it is at a bearing of W 20°, or E 340° as measured in a clockwise direction. Then 180° on the compass from W 20° would be E 160°. Again, use a straightedge to draw a line on your map from Mount Garfield in a direction of E 160°.

Where the two lines intersect is your location! Triangulation sounds easy, but it may take some practice. After doing this enough times, you may not even have to actually draw the lines anymore.

Navigating Using the Sun

You can also get a good sense of direction during the day by understanding the path of the sun across the sky at different seasons of the year. Picture an imaginary line that runs through the North and South Poles. As Earth orbits the sun, Earth rotates around that line, which we call Earth's axis of rotation. If Earth's axis of rotation were exactly perpendicular to the imaginary plane defined by Earth's orbit around the sun, there would be no seasons, the number of hours of daylight would be the same everywhere on Earth, and at any given latitude, the sun would rise and set at exactly the same positions on the horizon every day of the year. However, Earth's axis of rotation is not perpendicular to the plane of Earth's orbit around the sun; the axis is tilted at an angle of 23°27'.

That angle of 23°27' determines several things, including the northernmost and southernmost limits of the tropics. At latitude N 23°27', an imaginary line called the Tropic of Cancer circles Earth. The Tropic of Cancer represents two things:

1. It is the northernmost limit of the tropics

2. It is the northernmost latitude at which observers can ever see the sun directly overhead (at the zenith).

The Tropic of Cancer passes through northern Mexico, southern Florida, and the Pacific Ocean north of the Hawaiian Islands. The name Cancer is derived from the zodiac constellation, Cancer, also known as the Crab.

At latitude S 23°27', an imaginary line called the Tropic of Capricorn circles Earth. The Tropic of Capricorn is the southernmost limit of the tropics and passes through South America. The Tropic of Capricorn represents the southernmost latitude at which observers can ever see the sun directly overhead. The name Capricorn is derived from the zodiac constellation, Capricorn, also known as the goat.

The Solstices

At noon, when the sun passes through the zenith of an observer who is located at the Tropic of Cancer, people in the northern hemisphere celebrate the summer solstice (solstice means "high point"), which occurs on or around June 20. The summer solstice is the longest day of the year in the northern hemisphere; above the Arctic Circle, the sun doesn't even set. In the southern hemisphere, June 20 is the winter solstice and is the shortest day of the year.

In the northern hemisphere, when the sun is over the Tropic of Capricorn, the winter solstice occurs on or around December 21 and is the shortest day of the year. On that date, people living in the southern hemisphere are celebrating their summer solstice.

The Equinoxes

Twice a year—once in spring and once in fall—at noon, the sun passes through the zenith located at the equator. On two dates, on or around March 20 and September 22, there are exactly twelve hours of daylight and twelve hours of darkness everywhere on Earth. March 20 is the vernal equinox for inhabitants of the northern hemisphere; it is the autumnal equinox for inhabitants of the southern hemisphere. September 22 is the autumnal equinox for inhabitants of the northern hemisphere and the vernal equinox for inhabitants of the southern hemisphere.

Hiking Vocab

Equinox means "equal night," vernal means "spring," autumnal means "autumn."

Trail Wisdom

People living at the equator experience the same number of hours of daylight every day of the year. People who live at northern latitudes experience summers with more hours of daylight than night. People living above the Arctic Circle experience days in summer when the sun does not set and days in winter when the sun does not rise. Despite these differences, however, over the course of a year, the sun shines for exactly the same total number of hours at every location on Earth.

The Sun Is Due South at Noon

The direction of the sun at noon gives a method for knowing what direction is due south. The definition of noon may be a little ambiguous, however. You have to think in terms of solar, or local, time.

Solar noon is marked by the instant at which the sun reaches its highest point in the sky as observed from your location. This is probably different from the time indicated on your watch. What we usually call the time is actually standard time and is the average solar time for that time zone. Twelve o'clock noon standard time is at the same time everywhere in the same time zone, even though observers at different locations see the sun in different directions. What confuses things even more is daylight savings time. When daylight savings time is in effect, noon on a clock will be as much as an hour later than noon as determined by the sun.

Given the distinction between solar time, standard time, and daylight savings time, you have to estimate when solar noon is occurring at your location. One way to determine solar noon is to pound a stick into the ground and watch the stick's shadow. (Obviously, this method does not work on cloudy days.) The stick's shadow will be its shortest at the instant when the sun crosses your local meridian. At that instant you can say that the direction of the sun is exactly south. Once you know which direction is south, you can find west, north, and east.

Nature Note

In ancient times, various cultures around the world devoted considerable time and effort to identifying the exact dates of the equinoxes and solstices, so they would know when to plant and harvest crops. Several archaeological sites around the world were observatories, built specifically to identify when the equinoxes and solstices occurred. Ancient civilizations like the Mayans developed remarkably accurate calendars in the process.

Using the Sun and a Watch to Find South

An alternate method works only if you have a watch with hands—a digital watch won't work with this method. If your watch has hands, and assuming you are on standard time (not daylight savings time), point the hour hand directly at the sun. Imagine a line running between the center of the watch's face and the number 12. Divide the angle between that line and the hour hand in half. An imaginary line pointing at that angle from the watch's center indicates which way is south.

If your watch is set for daylight savings time, instead of using the hour hand, use an imaginary line running from the center of the watch's face through the hour one less than the current hour. Either way, you can find south if you forgot your compass.

Navigating Using the Stars

Everyone has heard of the North Star. You can find the North Star if you can find the Big Dipper. Use the two stars at the end of the bowl in the Big Dipper as pointer stars. They point directly to the North Star. Once you know which direction is north, you can find west, south, and east.

You can also find the latitude of your location by using the North Star. Imagine a line running from your feet directly toward the North Star. The angle between that line and the ground is called the North Star's angle of elevation, which is equal to your latitude. For most observers in the continental United States, the North Star's angle of elevation is between about 30° and 45°.

Nature Note

The North Star (Polaris) has not always been in the direction of true north. In the future it will again not be in the direction of true north. Earth's axis of rotation very slowly changes direction. Astronomers say that Earth's axis of rotation shifts, or precesses, so this change in direction is called the precession of the equinoxes.

The ancient Greeks would not have used Polaris as the North Star. They would have used a different star. At times there is no bright star exactly in the direction of true north. It will take about 24,000 years for Polaris to return to its current position.

Using Other Celestial Objects

There are a lot more stars in the sky that can be used for navigation than just the North Star. If you take the time to become familiar with prominent constellations and the brightest stars, and recognize the cycles they undergo during the course of a year, you can use them to identify the cardinal directions. For example, one of the most conspicuous winter constellations in the northern hemisphere is Orion, the hunter. Orion can be identified easily by the three bright stars that form the hunter's belt. Knowing that in winter Orion tends to be in the southern part of the sky during the hours of early evening shows you which direction is south. In summer, a prominent southerly constellation is Scorpio (the Scorpion).

Ancient observers knew at what times bright stars would rise on certain days of the year. Since all stars rise in the east, directions could be pinpointed fairly precisely that way. When

Polynesian mariners traveled thousands of miles across the Pacific Ocean, they found their way by following the stars. Experiments with birds suggest they also may use constellations when migrating.

Global Positioning Systems

A global positioning system (GPS) is an example of an electronic navigation aid (NAVAID). The GPS has been available to the general public since at least the early 1990s. Like early PCs, the first GPS units were pretty rudimentary; like modern PCs, today's GPS units are very sophisticated.

The GPS is based on twenty-four satellites orbiting Earth. The first satellite was launched in 1978 by the Department of Defense and was intended strictly for military use. The twenty-fourth satellite was launched in 1994. During the 1980s, the GPS became available for civilian use. Beyond the cost of the equipment, there are no fees for using GPS.

Each satellite orbits Earth twice a day at an altitude of roughly 12,000 miles (19,300 km). An individual satellite has a lifetime of about ten years, so satellites are constantly being replaced. Signal transmission strength is low, only about 50 watts. For a GPS unit to detect a satellite, the satellite must be above the observer's horizon and cannot be blocked by any solid objects, including rocks, buildings, mountains, or metal structures. Weather is not a limitation. A unit should be able to receive signals regardless of clouds or precipitation.

Trail Wisdom

The fact that satellite signals are blocked by rocks and mountains poses a problem when hiking in desert canyons. Canyon walls often block GPS signals.

A GPS unit has a built-in almanac of satellite locations at any given time, twenty-four hours a day. Each time a GPS is used, the unit needs to spend several minutes acquiring satellite data. If your current location is more than 500 miles (800 km) from the location at which the unit was last used, it may be necessary to program the unit for the state or country you are in. The unit has a pull-down menu with lists of states, Canadian provinces, and foreign countries. I sometimes find it necessary to initialize my current location when I change states and definitely when I travel overseas.

Using a GPS to Find Latitude and Longitude

A GPS unit requires simultaneous signals from a minimum of three satellites to fix an observer's latitude and longitude—what is called two-dimensional, or 2D, navigation. Location is fixed using triangulation from the satellites in a manner similar to triangulating one's position on a map. To also determine altitude—what is called three-dimensional, or 3D, navigation— requires simultaneous signals from a minimum of four satellites. Latitude and longitude are expressed very precisely, usually to a tenth of a second. The GPS unit's display gives an estimate of horizontal accuracy—the more satellite signals, the better the accuracy. Typically the minimum accuracy is 49 feet (15 m).

Trail Wisdom

The GPS demonstrates the effects of general relativity. According to general relativity, clocks run more slowly if the pull of gravity is weaker. At an altitude of 12,000 feet (3,658 m), the clock on a satellite runs more slowly than a clock at the surface of Earth. Therefore, in order to synchronize the two clocks, a relativistic correction has to be applied to the satellite's clock.

Using a GPS to Find Altitude

Some GPS units find altitude entirely by triangulation; others find altitude using barometric (atmospheric) pressure. Barometric pressure decreases with altitude. At an altitude of 3,280 feet (1,000 m), the pressure is 96 percent of the pressure at sea level. At 6,560 feet (2,000 m), the pressure is 93 percent of the pressure at sea level. At 9,843 feet (3,000 m), the pressure is down to 90 percent. Barometric pressure is 50 percent of the pressure at sea level at an altitude of 18,000 feet (5,486 m). With the exception of Mt. McKinley (Alaska) and Mt. Saint Elias (on the Alaska-Yukon border), that is higher than you can go in North America.

Using barometric pressure has its advantages and disadvantages. The advantage of using barometric pressure to find altitude is that you do not have to be in the line-of-sight of satellites. You can be inside a cave and still use barometric pressure.

The disadvantage, however, is that pressure varies not only with altitude, but with changing weather patterns. In good weather, a barometer reads a higher pressure; in stormy weather, it reads a lower pressure. Effective use of a barometer, therefore, requires that it be calibrated at a known altitude. For example, if the signpost at the trailhead indicates that the altitude at the trailhead is 4,237 feet (1,291 m), you can set the altitude at that reading. Assuming the weather does not change significantly during your hike, your altitude readings should be fairly accurate. However, you do not always have the advantage of knowing an initial altitude.

In contrast, the advantage of calculating altitude using satellite triangulation is that the calculation is completely independent of weather. But, as already mentioned, a significant disadvantage of using triangulation is that the lines of sight to satellites may be blocked. A satellite may be below the horizon, or there may be a cliff wall in the way.

Knowing your altitude probably is not as important as knowing your latitude and longitude. However, I think it's fun to know what altitude I am at. Knowing how high I am also gives me an appreciation of the heights of peaks around me.

An altimeter is an instrument for measuring altitude. If you have a topographic map, you probably don't need an altimeter. You can find the contour line corresponding to your location and the map tells you your altitude. I own a GPS unit and an altimeter, and I often carry a topo map. I frequently use all three and compare the results.

Conclusion

I rarely hike in an area where I have a chance of getting lost. For example, at the Grand Canyon it is pretty hard to venture far from some trails without falling over a 2,000-foot (610-m) cliff. In other areas, I am following a river or passing through a valley. Trails are well marked, and trail junctions are signed, so I know where forks in trails are going.

But, if you are worried about getting lost, the safest thing is to carry a compass and a topographic map. If you understand how to use both of them, it would be difficult to get lost. Since topo maps can be downloaded to most modern GPS units, you can even have your topo map and GPS, too!

I used to have a T-shirt that read "Don't get lost." That's always good advice. Carry a map and compass, and possibly a GPS. Learn how to use them properly, and you should never get lost.

CHAPTER 8

 # Health and Safety

---

In This Chapter

➤ Hypothermia

➤ Hyperthermia

➤ Don't let disasters happen to you

The world is full of hazards. Every day people are injured or die from automobile accidents, falls, drownings, poisonings, burns, cuts, assaults, or a myriad of other causes. We don't stop living our daily lives because of the risks involved.

Few people refuse to drive or ride in an automobile because of scary statistics about traffic fatalities. Many people enjoy riding motorcycles even though they know the dangers that are involved. Airplane passengers know that planes sometimes crash. People don't stop cooking because they might be burned. Hunters are unlikely to give up hunting because hunters sometimes are accidentally shot. And few people would never leave their homes because of fear of assault.

In our everyday lives, we learn to assess the risks that are involved in our activities and do our best to minimize those risks.

Responsible drivers stay within posted speed limits, stop at red lights, and generally maintain an awareness of the other traffic around them. Construction workers learn to use power tools and ladders safely. Cooks are careful with hot stoves and ovens. Many, many people enjoy target shooting and hunting, and do so in a safe, responsible manner by attending weapons safety courses, taking care of their weapons, and paying attention to their surroundings and fellow hunters. People learn what neighborhoods in their communities are safe and what neighborhoods are best avoided, especially at night.

All of the same attitudes and practices that we adopt—whether deliberately or subconsciously—apply on the trail and at the campsite as well. In fact, learning to take care of yourself in the wilderness can be fun and a source of pride. In this chapter you will learn about some of the hazards a hiker or camper might encounter and how to handle them.

Hypothermia and How to Avoid it

One of the first hazards persons engaged in various forms of outdoor recreation encounter involves abrupt changes of weather. How to read the skies and anticipate changes in weather is discussed in Chapter 10. In this chapter we are interested in what precautions to take to avoid potentially life-threatening situations.

Hikers and backpackers in North America may face a wide range of weather conditions that depend on latitude, elevation, and season. Let's look at one of the most common hazards associated with cold weather, hypothermia.

Hypothermia in Deserts

When most people think of deserts, they immediately picture very hot and very dry conditions. Depending upon the time of year, that image may be an accurate description, but not always. It would probably surprise many non-desert dwellers that as many (or more) people engaging in recreational activities in desert environments succumb to hypothermia, which is a decrease in core body temperature due to cold conditions, than to hyperthermia, which is an elevation in core body temperature due to becoming overheated.

Hiking Vocab

Hypothermia occurs when the body's core temperature has cooled to less than 95°F (35°C).

Hyperthermia occurs when the body's core temperature has increased to 100°F–101°F (37.8°C–38.3°C).

Both conditions can be life-threatening.

Your body likes a temperature of 98.6°F (37°C). A few degrees too high or too low could prove fatal. I want to devote a sizeable section of this chapter to hypothermia and hyperthermia because they are the leading causes of death normally described as due to exposure.

Probably the best explanation for the frequent occurrence of hypothermia is people go into the desert expecting it to be hot. They dress lightly, often wearing T-shirts and shorts even in winter. Assuming they are carrying sufficient supplies of liquids—including water and electrolyte replacements—they are probably fine during the day.

But then the sun sets and the temperature plummets. Before long, desert hikers could get very, very cold. If they don't have warm clothes to put on, some food to eat—the calories in food stoke the body's internal furnace—or the ability to return to someplace warm, there's a good chance that hypothermia will set in. What is deceiving is that the victim may not even recognize the symptoms, which are:

Trail Wisdom

It doesn't have to be the middle of winter for hypothermia to be a threat. Hypothermia can strike any time of year.

> ➤ Lethargy
> ➤ Sleepiness
> ➤ The desire to lie down and go to sleep

This is when they are in danger. Victims can die in their sleep if their core body temperature drops too low.

What happened? Why did it get so cold? The answer is the lack of water vapor (humidity) in the desert atmosphere. An important physical property of any substance is what scientists call the substance's specific heat. Basically, the specific heat of a substance is the number of calories of heat 1 gram of the substance absorbs when its temperature increases by 1° Celsius (1.8° Fahrenheit). Common metals like copper, iron, aluminum, and lead have low values of specific heat—generally less than 0.1 to 0.2 calorie per gram per degree.

A low specific heat means that the substance's temperature increases rapidly as it absorbs heat (or conversely, that its temperature decreases rapidly if it is giving off heat). Water, on the other hand, has a much higher specific heat than the common metals mentioned above—1 calorie per gram per degree Celsius. That means, for example, that if equal-size samples of copper and water absorb the same amount of heat, the temperature of the water will increase only about one-tenth as much as the temperature of the copper does.

The high specific heat of water makes water a great regulator of climate. Draw a line from Seattle to Boston. Seattle is situated on Puget Sound and has a relatively mild climate because the waters of Puget Sound absorb heat during the summer and release heat during the winter. That line passes through Montana, the Dakotas, and Minnesota, all of which have warmer summers and much colder winters than Seattle does. Without a large body of water to regulate temperature, both summers and winters at those locations are more extreme.

The same effect is true in the desert. With the desert's dry atmosphere, the air heats up quickly during a summer day, reaching temperatures well in excess of 100°F (38°C). It could become unbearable to people who are unused to it, but is likely to be very comfortable during the winter months.

As soon as the sun sets, since there is nothing in the atmosphere to retain the heat, the temperature drops dramatically. Compounding the problem is that a person's clothing is probably damp from perspiration. Wearing damp clothing has a cooling effect. You may have had the experience of soaking your T-shirt in water on a hot day, and then putting it back on. Your T-shirt acted like an evaporative cooler, wicking heat from your skin and cooling you off. That's great during the day, but not at night. At night, wicking heat from your skin makes you just that much colder, perhaps even dangerously so.

Nature Note

On a warm summer day, rocks and sand tend to be much hotter than any nearby water. Rocks and sand contain minerals (e.g., quartz) that have a low specific heat, so the energy in sunlight heats them up rapidly. Water in nearby ponds, lakes, or the ocean has a high specific heat, so its change in temperature is much less.

What should you do to avoid hypothermia? Here is a short list of suggestions:

➤ Stay hydrated. Don't wait to become thirsty; if you're thirsty, it means your body is already about a quart (liter) low on water.

➤ Snack regularly or eat regular meals. Just as a campfire dies out when it runs out of fuel, your body's internal fires die out if there's no food to fuel them.

➤ Change into dry clothing when you're through hiking for the day. The first thing I do when I reach my campsite is change into dry clothing. That's everything—shirts, pants, underwear, and socks. Depending upon the time of year and how cold it's likely to get, I dress in layers for the night.

➤ Set up your campsite while dinner is cooking. I set up my tent, roll out my sleeping bag, and do whatever else is necessary to make the campsite ready for the night. And if I'm feeling cold, I may even crawl into my sleeping bag while I'm waiting for dinner.

➤ Hiking companions should look after each other. Recognize the initial signs of hypothermia. If one of your companions begins to exhibit signs of seeming chilled or lethargic, get him or her warm as quickly as possible.

When I experienced an episode with hypothermia, my companions stuffed me into my sleeping bag and began heating water for hot chocolate. Of course, it was important that the hot chocolate wasn't too hot. It wouldn't have done me any good to burn myself, or to have been unable to drink it. So, warm enough to warm a person up again, but not so hot as to pose a hazard.

Warm clothing, warm food, and a warm beverage should be sufficient to offset the effects of hypothermia, or to prevent it in the first place.

One final word about hypothermia: an extreme case is life-threatening. If you have a companion who does not respond to the treatment just described, then he or she should be evacuated from the field and taken to a medical facility for treatment. If untreated, hypothermia can be fatal.

Hyperthermia and Staying Hydrated

If you carry sufficient clothing and keep it dry, handling cold weather is probably easier than handling hot weather. You can always add more layers if you're cold, but there is a limit to what you can take off if you're hot. Stripping to nakedness in the hot sun is not a good idea. Not only is it an invitation to extreme sunburn, but it also invites heat stroke or heat exhaustion.

The usual advice for hot weather is to avoid hiking between 10 a.m. and 4 p.m. Do all of your hiking during the early morning and evening hours, and take a siesta in the shade during the middle of the day. Or take a swim (still being careful of sunburn). Drink plenty of fluids.

Trail Wisdom

The human body consists of roughly 60 percent water by weight; that's 120 pounds (54.5 kg) of water for a 200-pound (91-kg) person The brain and lungs contain even higher percentages. Because so much of your health depends on staying well hydrated, it is absolutely essential to drink lots of liquids when hiking. Muscle aches, stomach cramps, vertigo, headaches, high blood pressure, and fatigue can all be signs that you're dehydrated. So drink up!

It's usually more obvious if you are suffering from hyperthermia than from hypothermia. With hyperthermia, you may feel really hot, your skin may be flushed, and you're definitely dehydrated. The best way to prevent hyperthermia is to stay hydrated. There are all kinds of rules of thumb people like to use. Here are some that I find useful:

➤ You should begin your hike each day fully hydrated. If it's the first day and you're driving to a trailhead, you should be sipping liquids all the way there.

➤ If you are camping overnight, you should drink plenty of liquids in the morning before hitting the trail. An indication that you haven't had enough to drink is if you don't need to urinate between the time you first get up and the time you're ready to start hiking. You're already dehydrated; drink something before you start.

➤ Depending upon the time of year, the temperature, and the difficulty of the trail you are on, you need to drink at regular intervals. Under some conditions, that may mean every fifteen minutes. Under other conditions, that may mean only every half hour or hour. But I would not go longer than that without drinking.

➤ The water you're carrying should be convenient to reach. Some hikers prefer a water bladder often called a camelback, which rides on their back and has a tube that goes over their shoulder. You can sip from the tip of the tube as often as you like without having to stop.

I carry a small water bottle that fits comfortably in my hand so that I can take sips frequently. If I leave the water in my pack and have to stop to take off my pack to get to it, I'm less likely to drink as frequently as I should. What seems to work well is to carry my liter-size bottles (34 fl oz, or a little more than 1 qt) in my pack, but carry a 16- to 20-ounce (0.5- to 0.6-liter) bottle in my hand. When I've emptied the smaller bottle, I just refill it from one of the larger bottles.

➤ Some people drink a quart of water every mile (or every hour) in hot weather, or carry 2 gallons of water (about 8 L) per person per day. Water requirements vary from person to person. Bigger people need more water than lightweight people. You need to keep track of how much you drink and how you feel, so you know what your personal requirements are.

➤ Each gallon of water weighs about 8 pounds (3.5 kg). You're carrying a lot of weight if you're carrying 2 gallons (8 L) of water—16 pounds (7.3 kg) in fact. Plan your day so that you can refill your water bottles at least once a day. If you know you are going to have a dry camp (one that isn't near a source of water), be sure to pack enough water to get you through the night and the next day to the next source of water. Also be sure to have a method to filter or disinfect natural water supplies (more on that later).

➤ The body tends to absorb cool water better than warm water. It may be difficult to keep your water supplies cool, but it's something to keep in mind. Of course, in very cold weather, drinking cold liquids might make you so cold that your body burns extra calories just to stay warm, in which case warm liquids are preferable.

➤ Some people prefer electrolyte drinks such as the sports drinks athletes buy. I think I probably get sufficient electrolytes when hiking by eating salty snacks. I also find that I drink more if I flavor the water a little. A flavored berry or grape mix works well. It is probably best, though, not to drink beverages that are too sugary when hiking—the purer the water, the better. In camp, I may make lemonade in warm weather or hot chocolate in cold weather.

➤ Drinking alcohol in camp may promote camaraderie or just be a nice ending to a good day on the trail, but alcohol contributes little to rehydrating the body. Don't let alcohol substitute for drinking plenty of water. What is true for alcoholic beverages is also true for caffeinated beverages. Both are diuretics; they cause you to lose more water when urinating than is desirable.

Trail Wisdom

I think the best rule I have ever heard for staying well hydrated is the advice given by the backcountry staff members at Philmont Scout Ranch in Cimarron, New Mexico. They say, "Urine should be clear and copious." That pretty much says it all. Dark brown or thick urine is a sure sign of dehydration. Urine should be clear or light yellow. And it should be produced in large (copious) amounts. Staying clear and copious will contribute significantly to your having a good time on the trail. Drink up!

You have probably heard stories of hikers who got lost, ran out of water, and drank their own urine trying to stay alive. That's not a good idea. A basic principle of biology is that no organism can live on its own waste products, and urine is a waste product. Don't put yourself in a situation where you might feel that drinking your urine is your only chance of survival. Plan ahead. Don't exceed your personal limits. I go hiking and backpacking to have fun, get some exercise, and commune with nature. I try to go into the field well prepared. That's my advice.

Hypothermia and Hyperthermia Risks for Children

Most adults can take care of themselves pretty well. It is children who need to be watched. Young children are less likely to recognize the symptoms of heat exhaustion or hypothermia, so their parents, or other adults, need to take care of them.

In hot weather, be sure they are wearing clothing that covers their head and skin, drinking plenty of fluids, eating foods that will replace electrolytes, and stopping to rest in the shade more frequently than an adult may require. A child's flushed face is a sign that he is too hot. It is time to stop and cool him down.

In cold weather, be sure children are wearing hats, scarves, and mittens. Children are unlikely to recognize the signs of frostbite.

Trail Wisdom

Children are less likely than adults to recognize when they are too hot, too cold, or dehydrated. Adults need to monitor the condition of children who are hiking with them and make sure they are staying well hydrated, cool in hot weather, and warm in cold weather. Take frequent rests, and watch for signs of any abnormal conditions.

Purifying Water in the Field

If you're day hiking, chances are you can carry sufficient water to get you through the day. If you're on the trail for multiple days, however, then you need to replenish your water supply.

In some parts of the world, people have to be concerned about hepatitis viruses, botulism, cholera, and typhoid that could be contracted from contaminated water supplies. These diseases are less of a concern in the United States and Canada, especially in wilderness areas. In North America, the major concern with water is the potential for harmful bacteria like Escherichia coli (E. coli) and protozoan parasites like giardia to be in the water.

The major symptoms of E. coli infection or giardiasis are intestinal problems—diarrhea, stomach cramps, bloating, nausea, vomiting, and weight loss. Both diseases may clear up on their own. If complications result, medical attention is required.

There are various ways to treat water to rid it of most contaminants. Let's take a look at them.

Boiling Water

Water can be brought to a boil. It doesn't actually have to boil very long. By the time it's boiling, any bacteria, protozoa, or viruses have been killed. There are at least three drawbacks to boiling:

1. Boiling consumes fuel. You've brought fuel on the trail for cooking; it could be a problem if you're also using it for disinfecting water.

2. Boiling removes air that's dissolved in water, leaving the water tasting flat.

3. You have to wait for the water to cool down to drink it.

Adding Iodine to Water

Water can be treated with iodine. Iodine is available in either tablet or crystal form. Tablets are easy to use but have a couple of disadvantages:

1. The tablets impart an iodine taste to the water; some people find that taste objectionable. Some packages also have a little vitamin C, which can be added to neutralize the excess iodine.

2. You have to plan ahead of time. It takes about an hour for a tablet to dissolve and kill any harmful microorganisms. One possibility is to treat all of your water before going to bed at night. That way it will be ready to drink when you get up in the morning.

Iodine is also available in crystalline form, which works more quickly, leaves less of an iodine aftertaste, and a supply can treat more water than the standard supply of tablets does. Iodine crystals are more expensive if you don't plan to use them very often. If you do extensive backpacking, however, they will pay for themselves in the long run.

Adding Chlorine Bleach to Water

Water can be treated with a few drops of chlorine bleach. But like iodine, chlorine leaves an aftertaste. Probably the biggest problem with using bleach is not knowing how much to add.

Filtering Water

Water can be filtered. Filtration is the method of choice for the majority of backpackers these days. Filtration systems have several advantages:

➤ They are reasonably compact and lightweight.

➤ There is no waiting period; water that has been filtered can be consumed immediately.

➤ Filtering leaves no aftertaste.

➤ A good filter can treat thousands of gallons of water.

The disadvantages of a filtration system include the following:

➤ The initial cost is much higher than the chemical treatment.

➤ The filters eventually have to be replaced, and they aren't cheap.

➤ Water has to be pumped by hand through the filter, and some people find pumping a nuisance.

Ultraviolet Light (UV)

A relatively new method on the market is to use a portable ultraviolet (UV) light to sterilize water. The cost of a UV system seems to be comparable to that of a filtration system. UV has the advantage in that pumping is not required. A potential disadvantage in using a UV system is that it is powered by a rechargeable battery. Having to recharge a battery could be a problem on a long trek.

At one time or another, I have used all of these methods, except the UV system, and my recommendation is to go with filtration. Just be sure that the filter is rated for removing viruses in case you travel to a place where viruses could be a problem. The UV system is a fairly new technology for backpacking, so ask about it when you're doing your other shopping. Maybe it will be all the rage someday.

Although it's recommended that drinking water be purified, I only purify the water I am going to drink cold. I don't purify wash water, and although I heat water for washing dishes (and myself), I don't heat the water to its boiling point. If I did, I wouldn't be able to put my hands in it. However, I do add a biodegradable detergent that kills any bacteria and protozoa that might be in the water. Also, I always set my dishes and utensils on a rock or log to dry in the sun. That's probably not enough UV light to sterilize them, but microorganisms don't survive in a dry environment. Giardia has to be in water or body fluids to survive. Once my dishes have dried out, giardia is no longer a potential problem.

I also don't bother to further purify water that I'm going to boil for hot chocolate or to cook with. Boiling water is sufficient to kill any microorganisms in it.

What's left is the water I'm actually going to drink. That may be a few quarts or liters a day—not enough to make filtering inconvenient.

Trail Wisdom

There are hikers and campers who end up suffering from diarrhea, stomach cramps, bloating, nausea, or vomiting. Some experts believe that the majority of those cases are due to poor personal hygiene, not to contaminated water supplies. People don't wash their hands after going to the bathroom. They handle each other's dishes and eating utensils. Sometimes groups cook one big pot of food, pass it around, and everyone in the group shares the same spoon. It only takes one person in the group to contaminate everyone else. Be safe. Wash your hands with soap before handling food.

Disasters on the Trail

Whole books have been written about people who have died in national parks. If I had read *Over the Edge: Death at Grand Canyon*, by Michael Ghiglieri and Thomas Myers before ever hiking the Grand Canyon, I probably would have been too scared to go! There certainly are a number of disasters that can occur in national parks, and national park records of deaths often go back to before a park was even established.

Visitors have perished on the trail in a variety of circumstances, including

➤ Falling while climbing

➤ Drowning

➤ Being killed or maimed by wild animals

➤ Dying from exposure (which usually means hypothermia or severe dehydration)

➤ Being struck by lightning

➤ Getting lost or wandering off and never being found

➤ Dying during volcanic eruptions

➤ Being buried by avalanches

➤ Dying in airplane or helicopter crashes

➤ Being murdered by various methods

➤ Dying of natural causes, which may have been due to overexertion or were unrelated to what they were doing in the park

➤ Committing suicide

➤ Dying while attempting rescues

When records from all the national parks in the United States and Canada are put together, the statistics are sobering. In 1997, there were 350 million visitors to national parks in the United States. (That figure duplicates visitors who went to the parks more than once.) Of those visitors, 14,000 required medical attention, 4,500 needed to be rescued, and 300 died in our national parks. Even with all the efforts to warn people against taking unnecessary risks, 187 people died in national parks in 2010. Those statistics may sound low, and they are, but low statistics don't matter if you happen to be one of the casualties.

The message here is don't take risks. Rangers at the Grand Canyon say that men in their twenties are the most likely to require backcountry rescues, more so than older men, and much more so than women. Men in their twenties think they're invincible, so they exhibit the riskiest behaviors.

Know your own limits. Don't attempt to hike farther in a day than you are physically fit to hike. Don't try to swim rivers with swift currents. And don't take shortcuts that can result in serious falls and injuries.

Trail Wisdom

The Greek philosopher Socrates said, "Know thyself." To that we can add, know your own limits. Hundreds of millions of people engage in various forms of outdoor recreation without mishap. Be one of them. Don't become one of the small number of casualties.

Conclusion

Hiking and backpacking are among the best ways to enjoy the great outdoors. Acting prudently and exercising common sense will permit many years of enjoyment. Be careful out there, and have a good time.

CHAPTER 9

First Aid in the Wilderness

In This Chapter

➤ What is first aid?

➤ First responses

➤ First aid scenarios

Accidents, burns, bites, stings, cuts, and scratches occur on the trail just as they do at home. Most first aid requires nothing more than just using common sense, just like you would at home. The difference on the trail is you can't just run to the medicine cabinet and grab a box of Band-Aids. On the trail, you have to carry all your medical supplies with you. This chapter is about the supplies you should have with you and how to use them.

The Definition of First Aid

What is first aid? A good definition is that first aid is emergency treatment administered to a sick or injured person. First aid is the first steps taken to assist a victim. First aid, however, is usually only temporary. In simple cases, first aid may be the only treatment a person needs: a cut or wound is cleaned, a Band-Aid is applied, warm fluids are given, the victim is allowed to rest. In severe cases, the purpose of first aid is to prevent further injury or additional aggravation of a problem that already exists until professional help can be obtained.

Trail Wisdom

First aid is using common sense to make an abnormal situation normal again. There's a saying among first responders: if the face is pale, raise the tail; if the face is red, raise the head.

Important Considerations

Being a first responder in an emergency is not the same in the wilderness as it is in the city. In the city, ambulances can be summoned; patients can be rushed to hospitals. In the city you can turn over care of your family member or friend to a health professional. That's not true in the wilderness.

In the wilderness you are on your own—most likely for at least several hours, but also possibly overnight or even for several days. If the injured person cannot be treated in the field, then he needs to be evacuated, usually by helicopter.

If you are carrying a cell phone and have coverage, you are really lucky. Unfortunately, in most wilderness areas, you likely will not have cell phone coverage. In that case, someone needs to hike back to the trailhead and drive to the nearest phone to get help.

This is why—unless you happen to be hiking on well-traveled trails—the rule of thumb is to hike in a group of at least four people. Why four? One person is injured. One person needs to remain behind with the injured person. Two people should go for help. Why two?

Suppose someone heads back alone to get help and he is injured. Now, not only is that person unable to obtain help, but he is also unable to inform the persons left behind that something has happened. The injured person and companion are going to sit there, possibly for days, wondering why help hasn't arrived. So, two people should go for help. Then if one of them is also injured, there is someone to help.

Trail Wisdom

Do not backpack alone into remote, lightly traveled wilderness areas. Travel with a group of at least four people. Give someone back home your itinerary, so if your group does not return on schedule, searchers will know where to look for you.

You might ask what happens if one or more members of the rescue party also become injured and cannot continue back to the trailhead to go for help? Obviously, the situation has now gone from bad to really bad. Fortunately, this kind of situation is pretty rare. The number of people who backpack into truly remote, isolated areas is fairly small. And people who do that are probably a cut above the rest of us in terms of their physical conditioning, planning, and skills, so they are less likely to run into problems (although it does happen!). The statistical odds of two people in a group of four both becoming too ill or injured to go for help are very, very low.

This brings up another rule of thumb: tell someone else where you are going and when you expect to return! That way, if you don't show up within a reasonable time, the appropriate authorities can be alerted and a search can begin for you. This suggests, also, that when you do get off the trail, phone the person who has your itinerary so he knows not to panic and phone the authorities needlessly.

Trail Wisdom

The math to calculate the probability of two people in a group both becoming sick or injured is actually very simple. Suppose the probability of one person becoming severely sick or injured on a backpacking trip is 1 in 100, or 0.01, which is probably an overestimate. Then the probability of two people in the same group becoming severely sick or injured is 0.01 times 0.01, or 0.0001, or only 1 in 10,000. The probability is not zero, but it is low enough that statistically you would have to do an awful lot of backpacking for it to happen.

First Responses

First aid is rendered when an abnormal situation occurs. The purpose of first aid is to try to restore the victim to normalcy.

Two admonitions to keep in mind are the following:

1. Do no harm

2. Do not place yourself in danger. In other words, don't make a bad situation even worse; you won't be able to alleviate the condition of an injured companion if you end up suffering an injury yourself.

Trail Wisdom

Hippocrates had it right. The first rule of first aid is to do no harm. Proceed carefully and cautiously. Don't compound an already bad situation by making it even worse.

Take Charge

When one member of a party is injured, this is no time for the other members to hang back and expect someone else to take charge. It should be understood ahead of time who should take charge. Remember: first aid needs to be immediate. There is no time to waste.

Approach the Victim in a Safe Fashion

It's common in first aid exercises to have someone playing the part of a victim lying on the ground in a variety of situations. The rescuers come upon the victim, access the situation, and presumably take necessary action.

I remember one such exercise in which I was participating that one of the victims was lying about 10–15 feet (3–4.5 m) on the downhill side of the trail. In his haste, the rescuer accidentally dislodged a rock that rolled down the hill and struck the victim in the head. The poor victim's original injury may not have been real, but he wasn't faking the pain in his head!

Let that be a lesson to would-be rescuers. When approaching a victim who is downhill from you, approach from the side, not from above. Watch where you step and be careful you don't accidentally kick any rocks or sticks onto the victim. If the slope is steep, tie a rope around your waist and tie the other end of the rope securely to a tree or log. If that's not possible, then tie the other end around the waist of another member of the party who secures himself in such a way that he isn't going to slide after you.

If the victim is on a ledge, there is the real danger that the victim—or the rescuer—could roll off the ledge. The rescuer must be secured to something immobile.

In Case of a Fall

If the injury is the result of a bad fall, there is always the possibility of a head or spinal injury. If in doubt, do not try to move the victim, unless moving him is absolutely necessary to get him to a safer position. If the victim is complaining of head or back pain, evacuation is probably required. If the victim is not breathing or his heart has stopped, CPR is required.

Check for Bleeding

It is absolutely essential that bleeding be stopped. Clean clothing can be placed on the wound and direct pressure applied. If an arm or leg is bleeding, elevate the limb.

Water Rescue

During a water rescue, there is always the danger of a double drowning. People who think they're drowning are likely to panic, and they may pull their would-be rescuers underwater with them.

Unless a victim is a child or someone much smaller than yourself, or you have been training in lifesaving techniques, avoid coming into contact with a drowning victim. Extend a stick or towel to the victim, and pull him ashore.

If the victim is awake and breathing throughout the ordeal, CPR isn't necessary once he's ashore. Wrap the victim in a warm blanket or sleeping bag, though, because hypothermia is probably present. If the victim is not breathing, CPR is required.

Treat the Victim for Shock

Most injured persons will suffer some state of shock and need to be treated for it. In cool weather keep the victim warm. Have the victim lie down and elevate his feet to help blood return to the brain and vital organs.

Hiking Vocab

If you've had CPR training, remember the ABCs of CPR:

➤ Airway

➤ Breathing

➤ Circulation

Check the victim's throat for obstructions. If there are no obstructions but the victim isn't breathing on his own and/or there's no pulse, administer breath and chest compressions.

If you've never had CPR training, sign up for a class the first chance you get.

Check for Additional Injuries

Bleeding, pain, lack of breathing, or lack of a pulse are obvious injuries that need immediate attention. Once the victim is stabilized, check for additional, less obvious, injuries. Look for bruises, other discoloration, and swelling. Compare the victim's arms and legs. Does it look like a limb is dislocated? How about the victim's eyes? Are the pupils dilated? Are the pupils the same size? How does the victim feel? Are there areas that are sensitive to the touch? Check the abdomen—does pressure cause pain? Is the victim suffering from nausea? Is the victim conscious or unconscious? If conscious, is the victim alert? Can the victim talk? Is he coherent or does he just mumble? Keep a log of your findings. At what time do symptoms appear? If paramedics need to be summoned to the scene, a log of symptoms and first aid that was administered will help them diagnose the situation and decide how to proceed.

You may not have the skill or medical equipment necessary to treat most of a victim's symptoms. However, a thorough examination will help you decide whether to call for help. Emergency medical personnel are going to want to know what the victim's symptoms are.

Trail Wisdom

Never leave a victim alone. The victim could panic and do harm to himself. Or, the victim's condition could worsen and no one would know.

First Aid Scenarios on the Trail

At least three first aid scenarios on the trail are possible:

1. Injuries are minor

2. The victim requires assistance to walk

3. The victim cannot walk at all

Let's consider each in turn.

Minor Injuries

Suppose the victim has been treated for an injury or illness and continues on the hike after he feels up to it. This is the most common situation. Perhaps the victim has twisted his ankle but has not actually sprained it. The pain will probably be temporary, and when it subsides the victim may announce that he feels capable of continuing. The victim's companions may help by carrying some of his gear for a while, until he feels that he has fully recovered.

Perhaps the victim arrives at camp at day's end with a throbbing headache. A little food, plenty of liquids, perhaps an over-the-counter analgesic like aspirin or acetaminophen, and a good night's rest are sufficient for the victim to awake in the morning fully recovered and fully capable of hitting the trail again.

Helping a Victim Walk

Let's say the victim's illness or injury is not particularly serious, but even after the victim has been treated, he feels unable to continue the hike. It may be that he has seriously sprained his ankle so he cannot put his full weight on it but is still capable of walking with assistance.

In that case, other members of the party can divide the victim's gear among them and take turns helping the victim walk out. The victim may need to lean on a stout walking stick for support, or he may need to drape an arm around the shoulder of a companion for support. Whether or not the victim can walk out in this manner will depend upon just how severe the injury is and on how far it is back to the trailhead. In some cases, a victim's companions may rig a stretcher and take turns carrying him.

Trail Wisdom

If a member of your party does suffer a sprained ankle, remember the acronym RICE:

➤ Rest

➤ Ice

➤ Compression

➤ Elevation

The biggest problem with a sprained ankle is swelling. Rest helps to prevent the ankle from getting worse. Ice, compression, and elevation all help to reduce swelling.

The Victim Cannot Walk at All

The victim has been treated for his illness or injury but is unable to walk. A severe situation is when a possible head or spinal column injury has occurred. Improperly moving a victim with a spinal column injury could result in permanent paralysis. Since any movement has the potential of making the injury even worse, the only movement that should be attempted is when moving the victim is necessary to prevent additional possible injury.

For example, the victim could be in water and running the risk of hypothermia. Or he could be dangerously close to a cliff and risks rolling or sliding over the edge. Although it would still be dangerous for the victim's companions to try to move the victim, they need to move him to safety. But they must do so as carefully as possible, being careful not to place any strain on the victim's head, neck, or back. Otherwise, the best the victim's companions can do for him is make him comfortable, treat him for shock, and arrange for a medical evacuation.

Burn Treatment

There are three types of burns:

1. First-degree burn

2. Second-degree burn

3. Third degree burn

In this section, we will learn about prevention and treatment of each type.

First-Degree Burns

First-degree burns are the most common and may or may not be serious. The main symptom is reddened skin that may be accompanied by pain and a feeling of being hot. The causes are either sunburn or coming in contact with a hot object. Sunburns can be easily prevented by taking a few simple precautions:

> ➤ Wear light clothing when hiking or performing other activities in direct sunlight. That includes a hat to protect the scalp, ears, and forehead. If the hat does not shade the back of the neck, wear a bandana or kerchief that covers the neck.

> ➤ Wear sunscreen on any exposed skin. Sunscreens are rated by Sun Protection Factor (SPF) values; the higher the SPF value, the better. If you are going to be in the sun all day, apply sunscreen more than once during the day.

> ➤ Apply lip gloss to the lips. The best lip glosses are ones that have sunscreen in them. Look for an SPF value on the label.

> ➤ Do not be fooled by the amount of cloud cover. The danger of sunburn is greater at higher elevations because of the greater exposure to ultraviolet radiation, but I have been burned at sea level on a cloudy day. Recognize, too, that sunlight reflected from sand, rocks, or snow can contribute to sunburn.

If sunburn does occur and is painful, applying aloe vera to the burned area can help relieve the pain. So can vaseline or other burn ointments on the market. If you are still active in direct sunlight, be sure to cover the burned area.

First-degree burns can also result from touching a hot stove, pan, or utensil. The best treatment is to soak the burned area in cold water. A national park backcountry ranger once told me that the most common accidents that had been brought to her attention that season had resulted from misuse of camp stoves. Be careful!

I carry a small hot pad with me or wear gloves when cooking. Remember that hot stoves do not look hot. After using one, be sure to let it cool down completely before touching the burner elements. Another stove accident can occur when victims spill hot water on themselves and are scalded. Again, the best prevention is to use a hot pad or wear gloves.

A mild sunburn or burn that does not result in blisters is an irritation and is not serious. Severe burns, however, are ones that produce blisters and may require more aggressive treatment, as described next.

Second-Degree Burns

Burns that result in blisters are second-degree burns. A second-degree burn can be a severe sunburn that blisters and eventually causes the skin to peel away. The biggest danger associated with a second-degree burn is that the blisters could break and become infected. It is better not to rub ointments on the blisters. The best treatment is to cover the blisters with a sterile gauze pad and tape the pad securely so it stays in place. Try to keep the gauze pad clean and dry until the blisters heal.

After you have returned home from your hike or backpacking trip, if the blisters do not seem to be healing—or if they become discolored or more painful—it is recommended that you have your doctor take a look at them.

Third-Degree Burns

The most serious are third-degree burns because they are potentially life-threatening. A third-degree burn is characterized by charred flesh. Prompt medical attention is required. Do not apply any creams or ointments to the burned area. Do not try to remove any clothing from around the charred flesh—the clothing could be sticking to the flesh. A real possibility is that the victim will go into shock, and this should be treated accordingly. Wrap clean clothing (or a sheet or blanket, if you have one) around the victim, and keep him warm if the weather is cool. Medical evacuation from the trail is necessary.

Tetanus

Anyone who spends any time at all outdoors, even if it's just puttering in the garden, needs to be immunized against tetanus. The recommended schedule is to receive booster shots at least every ten years.

Tetanus is carried by bacteria found in the soil. Entry of bacteria into the body is either by a laceration or a puncture of the skin. Punctures, as occur when a person steps on a dirty or rusty nail or other sharp object with bare feet, are especially hazardous. At least with a cut, you can thoroughly wash the cut and visually inspect the cut for dirt particles. On the other hand, with a puncture, dirt has likely gotten into the body under the skin where you can't see it or clean it out. Harmful punctures are not limited to the feet, however. Any puncture or laceration anywhere on the body needs to be treated. Animal bites or scratches are also potential sources of infection.

Tetanus symptoms may include muscle contractions at the site where the cut or infection occurred or over the whole body. The incubation period is five to twenty-one days. If untreated, tetanus can be fatal.

Another name for tetanus is lockjaw, because one of the most common symptoms is a stiff jaw that makes swallowing difficult. The stiffness may extend to the neck, arms, or legs. Fevers, headaches, and sore throats are common.

Blisters

Some people seem to be prone to blisters no matter what they do. Other people never get blisters. A blister is caused by repeated rubbing of skin. The best prevention is to wear shoes or boots that fit properly, lace them snugly, and change socks that are damp with sweat.

Usually before a blister actually forms, a hot spot develops on the foot. Wash and dry the foot and apply moleskin over the hot spot. That should take care of the problem. Moleskin is pretty sticky and will last a weekend or longer. Don't peel it off; just wait for it to naturally fall off.

Hiking Vocab

Moleskin is a self-stick padding for the feet that hikers use to prevent blisters. Moleskin can also be applied to a blister to ease discomfort.

If blisters do form, they will be one of two kinds:

1. Water blisters, which are clear

2. Blood blisters, which are red

Water blisters can be popped. Sterilize a needle by wiping it with alcohol or heating it with a match. Gently insert the needle until water drains out. Apply a little pressure to force out the water. At that point the blister should be a loose piece of skin. Do not pull or cut off the loose skin. Wipe it with alcohol or wash it with soap and water. Letting it air-dry is best. If the victim needs to continue hiking, tape a clean Band-Aid or gauze pad over the blister. Check it again later. It's common to have to drain water blisters more than once.

Blood blisters should not be popped—there's too much danger of infection. Do not apply moleskin directly on the blister. The usual method is to cut a hole in a piece of moleskin the size of the blister. Place the moleskin around the blister. Sometimes two or three layers of moleskin work well. The moleskin should prevent the blister from worsening.

Embedded Objects

Always carry tweezers when you're hiking or camping. Splinters and thorns usually can be removed fairly easily. Just be sure you don't accidentally break them off and leave part under the skin. After an object has been removed, squeeze the spot a little. Drawing a few drops of blood is a good thing, as blood will help flush the wound. After that, wash the wound and apply a clean bandage or dressing.

An object in the eye is another matter. Dirt or dust on the surface of the eye usually can be flushed out. Sometimes just blinking the eye is sufficient to wash out tiny particles. If that doesn't work, have the victim hold his eye wide open and wash it with water.

If a foreign object is actually embedded in the eye, do not try to remove it. Your attempt could permanently damage the eye and even result in loss of sight in that eye. Instead, tape a dressing across the eye and evacuate the victim. Get him medical attention as quickly as possible.

Bites and Stings

The chances in North America of being bitten or stung by a wild animal, poisonous insect, arachnid (spider or scorpion), or venomous snake are pretty slim. The two most common poisonous spiders are black and brown widows and brown recluses. Scorpions are common in desert environments. Venomous snakes include rattlesnakes and coral snakes.

Spider Bites

Poisonous spiders are most likely to be found in buildings. It doesn't hurt to check inside outhouses before using them. Bites may be painful, but medical care usually isn't required. In cases of extreme pain or difficult breathing, or if a child is bitten, the victim should see a doctor.

Scorpion Stings

Scorpions are nocturnal, so you are unlikely to even see one. Most scorpion stings are not deadly. Their stings may be painful, but they do not usually require treatment. Although the Arizona bark scorpion is poisonous, a healthy adult who is stung probably doesn't require treatment. Small children are a different story; they should see a doctor.

Snake Bites

Doctors recommend that you do not attempt to treat a poisonous snake bite yourself. Do not try to suck out the venom. Do not tie a tourniquet. Do not apply ice. Get to a doctor as quickly as possible. If you are bitten on an arm or leg, keep the extremity below the level of your heart. Your only course of action may be to walk back out to a trailhead. Either that, or have your friends carry you out. Either way, do so as quickly as possible; it usually takes a few hours for the effects of the venom to become serious.

The chances of dying from a poisonous snake bite are low; in the United States, there are only five to six recorded deaths annually. The odds are in your favor that you will survive.

Contents of a First Aid Kit

You may already have a first aid kit at home or that you carry in your car. A first aid kit you carry on the trail is similar but lighter in weight. Fortunately, most of the contents of a first aid kit weigh very little. The heaviest item in a home first aid kit is probably the container the kit is in. On the trail, you can substitute a lighter weight container. Sometimes I just put everything in a gallon-size ziplock bag.

Here are some of the essentials that belong in every first aid kit:

> ➤ Bandages of assorted sizes
>
> ➤ Adhesive tape
>
> ➤ Sterile gauze pads
>
> ➤ Tweezers
>
> ➤ Antiseptic wipes (rubbing alcohol works fine)
>
> ➤ Analgesics (aspirin, acetaminophen, ibuprofen, etc.)
>
> ➤ Scissors
>
> ➤ Moleskin pads

One cautionary note: some people may be allergic to aspirin or other analgesics. You probably know whether or not your own family members have allergies, but check with nonfamily hiking companions and be sure they are not allergic to a medication before you give it to them.

One thing that is important about all of the items in a first aid kit is that they are sterile. Even though bandages and gauze pads are wrapped in paper or plastic, they do not remain sterile forever. If you do most of your backpacking during only a few months of the year, it might be wise at the end of the hiking season to transfer bandages and gauze pads to your home or automobile first aid kits and restock the hiking kit next year at the beginning of the hiking season.

First aid supplies are inexpensive. If you know that the materials in your first aid kit have been there for years, I would recommend discarding them and restocking the kit with fresh supplies. Always check the contents of your first aid kit before any hike. A few moments ensuring that everything is there beats being in the field and discovering that you are missing something that you could really use.

Trail Wisdom

If you use any of your first aid supplies during a hike, don't forget to replenish them after you get home!

Conclusion

The majority of hikes take place without any of the situations described in this chapter arising. Nevertheless, they do sometimes occur, and you need to be prepared and willing to handle them.

CHAPTER 10

 **Weather**

In This Chapter

- ➤ The atmosphere
- ➤ Weather conditions
- ➤ Extreme weather
- ➤ Weather forecasting

Weather phenomena are caused by the sun heating different parts of Earth differently. What we call weather is the state of the atmosphere at a given time. Variables that affect the weather include temperature, cloud cover, humidity, wind speed and direction, and barometric pressure.

Weather and Its Effects on Hiking

Most of us probably prefer to do our hiking in mild conditions—weather that is not too hot or too cold; not too humid, not too stormy, and not too windy. Just as Goldilocks preferred her porridge not too hot or too cold, but just right, we outdoors types usually prefer weather that is not too hot or too cold, but just right. However, just as Goldilocks would probably have

Trail Wisdom

Weather is what is going on in the atmosphere where you are, right now. This is different from climate, which is the long-term trend in weather patterns over a large regional area. Climate tends to be determined by latitude, longitude, altitude, the distribution of land and sea masses, and topography.

gone hungry if she had not lucked upon a bowl of just-right porridge, we hikers would probably in a sense "go hungry" if we insisted that the weather were always perfect.

Weather affects all of us who enjoy spending time in the outdoors. Chances are that if the Weather Channel is predicting heavy rain or snow, most people are going to stay off the trail. This chapter is not about forecasting the weather before you are on the trail; you can let the professionals do that. Knowing what the forecast is, you should be able to prepare accordingly.

Nature Quote

"There's no such thing as bad weather, only unsuitable clothing"

–Alfred Wainwright, renowned British walker and author

Although weather is often predictable, sometimes the predictions are wrong. You need to be able to anticipate changes in the weather when you are already on the trail. Once you are in the field, you are on your own. Deciding to continue a hike or to hoof it back to the trailhead could be a life-or-death decision. The purpose of this chapter is to describe the signs that are indicators of changing weather, and advise on how to handle those changes.

Regions of the Atmosphere

As anyone who has traveled from sea level to the top of a mountain knows, the atmosphere becomes thinner with increasing altitude, which means that atmospheric pressure and density both decrease with increasing altitude. For our purposes we can divide the atmosphere into three regions based on altitude. In order from Earth's surface to the highest altitudes, these three regions are as follows:

1. The troposphere

2. The stratosphere

3. The ionosphere

Since weather does not occur in the ionosphere, we are not concerned with it here.

Hiking Vocab

An atmosphere (atm) is a unit of pressure equal to the pressure of the air at sea level. It can also be expressed as about 14.7 pounds per square inch or 1.01 bar (1,010 millibars).

The units used to measure atmospheric pressure are atmospheres (atm), millimeters of mercury (mm Hg), inches of mercury (in Hg), and bars or millibars (mbar). On average, atmospheric pressure is 1 atm at sea level (hence the unit of atmosphere), or 760 mm Hg.

At 5,000 feet (1,524 m), pressure drops to 630 mm Hg, and at 10,000 feet (3,048 m), it drops to 520 mm Hg. At the top of Mt. Everest in Nepal, which is at an altitude of 29,035 feet (8,850 m), the pressure is only 250 mm Hg. The summit of Mt. Everest pokes into the stratosphere.

As with pressure, the temperature decreases with altitude. The air is much colder on top of a 14,000-foot (4,267-m) peak in Colorado than at mile-high Denver, Colorado (5,280 feet, or 1,609 m), which in turn is usually cooler than the Great Plains to its east, which is much closer to sea level.

Pressure is so low in the stratosphere (only 1–10 mm Hg) that for all practical purposes the stratosphere is a vacuum. The stratosphere is significantly colder than the troposphere. It is so cold that liquid water does not exist there; water exists only as ice crystals.

You have probably observed jet trails from aircraft flying through the stratosphere, typically at altitudes of about 30,000 to 35,000 feet (9,140 to 10,670 m). Just as happens in the troposphere, the combustion of an aircraft's fuel produces carbon dioxide and water vapor in its exhaust. In the stratosphere, the water vapor instantly freezes and becomes a trail of ice crystals following the aircraft.

Because of the cold temperature of the stratosphere, very few weather phenomena occur there. The highest clouds are most likely to reach only as high as the tropopause, the boundary between the troposphere and the stratosphere.

The troposphere is where most water vapor is located, where the winds are, and where weather takes place. Consequently, the air in the troposphere tends to be well mixed. Unless you summit Mount Everest, all of your hiking and backpacking takes place in the troposphere. What is going on in the troposphere is what you need to be concerned about.

Nature Note

The tropopause is not a sharp boundary between the troposphere and the stratosphere. The height of the tropopause is a function of latitude and season of the year. The tropopause has its highest altitude at low latitude (over the equator) and its lowest altitude at high latitude (near the poles). The tropopause is also lower in winter than it is in summer.

Temperature Fluctuations

For a day hike lasting less than eight hours, you are unlikely to encounter unanticipated changes in wind or temperature. When backpacking it is advisable to always assume that there could be big differences in temperature between day and night, and that changes in temperature are often accompanied by windy conditions.

For years, I never carried a thermometer. If I felt hot, it was hot; if I felt cold, it was cold. It didn't really matter what the actual temperature was. When I would get back home, someone would invariably ask me how cold it got at night. My answer would be that I didn't know, I was just glad I had a warm sleeping bag, or that my water bottle had frozen during the night, so the temperature must have been below freezing.

Recently I bought an altimeter and it has a thermometer on it. Now that I have the thermometer anyway, I sometimes check to see what the temperature is, but the answer is usually about what I could have guessed anyway.

More important than knowing the actual temperature is being prepared to handle the highs and lows of temperature that naturally accompany spending time outdoors. One factor that greatly contributes to the feeling of being cold is the wind. A cold wind blowing on exposed skin makes you feel colder than an actual low temperature will.

Wind Chill

Meteorologists use the term wind chill to describe the effect of wind on temperature. Suppose a thermometer that is sheltered from the wind reads an air temperature of 40°F (4.5°C). If being in the wind makes it feel as though the temperature is actually 25°F (–4°C), then the wind chill factor is 25°F—the effect of the wind on your body is the same as if there were no wind, and the air temperature really is 25°F. In that situation, you should be dressed as you would be for the colder temperature.

How people react to high or low temperatures depends on age, weight, level of hydration, and mental attitude. Teenagers and young adults in good health seem to handle hot or cold temperatures more readily than persons of the same age who are not in good physical condition. Children are more affected by temperature extremes than adults are. Older adults may not have good circulation, so they feel colder, or hotter, than younger adults do.

Some people simply handle levels of discomfort better than other people because they have a more positive mental attitude. People who groan about every uphill step, about every pound of weight on their back, and how much farther they have to hike that day probably are going to complain about being too hot or too cold.

Wind

The wind blows when there is a difference in air pressure between two locations. Just as heat flows from a hot object to a cold object, air flows from high pressure to low pressure. Because of Earth's rotation, however, the direction of flow is a little more complicated than that. In the northern hemisphere, air tends to flow in a counterclockwise direction around areas of low pressure. Frictional forces eventually cause the difference in high and low pressure to equilibrate and the wind dies back down.

Nature Note

The deflection of air masses around a region of low pressure due to Earth's rotation on its axis is called the Coriolis effect, after the French scientist Gaspard-Gustave de Coriolis (1792-1843). The rotation causes any moving object—an air mass or a missile—to be deflected to the left. In the northern hemisphere, being deflected to the left causes counterclockwise rotation; in the southern hemisphere, it causes clockwise rotation.

The Beaufort Scale

It's pretty common for an increase in wind speed to indicate that a storm is approaching. Since it is helpful to be able to estimate wind speed, the Beaufort Scale was developed to correlate visual clues with wind speed. The scale has thirteen levels that measure the force of the wind. Wind speed is given in knots and kph. There is one Beaufort Scale for use on the ocean and another for use on land. Since we do our hiking and camping on land, here is the Beaufort Scale for use on land:

Force	Description	Events on Land	knots	kph
0	Calm	Smoke rises	below 1	below 2
1	Light air	Smoke shows direction of wind, but a wind vane does not	1-3	2-6
2	Light breeze	Wind is felt on the face; leaves rustle; wind vane points into the wind	4–6	7-11
3	Gentle breeze	Leaves and small twigs are in motion; small flags are extended	7-10	12-19
4	Moderate breeze	Wind raises dust; small branches move	11-16	20-30
5	Fresh breeze	Small leafy trees begin to sway; wavelets form on lakes	17-21	31-39
6	Strong breeze	Large branches move	22-27	40-50
7	Near gale	Whole trees in motion; difficult to walk into the wind	28-33	51-61
8	Gale	Twigs break from trees; walking is difficult	34-40	62-74
9	Strong gale	Heavy objects blow away	41-47	75-87
10	Storm	Trees are uprooted	48-55	88-102

Any wind less than a small breeze does not pose a problem. If the wind approaches gale force, you might want to find cover and wait until the wind dies down. Violent storms and tornadoes are most likely to occur over flat land like prairie or plains. I recommend seeking shelter if the wind has that much force. If you see a funnel cloud (tornado), definitely find shelter.

Camp Out of the Wind

When choosing a site to set up camp, wind needs to be taken into account—both the magnitude of the wind speed and the direction from which it is coming.

You may not have the opportunity to hike or camp above tree line very often, but if you are above tree line, adverse weather changes need to be considered. Above tree line there are no trees to provide shelter from the wind. If a particularly cold, windy night is anticipated, it is prudent to descend below tree line and find a grove of trees in which to camp, or at least look for a rocky outcropping that can provide a wind break.

Trail Wisdom

Everyone knows not to be out on water during a lightning storm. Lightning is attracted to metal and tends to strike the tallest object in an area.

Lightning is dangerous above tree line as well. People are the tallest objects. To make matters worse, pack frames, cooking utensils, some hiking poles, and other items are all made of metal. If there is any danger of lightning, move to a lower altitude. If you are up so high that lightning is striking below you, move quickly to an altitude lower than where the lightning is striking.

Recognizing Cloud Types

There are two broad categories used by meteorologists to describe clouds:

1. Heaped clouds: The familiar cumulus clouds that look like huge puffy balls of cotton; the term cumulus means "heap" or "pile." Cumulus clouds are fair weather clouds.

2. Layered clouds: Stratus clouds, which are indicative of relatively stable weather conditions; the term stratus means "stratified" or "layered."

Cumulus clouds are so common that they tend to be the ones people draw when depicting a cloudy sky. Sometimes people think they see familiar shapes in cumulus clouds. The tops of cumulus clouds tend to be white and the bottoms dark. How white and how dark depends on the amount of sunlight shining on them.

Cumulus clouds are heaped clouds that are frequently observed to be moving across the sky. Their movements are in response both to wind and to Earth's rotation. Cumulus clouds are formed by warm, rising air parcels. As long as the sky is filled with cumulus clouds, the weather tends to be fine, with little or no precipitation.

Stratus clouds are layered clouds that tend to fill the sky from the horizon upward and are uniformly gray and featureless. The sun cannot be seen through them during the day; the moon and stars cannot be seen through them at night. If they are cold enough, they will become saturated with water vapor, frequently resulting in at least light drizzles.

A blend of cumulus and stratus is called stratocumulus. There is more structure to stratocumulus clouds than to simple stratus clouds, but less space between them than between cumulus clouds. Stratocumulus clouds are often in horizontal layers with sunlight peeking through the layers.

Sometimes wispy, layered clouds are observed at extremely high altitudes—the top of the troposphere or the bottom of the stratosphere. These are cirrus clouds and are composed of ice crystals. The term cirrus means "a curling lock of hair"; cirrus clouds are sometimes called "mares' tails."

Storm clouds are typically of the cumulonimbus type; nimbus means "cloud." Cumulonimbus clouds look like massive cumulus clouds but are thicker and darker on the bottom. Another term for them is thunderheads. When you see thunderhead clouds forming from the fair-weather cumulous clouds, it is time to put on your rain gear or head for shelter. Cumulonimbus clouds are likely to bring heavy rain or snow showers, thunder and lightning, hail, fierce wind, and possibly a tornado.

Rain, Snow, Sleet, and Hail

The amount of water vapor air can hold depends on temperature; warm air can hold more water vapor than cold air. The dew point temperature (or just dew point) is the temperature at which air is cold enough that some of the water vapor condenses into liquid water. As temperature continues to cool, precipitation begins to fall.

Because of the risk of hypothermia, it is wisest to try to sit out heavy rain or snow storms. If you are carrying a tent, set it up, get inside and take a nap, play cards, read a book, or whatever. I carry a pack cover that fits snugly the full length of my pack. (A large trash bag works, too.) I put the cover on my pack and prop the pack against a tree, rock, or log, where it will stay dry.

If you do not have a pack cover, you might want to bring your pack inside the tent with you. Remember that the most important piece of your gear to keep dry is your sleeping bag. If there is any indication of stormy weather predicted before you leave home, you should wrap your sleeping bag tightly in a plastic bag.

Many backpacking tents have vestibules, usually part of the rain fly that projects a few feet out from the door of the tent. In inclement weather you can store gear under the vestibule. If you have to sit out a storm of particularly lengthy duration, you can even cook meals on a stove under the shelter of the vestibule.

I do not carry much freeze-dried food when I'm backpacking. However, I usually carry at least one pouch of food that can be prepared simply by adding a cup of boiling water and letting it seep for a while. During a storm, heating water to prepare a simple meal or hot drinks helps pass the time. Also, a little food and warm liquid help stave off the possibility of hypothermia.

If you are still cold, get inside your sleeping bag. Staying warm is vital. Food stokes the body's internal fires, but food alone may not be enough to keep you warm. Wearing a knit cap while in your sleeping bag may also be good idea. Your body loses a lot of heat through your head because it's important to keep your brain cool. Losing too much heat is not good, though, and a cap helps prevent that from happening.

If the storm does not let up, you may decide to return to the trailhead.

In high country, snow is particularly hazardous. Trying to walk in deep snow, especially while carrying a heavy pack, can be extremely fatiguing. Better to get out, or at least to a lower altitude, before the snow gets too deep.

Heavy rains increase the depth and speed of flow of streams and rivers. The stream you easily waded across or forded two days earlier may be a foot or two deeper today and flowing several times more rapidly. If it is flowing too swiftly, you may not be able to ford it safely. Again, better to get out while you still can.

Extreme Weather

Funnel clouds hang down from thunderclouds and do not touch the ground. If a funnel cloud is touching the ground, then it is called a tornado.

Tornados result from a large-scale rotation of air masses with strong updrafts and downdrafts. You know when a funnel cloud has touched the ground and become a tornado because dust and debris are lifted from the ground and swirled around with the funnel.

Tornados are most likely to form in flat, open country where there are few natural shelters. If you see a tornado approaching and are caught on open ground, move out of the tornado's direct path. Find a depression in the ground and lie as flat as possible. Protect your head from falling objects. Tornados usually touch down only briefly and the path of destruction is usually narrow.

Weather Forecasting

Changes in weather usually occur when two different kinds of air masses encounter each other and form a front. The term front is derived from military terminology where two opposing armies meet at the front in a battlefield.

In a warm front, warm air is advancing and replacing a cold air mass. Warm fronts are associated with stratus clouds and light rain or snow.

In a cold front, cold air is advancing and replacing a warm air mass. Cold fronts often develop cumulonimbus clouds, causing thunderstorms and heavy rain or snowfall.

If you're experiencing fair weather and there's little or no wind, it's unlikely the weather is going to change any time soon. If wind suddenly picks up, look for clouds moving your way.

It's a good sign that a storm is approaching, and you might want to look for shelter.

Predicting the weather can be tricky in the mountains. I have often been hiking through a valley between two mountain ridges when the wind has picked up and it's clear that foul weather is approaching. What often happens is the storm will blow down the other side of one of the ridges leaving the valley I'm in completely dry. Or, from a mountain on which I'm standing, I can see rain falling on a nearby mountain. You never really know. One time you may experience no rain at all, and the next time you get drenched. So be prepared; stay alert to what's going on around you.

Conclusion

I have been on backpacking trips that have been cut short by storms that moved in after we were already on the trail. I have also been on trips where we sat out a day or two of rain and then continued on. If you carry proper clothing and the right equipment, you should be able to handle adverse weather. Know the signs to watch for and know how to respond.

PART THREE

Major Regions of North America

CHAPTER 11

 **Mountains and Tundra**

> **In This Chapter**
> ➤ Ecosystems
> ➤ Mountains
> ➤ Above tree line

North America has an incredible diversity of scenery, terrain, climate, vegetation, and wildlife. When you're hiking in North America, it makes sense to be knowledgeable about the geographic regions in which you find yourself. Beginning with this chapter, you will be learning about the characteristics of the various ecosystems of North America.

Kinds of Ecosystems

An ecosystem consists of a community of living organisms—the plants and animals that comprise the biotic (living) part of the environment—and the abiotic (nonliving) components of the environment—air, water, rocks, and soil. An ecosystem can be small—a pond, for example—or large—a mountain range or prairie covering thousands of square miles.

Terrestrial ecosystems are ecosystems that occur on land; aquatic ecosystems are ecosystems that occur in watery environments—lakes, streams, estuaries, oceans. Because this book is about hiking and backpacking, activities in which we engage on land, not on water, my emphasis here is on terrestrial ecosystems.

Nature Note

An ecosystem is an ecological community composed of living organisms and their environment. A biome is a larger classification, describing a type of ecological community such as a desert or tundra.

Ecologists use the term biome to refer to ecosystems on a large scale that might cover several states or provinces. When observed on a large scale, a biome looks uniform in composition. Looked at on a small scale, however, there may be a diversity of ecosystems. We are ignoring the small scale for now and focusing on the general characteristics of whole states or regions of North America.

A biome is described by the dominant kinds of plants found in it and the climatic regime to which those plants are adapted. The two major factors that determine climate are:

1. Annual temperature ranges

2. Precipitation

A desert is warm and dry; tundra is cool and dry. A tropical rain forest is hot and wet; a temperate rain forest is cool and wet. A deciduous forest may have cold winters, warm summers, and precipitation year-round in the form of snow and rain.

Total sunlight is also a factor. Incoming sunlight can be reflected, absorbed, or scattered. The albedo of a surface measures the degree to which sunlight is reflected from that surface; albedo is high for snow, sand, and ice fields and low for forests and grasslands.

There is a balance between the energy in the solar ultraviolet, visible, and infrared radiation incident on Earth and the energy in the infrared radiation emitted back into space by Earth. This balance helps determine overall climate. Seasons occur because the amount of incident solar radiation is different at different times of year due to the tilt of Earth's equator to the plane of Earth's orbit around the sun.

Most of North America lies within temperate latitudes. In the northern hemisphere, the term temperate refers to the region that lies between the Tropic of Cancer and the Arctic Circle. The region north of the Arctic Circle is the Arctic. The Arctic Circle passes through Alaska north of Fairbanks and the northern territories of Canada.

The region south of the Tropic of Cancer is the tropics. In the United States the southern tip of Florida is subtropical; the Hawaiian Islands are tropical. Canada does not have tropics. Since the focus of this book is on hiking and backpacking in the United States and Canada, most of the discussion in these chapters relates to temperate regions.

The Effect of Elevation

When considering the ecology of large geographical regions, you should keep in mind the combined effect of latitude and elevation, referred to as geographical and vertical zonation.

At latitudes typical of the continental United States, tree line tends to be at elevations of about 9,000 to 10,000 feet (2,700 to 3,000 m). Farther north, tree line gradually drops in elevation until it is at sea level above the Arctic Circle.

Nature Note

The major ecosystems that characterize North America are the following:

> ➤ Mountains
> ➤ Deciduous forest
> ➤ Coniferous forest
> ➤ Desert
> ➤ Plains and prairies

There are also two minor ecosystems found in North America: temperate rain forest and tundra.

Hiking Vocab

Tree line is the elevation above which trees don't grow. Any "trees" growing just above tree line tend to be stunted, short shrubs.

Climbing a mountain in the Rockies or Sierras involves the same kind of biome changes as a trip from the Gulf of Mexico to the Arctic Circle. In Arizona, for example, if you travel from Phoenix to the summit of Mount Humphrey (the highest peak in Arizona), the changes in climate and prominent vegetation types are similar to what you would observe if you traveled from Phoenix to Fairbanks, Alaska!

Mountains in North America

Broadly speaking, you can divide the United States and Canada into three large regions: West, Central, and East. The dominant geological feature of the western United States and Canada is the Rocky Mountains, which are located in the following states and provinces:

➤ British Columbia

➤ Alberta

➤ Idaho

➤ Montana

➤ Wyoming

➤ Colorado

➤ New Mexico

The dominant geological feature of the eastern United States and the maritime Canadian provinces are the Appalachian Mountains. The Appalachians are located in the following states and provinces:

➤ Quebec

➤ New Brunswick

➤ Maine

➤ New Hampshire

➤ Vermont

➤ New York

➤ Pennsylvania

➤ West Virginia

➤ Virginia

➤ Maryland

➤ Kentucky

➤ Tennessee

➤ North Carolina

➤ South Carolina

➤ Georgia

➤ Alabama

If you study a map of North America, you can't help but notice that the Rockies, Appalachians, and most other mountain ranges have a north–south orientation, a feature that makes them important in determining regional weather patterns.

Because the Rockies and Appalachians are so large in area, sections of them have local names. For example, the Alleghenies in Pennsylvania, the Smoky Mountains of Tennessee and North Carolina, the Green Mountains in Vermont, and the White Mountains of New Hampshire are all part of the Appalachian range.

The dominant feature of the central region of the United States and Canada is prairie. I discuss prairies in Chapter 12.

The Appalachians are much older than the Rockies; since the Appalachians have been weathering for a longer time, they are lower in elevation. Elevations in the eastern United States are less than 6,700 feet (2,040 m). Because the Rockies are relatively young—geologically speaking—they are much higher; peaks of 13,000 to 14,000 feet (4,000 to 4,270 m) or higher are common.

Other Mountain Ranges

Although the Rockies and the Appalachians are the two major mountain ranges in North America, there are other ranges, nearly all of which have a north-south orientation. I'm giving only a partial listing here; other ranges are referred to in part four where I describe recommended trails throughout the United States and Canada.

Some of the larger mountain ranges in North America are the following:

➤ The Olympic Mountains are on the Olympic Peninsula of Washington. The Olympics are important because they are home to Olympic National Park and the only temperate rain forest in the lower forty-eight states.

➤ The Cascades span northern Washington to northern California. The Cascades consist of a string of volcanoes; the southernmost volcano is Mount Lassen. Mount Rainier National Park in Washington is perhaps the best-known national park in the Cascades.

➤ The Sierra Nevadas begin in northern California, where the Cascades end and cover most of eastern California. The best-known national park in the Sierras is Yosemite; together with Sequoia and Kings Canyon National Parks, Yosemite is home to groves of giant Sequoia trees.

➤ The Black Hills of western South Dakota rise out of the plains. Mount Rushmore, with its famous carvings of four US Presidents, is found in the Black Hills.

➤ The Ozarks are located in Arkansas and Missouri and are popular recreation areas in those states.

All of these mountain ranges offer superb opportunities for outdoor recreation that includes hiking, backpacking, camping, fishing, and boating.

Montane Forests

Below tree line, most mountain ranges are heavily forested. The term montane forest is used to refer to these forests. Montane forests are usually characterized by conifers—pines, spruces, firs, larches, and hemlocks. Lakes, ponds, and subalpine meadows round out the landscape. Because of the trees, meadows, lakes, and rugged mountain backdrops, mountains are my favorite places to go hiking.

Nature Note

Common mammals in the Arctic tundra include the following:

➤ Caribou

➤ Musk oxen

➤ Arctic hares

➤ Arctic foxes

➤ Wolves

➤ Grizzly and polar bears

Snowy owls are characteristic birds of the Arctic, but there are no reptiles or amphibians; it's too cold for them.

Arctic Tundra

The northernmost biome in North America is the Arctic tundra, which dominates the latitudes between the Arctic Circle and the Arctic Ocean. The tundra begins where the mountains end. Unless you are truly adventuresome, your travels may not take you to regions of Arctic tundra. I include it here so I can compare it to the alpine tundra.

The Arctic tundra is characterized by vast treeless plains. Rainfall is as low as in desert climates, but the annual mean temperature is also low. A prominent feature of tundra is permafrost—soil that remains frozen year-round. Trees don't grow in permafrost. Plants that do grow include lichens, mosses, grasses, sedges, willows, and heath.

The tundra is ecologically important because millions of waterfowl—ducks, geese, and swans—migrate from southern latitudes (where they spend the winter) to the tundra to breed. Because the tundra is north of the Arctic Circle, one of its important features is the change in amount of daylight over the seasons.

Winters are characterized by few hours of sunlight and long hours of darkness. Summers are the opposite; the sun may set just briefly for a couple of hours and the rest of the time is daylight. In fact, it may never actually get dark in summer; nights are just a couple of hours of twilight.

Tundra and desert can be compared and contrasted. They have one thing in common: precipitation is low at both, usually less than 10 inches (25 cm) a year. Because of low precipitation, both are fragile environments; if disturbed, both can take a century to heal. The difference is that the desert is hot and dry; the tundra is cold and dry.

Alpine Tundra

Just as the Arctic tundra refers to tundra north of the Arctic Circle, alpine tundra refers to tundra at latitudes south of the Arctic Circle and at altitudes above tree line. At mid–latitudes, alpine tundra is typically found above about 12,000 feet (3,6605 m) in elevation. Plant species are similar to those found in the Arctic tundra, but mountaintops lack most of the mammals characteristic of the Arctic.

Because of the fragility of alpine tundra, extra care needs to be taken when crossing it. Stay on any existing trails; try very hard not to trample vegetation along the trails. If you need to camp above tree line, find a rocky or gravelly area where you aren't crushing any plants. Most important, practice Leave No Trace principles (see Chapter 6).

Conclusion

Many of the destinations described in part four are located in mountainous areas. There's a good reason for that; mountains attract hikers and campers. John Muir said it best: "Going to the mountains is going home."

CHAPTER 12

Plains and Prairies

In This Chapter

➤ Plants and animals of the prairies and plains

➤ Tallgrass prairies

➤ Shortgrass plains

➤ Mixed-grass prairies

The extensive grasslands of central North America are zones where fire and grazing animals have worked together to prevent the spread of trees. States along the Mississippi River receive a large amount of precipitation; the result is tallgrass prairies. As you move westward towards the Rocky Mountains, precipitation declines, and tallgrass prairies give way to shortgrass plains.

The hundredth meridian (the 100° line of longitude) marks a boundary important to farmers. East of the hundredth meridian, there is sufficient rainfall that farming can be practiced without irrigation. West of the hundredth meridian, it is so dry that farmlands must be irrigated.

Hiking Vocab

Most people use the terms plain and prairie interchangeably. In this book I am distinguishing the two. Both refer to an extensive level region where trees are notably absent and grasses predominate. I am using the term plain if vegetation consists primarily of shortgrass, and prairie is used when the vegetation is primarily tallgrass. The term prairie is used to refer to plains and prairies collectively.

In this chapter we will be looking at general features of grasslands you're likely to notice when hiking.

Plants and Animals

Grasses are perennials. They grow from the base of the plant rather than from the tip, so animals can graze without damaging the grass; it just keeps growing. Grazing animals return grasses' nutrients to the soil when they defecate. Over thousands of years the grasslands of central North America built up deep topsoil. Grassland soils are rich with abundant humus, which is dark, decomposed organic material derived from both plants and animals.

Prior to the arrival of humans in North America, the continent's grasslands supported megafauna (large animals) as diverse and numerous as found on the present-day Serengeti in eastern Africa. For thousands of years, mammoths, mastodons, and saber-toothed tigers flourished, but they became extinct shortly after the arrival of humans. Whether the animals were hunted to extinction or died because of climate change is open to debate.

With the disappearance of larger grazing animals, bison became the keystone species that ruled the grasslands. A keystone species dominates an ecosystem and can be a carnivore (meat eater) or herbivore (plant eater). As late as the nineteenth century, the bison population was estimated to be between 20 and 70 million. In the late nineteenth century, hunting reduced that number to fewer than 1,000 individuals before conservation efforts were instituted to save the remaining bison before they became extinct.

Bison played such an important role in the lives of Native Americans that they regularly set fires to burn large areas of grassland. Fire suppression leads to invasion by woody plants; recurrent fires kill most woody species above ground while leaving grasses intact.

There are two species of bison in North America. What most people are familiar with are plains bison; at one time plains bison were found as far east as Pennsylvania and West Virginia and as far south as Texas, Louisiana, and Mississippi. Farther north, in Alaska and the Yukon, a different species is still found—wood bison. In some areas wood bison are wild.

Hiking Vocab

Some people mistakenly call bison buffalos and pronghorns antelopes. Bison are not buffalos; buffalos are found in Africa and Southeast Asia. Pronghorns are unrelated to the various species of antelopes found in Africa; they are the sole species of a family of mammals unique to North America. Wyoming is the best state in which to see large herds of pronghorn.

Along with bison, other animals were widespread throughout the grasslands:

- ➤ Prairie dogs
- ➤ Black-footed ferrets (which prey exclusively on prairie dogs)
- ➤ Pronghorns
- ➤ Coyotes
- ➤ Wolves
- ➤ Foxes
- ➤ Bobcats
- ➤ Badgers
- ➤ Squirrels
- ➤ Voles
- ➤ Mice

Estimated numbers of these animals help us appreciate the fecundity of the prairies. Before the encroachment of civilization, in addition to the huge number of bison, the pronghorn population was probably in the tens of millions. Such large numbers of grazing animals would have supported a sizeable population of predators; there may have been 0.75 million gray wolves ranging the prairies.

Prairies are so windy that most insects and birds do little flying. Prairie chickens and sage grouse are examples of birds that spend virtually all their time on the ground.

Farming, ranching, and urbanization have resulted in a large decline of birds nesting in grasslands. Prairie marshes and potholes have long been among the major habitats of breeding waterfowl—ducks, geese, and swans—in North America. Other birds that are characteristic of grasslands include sparrows and meadowlarks.

Grasshoppers are common insects, as are chiggers, which tend to be the bane of hikers and campers in prairie country.

Nature Note

In wooded areas birds perch in high places to sing so their voices will carry. What about birds that live in grasslands, where there are no trees? Birds skylark. They fly in a large circle as though they're going around a Ferris wheel; at the peak of the circle they sing their hearts out.

Reptiles, fishes, and amphibians are widespread in the prairies. Most people think of rattlesnakes as reptiles exclusive to the desert, but prairie dwellers know that rattlesnakes are common there, too. Bull snakes are also common, but they're not poisonous. Another common reptile is the box turtle. More than two hundred species of fish live in the lakes, ponds, streams, and rivers of the prairies. Warm-water fish that thrive there are carp and catfish. Spadefoot toads and leopard frogs are among the species of amphibians found in prairie ponds.

Westward Expansion

Several major rivers and their tributaries traverse the prairies. The most prominent ones are the Mississippi, the Missouri, and the Platte. As pioneers moved west, the first large cities were established along these rivers.

When the migration west began, settlers discovered that the prairie soil, which was ideal for bluestem, the dominant grass of the original tallgrass prairies, was also ideal for growing corn; the central states and provinces became the breadbasket of the United States and Canada. Nebraska, Iowa, and Illinois are the center of the Corn Belt; wheat is grown in Kansas, Saskatchewan, and Manitoba; soybeans are a major crop throughout the Midwest.

Local History

Several authors have written movingly about pioneer life on the prairie. The books of Laura Ingalls Wilder were the basis for the popular television series "Little House on the Prairie." Willa Cather is known for books such as *My Antonia*, that are about life on the prairie. Ole Rölvaag's *Giants in the Earth* is a classic about Norwegian immigrants on the prairie.

In North America, humans have done more to obliterate grasslands than they have to obliterate any other ecosystem. Huge expanses of central America's grasslands have been plowed under. Pavement covers many hundreds of square miles as a result of urban sprawl. Where irrigation is too expensive to make farming economical, cattle ranches are found.

Remnants of prairies remain, however. Former farmland has been restored to prairie; tallgrass prairie preserves are found in several Midwestern states. In my travels, I've come across some cases of restored prairies that are only a few acres in size. Size is less important than the pride felt by local communities.

Hiking through a restored prairie in summer is a delight; acres and acres of wildflowers are simply breathtaking. Many preserves and state and federal parks have nature trails with signage to help visitors identify the flowers they're seeing and understand the ecological relationships that make grasslands special.

Tallgrass Prairies and Hiking Sites

Before agriculture, tallgrass prairies extended from Alberta and Manitoba in southern Canada through North Dakota to Texas, from Minnesota to Missouri along the Mississippi River, and from Wisconsin to Illinois, Indiana, and Ohio east of the Mississippi. Today, tallgrass prairies occur mainly in the eastern Dakotas, in western Minnesota, and in remnants of Nebraska, Iowa, and Kansas.

The grasses most characteristic of tallgrass prairie are species of bluestem, which can grow to heights of 8 feet (2.4 m) or more. Nineteenth-century pioneers recorded that when they rode their horses through the prairies, sometimes they couldn't even see over the top of the grasses. The prairie grasses are not only tall, they also have deep root systems—often 6 feet (1.8 m) deep.

Recommended Tallgrass Prairie Sites

I highly recommend that you visit the Neal Smith National Wildlife Refuge in central Iowa east of Des Moines. Hiking trails take you through the tallgrasses and a profusion of coneflowers and Black-eyed Susans in summer. The Tallgrass Prairie Preserve south of Manhattan, Kansas, is also a recommended destination to see how tallgrass prairies looked to early settlers.

Nature Note

The Neal Smith National Wildlife Refuge and Prairie Learning Center in central Iowa has an excellent visitors center with informative exhibits about the ecology of tallgrass prairies. It is well worth the visit.

There are a large number of other locations where you can visit tallgrass prairie habitats. The most recommended ones are the following:

➤ Ayers Sand Prairie Natural Preserve in northwestern Illinois

➤ Fults Hill Prairie Natural Preserve in southwestern Illinois

➤ Midewin National Tallgrass Prairie south of Chicago

➤ Broken Kettle Grassland Preserve on the Missouri River just north of Sioux City, Iowa

➤ Hayden Prairie State Preserve in northeastern Iowa

➤ Konza Prairie just west of Manhattan, Kansas

➤ Bluestem Prairie Scientific and Natural Area southeast of Moorhead, Minnesota

➤ Wallace C. Dayton Scientific and Natural Area in the extreme northwest corner of Minnesota

➤ Hole-in-the-Mountain Prairie in southwestern Minnesota

➤ Prairie State Park north of Joplin, Missouri

➤ Osage Prairie Conservation Area also north of Joplin, Missouri

➤ Wah' Kon-Tah Prairie in western Missouri

➤ Homestead National Monument south of Lincoln, Nebraska

➤ Lyndon B. Johnson National Grassland in northern Texas

➤ Attwater Prairie Chicken National Wildlife Refuge near Houston, Texas

Shortgrass Plains and Hiking Sites

The reason less precipitation falls in the western plains is because they lie in the rain shadow of the Rocky Mountains. As moist air masses from the Pacific Ocean move across the United States, they encounter several mountain ranges—the coastal range, the Cascades, the Sierra Nevadas, and the Rockies.

As an air mass moves up each mountain range, it dumps its rain and snow, resulting in the western slopes being wetter and covered with more vegetation than the eastern slopes. By the time the Rocky Mountains have been traversed, there is little moisture left to water the plains; eastern Montana, Wyoming, and Colorado are relatively dry compared to the western sides of those states.

> ### Local History
>
> The plains are cowboy country. Unsuitable for farming without irrigation, the plains are natural for cattle ranches. Water is the limiting factor for survival on the plains. It has been said that the history of the West is the history of water.

Precipitation doesn't end abruptly; you can't face north and say tallgrass prairie only occurs to your right and shortgrass plains to your left. The change is gradual. From the western Dakotas south to Texas, the transition zone is sometimes called mixed-grass prairie, where wheatgrasses, needlegrasses, and grama grasses are the dominant grasses.

Recommended Shortgrass Plains Sites

Here are some shortgrass plains habitats I recommend that you visit:

> ➤ Pawnee National Grassland in northern Colorado
>
> ➤ Comanche National Grassland in southeastern Colorado
>
> ➤ Cimarron National Grassland in the southwest corner of Kansas
>
> ➤ Charles M. Russell National Wildlife Refuge northeast of Lewistown, Montana
>
> ➤ Kiowa and Rita Blanca National Grasslands in northeastern New Mexico
>
> ➤ Las Vegas National Wildlife Refuge just east of Las Vegas, New Mexico
>
> ➤ Black Kettle National Grassland in western Oklahoma
>
> ➤ Rita Blanca National Grassland in the Texas Panhandle
>
> ➤ McClellan National Grassland in the Texas Panhandle
>
> ➤ Thunder Basin National Grassland in northeastern Wyoming

Mixed-Grass Prairies

Mixed-grass prairies are transition zones between tallgrass and shortgrass ecosystems that run from Saskatchewan to Oklahoma. Most of North and South Dakota, central and western Nebraska, and central Kansas and Oklahoma are best described as mixed-grass environments.

Recommended Mixed-Grass Prairie Sites

Here are some mixed-grass plains habitats I recommend that you visit:

➤ Cheyenne Bottoms Wildlife Area in central Kansas

➤ Quivira National Wildlife Refuge southeast of Cheyenne Bottoms in central Kansas

➤ Rowe Sanctuary southwest of Grand Island, Nebraska

➤ Agate Fossil Beds National Monument in the northwest corner of Nebraska

➤ Valentine National Wildlife refuge in northern Nebraska

➤ Niobrara Valley Preserve in northern Nebraska

➤ Oglala National Grassland in the northwest corner of Nebraska

➤ Theodore Roosevelt National Park in western North Dakota

➤ Little Missouri National Grassland in the northwest corner of North Dakota

➤ Sheyenne National Grassland in the southeast corner of North Dakota

➤ Fort Pierre National Grassland just south of Pierre, South Dakota

➤ Badlands National Park in western South Dakota

➤ Buffalo Gap National Grassland adjacent to Badlands National Park in western South Dakota

➤ Grand River National Grassland in the northwest corner of South Dakota

Personal Anecdote

Kansas was experiencing a serious heat wave when I visited Cheyenne Bottoms Wildlife Area. In summer, Cheyenne Bottoms seemed pretty desolate, but I saw great birds there and added three species to the list of birds I have seen in my life (my "life list"). I was also fascinated by what seemed to me to be very large, long water snakes.

Canadian Prairie

The prairies of the United States continue northward into Manitoba, Saskatchewan, and Alberta. They end where the boreal forest begins. Canadian prairies tend to be very cold, so plants have a short growing season.

Recommended Canadian Prairie Sites

In Canada, prairie systems can be visited at the following locations:

> ➤ Head-Smashed-In Buffalo Jump in Alberta

> ➤ Hand Hills Ecological Reserve in Alberta

> ➤ Manitoba Tallgrass Prairie Preserve in the southeast corner of Manitoba

> ➤ Yellow Quill Prairie in southwestern Manitoba

> ➤ Grasslands National Park in southwestern Saskatchewan

> ➤ Old Man on His Back Prairie and Heritage Conservation Area in the southwest corner of Saskatchewan.

Conclusion

Grasslands, which cover a large region of central North America, mark transitions between mountains and deserts. In the next chapter you will learn about the deserts of North America.

CHAPTER 13

The Deserts of North America

In This Chapter

➤ What makes a desert
➤ Desert characteristics and climate
➤ Desert ecology
➤ Sonoran, Chihuahuan, Mohave, and Great Basin Deserts

Deserts are defined as regions of low annual precipitation and high summer temperatures. Annual precipitation is less than 10 inches (25 cm). At low elevations, precipitation is entirely in the form of rain; at higher elevations, deserts get at least a dusting of snow throughout the winter.

Summer desert temperatures can be brutal; 120°F (49°C) is common. Highs greater than 130°F (54°C) have been recorded at Death Valley, California. What surprises people is that winter lows often go below freezing. In the desert, there can be large fluctuations in temperature between day and night because of the dry air; without water vapor to trap heat, days warm up quickly and nights cool down quickly.

In general, the world's deserts are located approximately between latitudes of about 35° north and south of the equator. When one thinks of the great deserts of the world, the Sahara in northern Africa probably is the first desert that comes to mind. The Sahara is huge; its area is roughly the size of the entire continental United States. There are also the Gobi Desert in northern China and southern Mongolia, the deserts covering western and central Australia, the Arabian Desert in the Middle East, the Kalahari Desert in southern Africa, and regions of desert along the western coast of South America.

In this chapter we will be looking at general features of deserts you're likely to notice when hiking in North America.

The Large Deserts of North America

In North America, there are several large deserts, each characterized by its own vegetation types:

➤ The Sonoran Desert: Includes much of Arizona from Phoenix south and west to the Colorado River, and extends into Baja California and the Mexican state of Sonora.

➤ The Chihuahuan Desert: Includes Arizona southeast of Tucson, southern New Mexico, western Texas, and extends throughout the Mexican state of Chihuahua. In general, elevations in the Chihuahuan Desert are higher than in the Sonoran Desert.

➤ The Mohave Desert: Encompasses southeastern California and southern Nevada. Parts of the Mohave Desert are called the high desert and are at elevations ranging between 3,000 and 4,000 feet (9,100 and 1,200 m), which contrast to areas at lower elevations along the Colorado River.

➤ The Great Basin Desert: Begins in eastern California and Oregon, and includes southern Idaho, much of Utah, and most of Nevada. The Great Basin lies in the rain shadow of the Sierra Nevada and Cascade mountain ranges, and has the highest elevation of North American deserts—generally above 4,000 feet (1,200 m). Unlike the deserts lying at lower elevations, the Great Basin is a cold but relatively dry desert, with snow and freezing temperatures prevailing in the winter.

In terms of relative size, the Chihuahuan Desert encompasses a little over one-third of the total desert area in North America. The Great Basin Desert is the next largest in size, followed by the Sonoran Desert, and finally the Mohave Desert, which is the smallest of the four, comprising only about 10 percent of the total desert area.

Some desert ecologists define smaller desert regions. For example, the region in California and Arizona directly along the Colorado River and extending into the Grand Canyon may be called either the California Desert or the Colorado Desert and is treated separately because it represents a transition between the Mohave and Sonoran Deserts. For our purposes, however, we will stick to the four deserts listed above.

General Characteristics of a Desert

People think of deserts in varying ways. I suppose many people think of deserts as wastelands where nothing lives. Images of the Sahara certainly tend to reinforce that opinion—hundreds of miles of sand dunes, rocky plateaus, gravelly plains, a few scattered oases, and cultivated land mainly along the Nile River in Egypt. Life in the Sahara—both human and animal—congregates around fewer than one hundred large oases and many very small oases scattered through the region.

North American deserts are not like that, however. There are some sand dunes, and water generally is scarce, but vegetation covers the landscape; the deserts are filled with abundant wildlife that includes mammals, birds, reptiles, amphibians, fish, and numerous invertebrates (insects, spiders, scorpions, etc.). If people aren't seeing a desert's wildlife, it is most likely because they are active on the desert during the day when the animals and insects are burrowed away from the sun. Venture onto the desert at night, however, and the desert is bustling with living creatures.

Nature Note

When is an insect not an insect? When it has more than six legs. Insects comprise a class within the animal phylum called arthropods. Spiders and scorpions have eight legs and belong to a class called arachnids. Ticks, mites, and harvestmen (daddy longlegs) are also arachnids.

Centipedes and millipedes belong to the classes Chilopoda and Diplopoda, respectively. Centi-pede means "one hundred legs"; milli-pede means "one thousand legs." Centipedes can have more or fewer than a hundred legs. No millipede has one thousand legs. Centipedes have one pair of legs per segment and millipedes have two pairs per segment, which is why millipedes look like they have so many legs.

There are a number of national parks, monuments, and recreation areas (as well as state parks and recreation sites) located in deserts that can be enjoyed at just about any time of year, including the following:

➤ Death Valley and Joshua Tree in California

➤ Great Basin in Nevada

➤ Zion and Canyonlands in Utah

➤ Saguaro in Arizona

➤ Guadalupe and Big Bend in Texas

> ➤ Lake Mead National Recreation Area bordering Nevada, Arizona, and Utah

> ➤ The bottom of the Grand Canyon along the Colorado River in northern Arizona.

In their own way, deserts are just as beautiful as any other kind of landscape. To many people, deserts are perhaps more beautiful—vast skies, spectacular sunsets, and acres upon acres of spring wildflowers. Best of all, deserts can be enjoyed during those times of year when much of the rest of North America lies dormant under a mantle of snow and ice.

Nature Quote

"The desert is the environment of revelation, genetically and physiologically alien, sensorily austere, esthetically abstract, historically inimical... . To the desert go prophets and hermits; through deserts go pilgrims and exiles. Here the leaders of the great religions have sought the therapeutic and spiritual values of retreat, not to escape but to find reality."

–Paul Shepard, in *Man in the Landscape: A Historic View of the Esthetics of Nature.*

Desert Climates

Deserts tend to have dry summers and wet winters, although the Sonoran Desert also has a wet monsoon season in July and August. Because the air is so dry much of the year, diurnal temperature fluctuations can be extreme.

During the daytime in winter, you may be comfortable in a T-shirt and shorts, only to have the nighttime temperature plummet to below freezing. In summer, daytime temperatures usually exceed 100°F (38°C), but temperatures can still drop at night to 50°F (10°C).

High temperatures lead to the quick evaporation of water. Desert plants have adapted to the high temperatures by growing needles or spines instead of leaves in order to conserve water. Plants lose water through openings called stomata on the undersides of their leaves in a process called transpiration. You can think of a cactus needle as a leaf that has curled up on itself. A needle has much less surface area than a leaf does, so the rate of water loss through transpiration is greatly decreased.

Although many desert plants are cacti, not all desert plants are. There are also yuccas, agaves, palm trees, sage brush, and even water-loving trees like cottonwoods that grow in places where water is present year-round, even if only below the surface.

Just because low deserts can be very hot in summer and high deserts can be very cold in winter should not deter you from venturing into deserts during milder times of year, any more than severe winter weather in mountainous areas would keep you from going to the mountains in the summer. Springtime flowers can be spectacular, even in a regime as seemingly desolate as Death Valley. Spring and fall weather in the desert tend to be comparatively mild.

Hiking Vocab

The word cactus has three plural forms. You can refer to more than one cactus as cacti, cactuses, or cactus.

I often head into the desert in early spring when higher elevations are still snowed in, or hike in the desert into late fall when snowfall has begun to cause mountain trails to close. I avoid backpacking to the bottom of the Grand Canyon in summer when temperatures usually exceed 110°F (43°C) during the day and remain too high at night for me to sleep comfortably. But unless a winter storm happens to hit, canyon hiking is great from October through April. In summer, I head for the Sierras or the Rockies. So with proper timing—and assuming you have some flexibility in your own schedule—somewhere in the United States or Canada there is good hiking 365 days a year!

Ecology of North American Deserts

As has been pointed out already, North American deserts differ in elevation, amount of rainfall, and annual temperatures. All of these elements determine the plants and wildlife characteristic of each desert.

The Sonoran Desert

The northern half of Arizona is described as high plateau and includes areas such as the Colorado Plateau, the Mogollon Rim, and the White Mountains. Elevations in the northern part of the state typically range from about 3,000 feet (914.5 m) to 10,000 feet (3,048 m), with the state's highest elevation on Mount Humphrey, which is just north of the city of Flagstaff and peaks at 12,633 feet (3,850.5 m). At much lower elevations, south and west of the plateaus and mountains lies the Sonoran Desert. As mentioned previously, the Sonoran Desert is our second largest desert.

The Sonoran Desert is part of the low desert, with elevations ranging from sea level to about 1,500 feet (457 m) above sea level. The signature plant of the Sonoran Desert is the saguaro cactus.

Rainfall and Floodwaters

Although the Sonoran Desert does not receive much rainfall on an annual basis, the rain it does receive tends to fall in two seasons—winter and summer. Snow is rare, but some snow does fall every few years. And desert rainstorms tend to be violent but brief.

Even rain that falls miles away from you can affect you. Rains can be so torrential that the runoff swiftly fills washes, and the floods that result can carry away every object, living or otherwise, that is in the wash.

The floodwaters can appear swiftly and without warning. Desert dwellers know to avoid washes at any sign of rain. You should avoid washes as well. Never camp in a wash, and always camp on high ground. Desert floods are sudden, but they are also short-lived. Before long, the water will run its course, soak back into the ground, and life in the desert will return to normal.

The Saguaro Cactus

The iconic plant species of the Sonoran Desert is the saguaro cactus (pronounced sah–*wah'*–ro). The saguaro with its beautiful white flowers that blossom in May and June is the state flower of Arizona. Saguaros can withstand some freezing temperatures but not prolonged freezes.

Just as alpine regions of mountains are marked by a tree line above which trees do not grow, the boundaries of the Sonoran Desert are marked by a saguaro line above which saguaros do not grow. It is a fairly well-demarcated line. As you drive in any direction from Phoenix or Tucson in which you are gaining elevation, saguaros can surround the highway one moment, and then be completely absent just moments later.

Nature Note

One of the best places in Arizona to see saguaros is at Saguaro National Park. Saguaros grow very slowly; it may be seventy years before the first branch forms. When you see saguaros with multiple branches, you know they are very old.

Cactus Species

Along with the saguaro cactus, many other cactus species are found in the Sonoran Desert, including the following:

➤ Chollas

➤ Barrel cacti

➤ Prickly pears

➤ Organ pipe cacti, a many-armed cactus characteristic of Mexico and Organ Pipe National Monument in southwestern Arizona

All the plant species of the Sonoran Desert are too numerous to list, but some of the noteworthy species that are not cacti include the following:

➤ Ocotillos

➤ Mesquites

➤ Creosotes

➤ Ironwoods

➤ Paloverdes

➤ Yuccas

➤ Agaves

Mammals

Contrary to what many people might think, the Sonoran Desert is teeming with wildlife. Mammals include the following:

➤ Desert bighorn sheep

➤ Bobcats

➤ Coyotes

➤ Kangaroo rats

➤ Wood rats

➤ Mice

➤ Bats

➤ Jackrabbits

➤ Desert cottontails

➤ Ground squirrels

➤ Kit foxes

➤ Collared peccaries (also known as javelinas)

Birds

Species of birds are numerous and include species that regularly migrate through as well as the following full-timers:

➤ Cactus wrens (Arizona's state bird)

➤ Turkey vultures

➤ Harris's, zone-tailed, and red-tailed hawks

➤ Gambel's quail

➤ White-winged, Inca, and mourning doves

➤ Greater roadrunners

➤ Elf, great horned, and burrowing owls

➤ Nighthawks

➤ Poorwills

➤ Anna's, Costa's, and broad-billed hummingbirds

➤ Gila and ladder-backed woodpeckers

➤ Gilded flickers

➤ Mockingbirds

➤ Flycatchers

➤ Verdins

➤ Curve-billed thrashers

➤ Gnatcatchers

➤ Vireos

➤ Northern cardinals

➤ Pyrrhuloxia

➤ Sparrows

➤ Warblers

➤ Finches

Reptiles and Amphibians

The desert certainly has its share of herps—reptiles and amphibians. Everyone associates deserts with rattlesnakes, and the Sonoran Desert has its share of those—western diamondbacks, sidewinders, and black-tailed. Rattlesnakes belong to the family of snakes called pit vipers because they have a small pit on each side of the head and poisonous venom that is injected through their fangs.

I have encountered my share of rattlesnakes while hiking over the years, but have never been bitten. Nor do I know anyone else who has been bitten. Generally speaking, about the only times people are bitten by rattlesnakes is when they try to handle the snakes or annoy them in some other way. Snakes bite humans in self-defense. Humans are not on a rattlesnake's menu.

Rattlesnake bites are rarely fatal, although in the event that a bite does occur, medical attention should be sought, especially in the case of small children and the elderly. To avoid snake bites, never blindly put your hands into crevices and do not step in places you cannot see.

Besides snakes, other desert reptiles include the following:

> ➤ Tortoises
>
> ➤ Collared lizards
>
> ➤ Chuckwallas
>
> ➤ Horned lizards
>
> ➤ Geckos
>
> ➤ Gila monsters

Nature Note

Gila monsters are one of only two poisonous lizards in the world (the other being Mexico's beaded lizard). Gila monsters have an extremely powerful bite that can be difficult to dislodge. But, like rattlesnakes, gila monsters are unlikely to bite humans, and will do so only if provoked. Their venom is painful, but death is rare.

Desert amphibians are mostly found around water, and include various species of frogs and toads. Unlike reptiles, which do not need to live near water, amphibians must spend at least part of their lives in or around water.

Most species spend most of their lives burrowed deep underground. When rains come and ephemeral ponds are temporarily filled with water, frogs and toads will emerge, mate, and lay eggs, which hatch within a few days. Tadpoles mature rapidly. When ponds dry up, frogs and toads burrow underground again and wait for the next rain.

Fish

Fish can live only where there is permanent water. Native Sonoran desert fish tend to be very small species, usually only 2 inches (5 cm) in length, but there are over eighty species found in the Sonoran Desert. An example is the desert pupfish, which reaches a length of only 2.5 inches (6.4 cm). Larger fish may be found in the Colorado River and its tributaries, although game fish like bass or trout are likely to be introduced species.

Scorpions and Tarantulas

Deserts are also known for their invertebrate species, and the Sonoran Desert has its share of scorpions and spiders, including tarantulas.

Scorpions tend to be active mostly at night. A good way to find scorpions is to walk across the desert floor after dark shining a black light (which shines in the ultraviolet region of the spectrum) on the ground. Parts of scorpions fluoresce, just like some minerals do.

Scorpion stings can be painful but are rarely harmful. The Sonoran Desert does have one genus of scorpion, Centruroides, with a sting that requires medical attention. I have encountered scorpions on my trips, the largest specimen being one that spent the night under my inflatable sleeping pad. When I picked up the pad in the morning, the scorpion simply scooted away to a nearby rock crevice. I have never been stung by a scorpion, however, nor have I hiked with anyone who has ever been stung.

Scorpions can be clinging to the underside of any rock or stick, so be careful when picking up anything. If you go hiking in Mexico, be even more careful. There are scorpions there with venom that is much more toxic than the venom of species found in Arizona.

Tarantulas are harmless to people. In fact, some people keep tarantulas as pets. Ants, wasps, and beetles are also found in the desert. Their bites or stings can be painful but can be avoided.

Hiking in the Sonoran Desert

The area in and around Phoenix is marked by several low mountains. Hiking trails are numerous and are used year-round, although in the summer hiking is best done in the very early morning or in the evening just before sunset. The Tucson area enjoys similar hiking trails, especially in Saguaro National Park, which is divided into two districts— the Tucson Mountain District, which is west of Tucson, and the Rincon Mountain District, which is east of Tucson.

Excellent hiking from late fall through early spring is found in the Superstition Wilderness, an area of rolling hills, saguaros and other cacti, and both permanent and ephemeral springs that is east of the Phoenix metropolitan area.

Topographic maps indicate the locations of springs, but they are best found by watching for cottonwood trees or other green vegetation, usually a sure sign of water in the desert. Or, if in doubt, there are usually enough hikers on the trails that someone will be able to point out where to expect water. Purify any surface water you use; livestock and wildlife often make use of the same springs.

In a year of high rainfall, the wildflowers can be especially spectacular. The Superstitions are situated east of Apache Junction about an hour's drive east of Phoenix on the Superstition Freeway (Highway 60). For most of the loop trails, a three-day backpacking trip is just about right, with loops typically being about 20 miles (32 km) in length. Unless a winter storm happens to hit—which could produce heavy rains and even heavy snow—winter daytime temperatures are warm enough for T-shirts and shorts, with nighttime temperatures remaining above freezing.

An important feature of the Sonoran Desert is the presence of sky islands—mountains that rise from the desert floor like islands rising from the ocean floor. The Sonoran Desert's principal sky islands that attract hikers are Mount Lemmon, northeast of Tucson; and Mount Graham, on the eastern side of Arizona. Residents of Phoenix and Tucson seek refuge from the summer heat and head to higher elevations to enjoy environments marked by much cooler temperatures, forested mountainsides, and hiking trails enjoyable all summer long.

The Chihuahuan Desert

The Chihuahuan Desert begins just southeast of Tucson, includes some of southern New Mexico, the very western part of Texas, and then the state of Chihuahua, Mexico.

Drive south on Interstate 10 from Phoenix to Tucson, and continue through the hills immediately surrounding Tucson, and you will find yourself in the land of saguaro cacti.

Continue in a southeasterly direction on I–10, however, and you will leave the saguaros behind. You have entered the Chihuahuan Desert.

Higher in elevation than the Sonoran Desert, parts of the Chihuahuan Desert exceed 4,000 feet (1,200 m). Rainfall patterns are different from those of the Sonoran Desert, with relatively dry winters and most rain falling in the summer.

There are several popular destinations in southeastern Arizona—Madera Canyon in the Santa Rita Mountains, southeast of Green Valley; the Huachuca Mountains a little farther to the east near Sierra Vista, which include Coronado National Monument on the Mexican border; and Chiricahua National Monument in the Chiricahua Mountains still farther east, very close to the New Mexico state line. These are the sky islands of that portion of the Chihuahuan Desert found in Arizona and are all north-south mountain ranges.

These mountains are meccas for birders from all over the United States and Canada, since many Mexican species breed in these mountains and nowhere else north of the border. Some of the non-bird species of animals are also more representative of Mexico than they are of the United States. It is not very often that a confirmed sighting of a jaguar or ocelot occurs, but sightings are occasionally reported on this side of the border.

All of West Texas is part of the Chihuahuan Desert ecosystem. Two national parks are found here—Guadalupe, on the New Mexico state line, and Big Bend on the Rio Grande River, which marks the border between the United States and Mexico. The uniqueness of the plant and animal species found in these parks and in the rest of West Texas makes these national parks popular destinations.

An agave called lechuguilla, is the indicator plant of the Chihuahuan Desert, although I personally find the sotols to be more eye-catching. Sotols produce a large flower stalk each spring and add a lot of beauty to the desert.

In Big Bend National Park, the Chisos Mountains are sky islands. Rising out of the desert floor, the Chisos range from 5,000 to 7,000 feet (1,500 to 2,100 m) in elevation, with several peaks rising over 7,000 feet. The highest elevation in the park is on Emory Peak at 7,825 feet (2,385 m). Emory is the most prominent peak in Texas and on clear days has outstanding 360° views of Texas and across the Rio Grande into Chihuahua, Mexico.

The Mohave Desert

The Mohave is America's smallest desert. It is squeezed between the Sonoran and Great Basin Deserts. The way I always know I am in a section of the Mohave Desert is that I begin seeing Joshua trees, which is the signature plant of the Mohave Desert. Joshua trees are a type of yucca, a member of the agave family. The Mohave Desert is the only place in the world that Joshua trees are found.

Joshua Trees

There are a couple of stories of why Joshua trees were so named. The name Joshua in Hebrew becomes Jesus in Greek. Some people think a Joshua tree looks like the cross on which Jesus was crucified, so it can be thought of as the Jesus tree. Another story is that the tree reminded Mormon pioneers of Joshua in the Old Testament.

Landscape and Location of the Mohave Desert

Elevations in the Mohave Desert generally vary between 2,000 and 5,000 feet (600 and 1,500 m). However, Death Valley is part of the Mohave Desert, and sections of Death Valley are below sea level. The reason this desert is so dry is that it lies in the rain shadow of the southern Sierras, the Tehachapi Mountains, and the San Bernardino Mountains.

Two small sections of the Mohave Desert protrude into Arizona. The Colorado River corridor is characterized by Mohave Desert vegetation, which means that the bottom of the Grand Canyon is Mohave Desert. A second section is traversed by Highway 93 between Wickenburg and Kingman. On the edge of the Sonoran Desert, Joshua trees almost mingle with saguaros.

Two very large areas of the Mohave Desert have been set aside to preserve this unique ecosystem. Interstate 40 runs east-west through the desert and roughly cuts the desert in half. On the north side of I–40 is the Mohave National Preserve, which covers 1.6 million acres (6,500 sq km) of desert and is the third largest unit of the national park system in the continental United States.

Visitors are attracted to the preserve to hike, backpack, and camp, and to go horseback riding and four-wheeling. Because it is a national preserve, not a national park, hunting of game such as quail, chukar partridge (an imported game bird), mule deer, bighorn sheep is permitted in season. There's also some interesting history to the preserve, especially at the Kelso Depot Visitor Center and railroad museum.

Joshua Tree National Park is on the south side of Interstate I–40, and is bounded by Highway 62 on the north and Interstate 10 on the south. Because it is a national park, hunting is not allowed.

Joshua Tree covers about 800,000 acres (3,240 sq km) of desert and has several campgrounds and hiking trails. My favorite area of the park is Cottonwood Spring, which is close to one of the visitor centers and a campground.

Both Mohave National Preserve and Joshua Tree National Park get most of their visitors during the cooler months of the year, since summer daytime temperatures can be pretty brutal.

Animals of the Mohave Desert

Two species of animals are closely associated with the Mohave Desert. One of the best places to find desert tortoises is in the Mohave. Tortoises are on the endangered species list, and both government and nonprofit organizations are working hard to preserve it.

Desert bighorn sheep are an icon of the desert. At one time there were about 2 million bighorn sheep. There are only about 20,000 today. Although that's not a large population, some hunting is permitted.

Nature Note

Members of the deer family, which includes deer, moose, elk, and caribou, shed their antlers each fall and begin growing new ones the next spring. These animals tend to live in areas that can have heavy snowfall. If they didn't shed their antlers, the weight of snow the antlers would collect would be extremely cumbersome. Shedding their antlers presumably is nature's way of helping deer survive the winter. Desert bighorn sheep don't have to cope with snow, so they don't shed their horns. Instead, their horns continue to grow throughout their lifetime.

Great Basin Desert

The Great Basin Desert is the northernmost and largest desert in North America. It covers most of Utah and Nevada, with parts extending into the adjoining states of California, Oregon, Idaho, and Arizona. Its western boundary is the Sierra Nevada Mountains in California; its eastern boundary is the Wasatch Mountains in Utah. The reason the desert exists is that it lies in the rain shadow of the Sierra Nevada Mountains to the west. Moist air masses blown inland from the Pacific Ocean deposit rain and snow on the Sierras. By the time the air masses have crossed the mountains, they are dry; little precipitation falls in the Great Basin.

Plants and Animals

The Great Basin Desert is the coldest of North America's deserts. Most of it lies at elevations above 4,000 feet (1,219 m), so it snows regularly in winter, and freezing temperatures are common. Moist precipitation falls in winter and spring.

Because of freezing conditions in winter, cacti are not common in the Great Basin; the signature plant is sagebrush. At lower elevations, miles and miles of sagebrush and rabbit brush predominate. Conifers grow at higher elevations. The importance of sagebrush shows in the names of common birds and animals associated with it:

➤ Sage sparrow

➤ Sage grouse

➤ Sage thrasher

➤ Sagebrush chipmunk

➤ Sagebrush lizard

Ground squirrels, coyotes, bobcats, badgers, pronghorns, and foxes are also common.

Salt Lakes

Salt lakes occur in the Great Basin, the best-known being the Great Salt Lake in Utah and Mono Lake near Lee Vining, California. Rivers and streams carry dissolved salts. Normally, they flow to the sea and deposit their salts there. Salt lakes have no outlets, so salt accumulates. Salt lakes are often saltier than the ocean.

The principal national park in the Great Basin is Great Basin National Park in eastern Nevada. Mountains rise out of the desert, providing cool relief for hikers.

Conclusion

Deserts may seem stark and monotonous to some people in comparison to mountains or prairies. I encourage you, however, to include them in your travels. Some of that stark scenery can be absolutely breathtaking.

CHAPTER 14

Public Lands, National Parks, and Forests

In This Chapter

➤ National parks and forests

➤ Wildlife refuges

➤ State parks and services

➤ Canadian public lands

Unless you are personally acquainted with private land owners, your outdoor experiences likely will be entirely on public lands. These lands can be under the jurisdictions of a wide diversity of government agencies. There are many reasons why they have been preserved from further development. They may have exceptional scenery, unique geological features, a diversity of wildlife, outstanding recreation potential, historical significance, or other values.

Sizes of parks and recreation areas vary widely, from millions of acres in national parks, forests, and wildlife refuges to a single building, as is the case with the National Jazz Historic Site at New Orleans, Louisiana.

The purpose of this chapter is to acquaint you with the major classifications of public lands at the national, state or provincial, and local levels. Understanding the important features of different types of public lands helps a person understand what recreational and educational opportunities are available on those lands.

National Parks

The United States has a distinguished record of setting aside lands. Wyoming's Yellowstone National Park was created in 1872 as the world's first national park, but it wasn't the first park established by the federal government.

What eventually became Arkansas' Hot Springs National Park was originally a federal reservation set aside in 1832 by President Andrew Jackson. It was not until 1921 that Hot Springs attained national park status. The Adirondack Mountains in northeast New York was also set aside early and is now the largest state park in the United States.

California's Yosemite National Park had its beginning in 1864 under the administration of President Abraham Lincoln as a land grant from the federal government to the state of California. Yosemite originally consisted of Yosemite Valley and the Mariposa Grove of sequoia trees. In 1890, when Yosemite was deeded back to the federal government and made a national park, the size of the park was enlarged to include much of the present holdings within the park.

Founding National Parks

A national park like Yosemite is a good example of what dedicated citizens can accomplish if they work hard enough.

Several national parks have been established because of the tireless efforts of someone who has championed the cause:

➤ John Muir (1838–1914): Scottish immigrant and naturalist who championed Yosemite National Park

➤ Enos Mills (1870–1922): Naturalist and public speaker who established Rocky Mountain National Park in northern Colorado

➤ John D. Rockefeller, Jr. (1874–1960): Philanthropist who donated 35,000 acres (141.5 sq km) of the Grand Teton National Park in northwestern Wyoming and contributed generously to the Acadia National Park on the southeastern coast of Maine by financing the construction of a network of carriage roads and granite bridges, many of which are in use today

➤ Charles Eliot (1834–1926): Nineteenth-century landscape architect who provided the inspiration for the creation of Acadia National Park on the southeastern coast of Maine

➤ Marjorie Stoneman Douglas (1890–1998): Journalist, writer, and crusader for the conservation of nature who was the champion for Everglades National Park in southern Florida

➤ William Gladstone Steel (1854–1934): Struggled for seventeen years to establish Crater Lake National Park in southern Oregon as a national park

Some national parks were established due to the efforts of more than one person. Fearing complete logging of northern California's coastal redwood trees, the Save the Redwoods League was established in 1918 by Henry Fairfield Osborn (1857–1935), a paleontologist with the American Museum of Natural History; Madison Grant (1865–1937), a physical anthropologist with the New York Zoological Society; John C. Merriam (1869–1945), a paleontologist at the University of California at Berkeley; and Frederick Russell Burham (1861–1947), a scout and tracker with the United States Army. Their efforts resulted in the creation of Redwoods National Park and several California state parks that contain stands of redwood trees.

In addition to Yellowstone and Yosemite, several other national parks were established before 1900, including the following:

➤ Sequoia National Park, south of Yosemite: 1890

➤ Glacier National Park, in northern Montana: 1897

➤ Olympic National Park, on Washington's Olympic Peninsula: 1897

Two national military parks—Gettysburg, in southern Pennsylvania (1895)) and Vicksburg, in Mississippi (1899))—were established to commemorate significant battlefields of the Civil War. The creation of all of these parks required acts of Congress.

Antiquities Act

It was the Antiquities Act of 1906 that gave the President of the United States the authority to set aside public lands without the approval of Congress. Officially entitled "An Act for the Preservation of American Antiquities," the Antiquities Act was signed into law by President Theodore Roosevelt and was intended to protect natural areas with significant historic and scientific interest. These areas were called national monuments.

It is important to note that national monuments have a lower level of protection afforded them than national parks do. However, it is also true that many national parks have had their beginnings as national monuments. Grand Canyon and Grand Teton are notable examples.

Nature Note

While President, Theodore Roosevelt established 150 national forests, 4 national game preserves, 5 national parks, and 18 national monuments. No wonder he is often called the conservation president!

The President of the United States still cannot establish national parks without the approval of Congress, but Congress doesn't have a say in the establishment of national monuments.

Using the authority given him under the Antiquities Act, President Roosevelt established the first national monument—Devil's Tower in the northeastern corner of Wyoming. By the time Roosevelt's presidency ended in 1908, he had established eighteen national monuments.

Presidents still use the Antiquities Act, often as last acts before leaving office. In 2000, President Bill Clinton set aside the Grand Staircase-Escalante National Monument in southern Utah shortly before the expiration of his second term of office. In November 2011, President Barack Obama used his authority to establish Fort Monroe National Monument in Virginia, and in April 2012, he established Fort Ord National Monument in California.

National Park Service Organic Act

Although national parks had been in existence in the United States for several decades, as of 1910, no federal agency existed with the primary responsibility of protecting and administering the parks. Early protection of the parks was assigned to the United States Cavalry, in part because the western Indian Wars were coming to an end and troops were available for national park assignments.

In 1916, Congress passed the National Park Service Organic Act that established the National Park Service (NPS). President Woodrow Wilson signed the bill into law. The organic act specifically gave the NPS authority over the national parks and monuments that existed at that time, as well as over the federation reservation at Hot Springs.

The first director of the NPS was Stephen Mather. The Park Service itself was put under the authority of the Department of the Interior (DOI). The position of national park ranger was created to replace the army troops in protecting and administering the parks.

Historical Quote

The wording of the National Park Service Act has been an inspiration to generations of park rangers and visitors: "[the purpose of the parks and monuments is] to conserve the scenery and the natural and historic objects and the wildlife therein and to provide for the enjoyment of the same in such manner and by such means as will leave them unimpaired for the enjoyment of future generations".

National Forests

The bill authorizing the establishment of national forests was passed by Congress in 1891 and signed into law by President Benjamin Harrison. Harrison set aside 13 million acres (53,000 sq km) of land into forest reserves. He was followed by President Grover Cleveland, who set aside 25 million acres (101,171 sq km), and President William McKinley, who during his short administration added 7 million acres (28,000 sq km).

At first, national forests were placed under the oversight of the Department of the Interior (DOI). In 1905, jurisdiction was transferred to the United States Department of Agriculture (USDA), where it still resides today within the National Forest Service.

The country's first national forest was Mt. Hood National Forest in northern Oregon, established in 1893. One of the earliest, and most colorful, directors of the United States Forest Service (USFS) was Gifford Pinchot (1865–1946).

Theodore Roosevelt (1858–1919) added a remarkable total of 150 national forests during his presidency (1901–1909). Today there are 155 national forests and 20 national grasslands administered by the United States Forest Service. Most national forest land—87 percent—is located west of the Mississippi River. National forests in the United States encompass 190 million acres (769,000 sq km).

The Wilderness Act

In 1964, President Lyndon Johnson signed into law the Wilderness Act, which was the result of many years of hard work on the part of conservationists. Two prominent proponents of establishing wilderness areas were University of Wisconsin wildlife biology professor Aldo Leopold (1887–1948) and forester Bob Marshall (1901–1939), although neither of them lived to see the law enacted. The act created the National Wilderness Preservation System (NWPS).

The wording of the Wilderness Act still provides the working definition of wilderness: "a wilderness, in contrast with those areas where man and his own works dominate the landscape, is hereby recognized as an area where the earth and community of life are untrammeled by man, where man himself is a visitor who does not remain."

The Wilderness Act provided for the initial establishment of 9.1 million acres (36,800 sq km) of wilderness in national forests. As of 2011, the total area comprising the NWPS was almost 108 million acres (437,000 sq km). To put that number in perspective, 108 million acres represents almost 5 percent of the total area of the United States.

Approximately half of America's wilderness areas are under the jurisdiction of the NPS, with the remaining lands under the jurisdiction of the Forest Service, the US Fish and Wildlife Service (USFWS), and the Bureau of Land Management (BLM).

One of the distinguishing features of wilderness areas is that—in contrast to all other federal lands—no motorized vehicles are allowed. In many wilderness areas, even aircraft are not permitted to fly below a certain ceiling unless necessary for rescue operations. In some instances, activities such as mining, livestock grazing, and other commercial operations that had existed in the area before it was designated as a wilderness area—and that presumably have minimal impact on the wilderness area as a whole—have been grandfathered and continue to occur.

Wilderness areas are among the most popular destinations of backpackers. Because there are no roads passing through them, fewer people use wilderness areas. However, that also means that people who go there need to be more experienced than casual backpackers and better equipped to handle emergencies that could arise on the trail.

National Wildlife Refuges (NWRs)

Enter Teddy Roosevelt again. In 1903, Roosevelt established Pelican Island in Florida as America's first national wildlife refuge. NWRs are administered by the United States Fish and Wildlife Service (USFWS), an agency within the Department of the Interior.

Unlike national parks or monuments, wildlife refuges serve a more utilitarian purpose. Rather than the preservation of sites of spectacular scenery or historical significance, wildlife refuges aim to maintain habitat for wildlife such as game mammals, fish, and migratory waterfowl. Also unlike parks or monuments, hunting is allowed on wildlife refuges. Much of the funding for wildlife refuges is derived from the sale of hunting and fishing licenses.

Today there are 556 units within the National Wildlife Refuge System, totaling over 150 million acres (600,000 sq km). Over 20 percent of refuge lands—mostly in Alaska—are wilderness areas.

To protect wildlife, especially during breeding season, much of the acreage of wildlife refuges is off limits to visitors. Additionally, if the focus is on waterfowl conservation, much of the acreage may consist of wetlands that are largely inaccessible.

During hunting season, sections of refuges could be dangerous for casual recreation. At some of the smaller refuges, that may leave little or no room for hiking trails. However, at the larger refuges, hiking trails still exist. It pays to inquire in advance as to what recreational opportunities are available.

Bureau of Land Management (BLM)

When I think of federal lands and subtract the national parks, national monuments, national forests, and military reservations, I usually figure that what are left is BLM holdings. The

BLM administers 264 million acres (1.1 million sq km) of land, mostly in the western United States. To put that in perspective, 264 million acres is approximately one-eighth of the total landmass of the United States.

The BLM is an agency of the Department of the Interior, but BLM designation provides the least amount of preservation compared to national parks and monuments. Unlike national parks and monuments, BLM land is open to grazing and mining. Usually, there is very little development on BLM land—fewer campgrounds, maintained trails, and organized centers of recreation. However, there are still plenty of recreational opportunities available. Considering how much of the western United States is BLM land, it is worth looking into what is available on BLM lands through which you might be traveling.

National Recreation Areas (NRAs)

National recreation areas are large tracts of land often centered on reservoirs that are intended for recreational purposes rather than preservation. The NPS administers eighteen national recreation areas, the BLM administers eleven, and the USFS administers twenty-six. Although most visitors are attracted by aquatic sports, most recreation areas also have systems of trails.

State and Local Parks

Every state has state parks; in the eastern United States, state forests are also widespread. There are regional, county, and city parks at the local level. These parks can be convenient if you're looking for a weekend day hike and do not have the time to travel to a trail that's far from home.

Canada

There are forty-one national parks and national park reserves in Canada. A national park reserve is on its way to becoming a national park pending the settlement of land issues with First Peoples. Two of the most popular national parks are Jasper and Banff, located in the Canadian Rockies. Established in 1885, Banff was Canada's first national park. Canada is expanding its national park system and expects to add up to ten new parks in the next few years.

Hiking Vocab

In accordance with use in Canada, I am using the term First Peoples to refer to the aboriginal people who occupied Canada prior to the arrival of Russians or Europeans. The term is analogous to Native Americans used in the United States.

A Wild Country

Instead of states, Canada is divided into thirteen provinces and territories. There are more than three hundred provincial and territorial parks; that's an average of over twenty parks per province or territory.

Canada has only nine cities with populations greater than 0.5 million. Four of the largest cities—Toronto, Montreal, Quebec, and Ottawa—are in the east; the remaining four—Vancouver, Calgary, Edmonton, and Winnipeg—are in western and central Canada. With the exception of Calgary and Edmonton, which are located in the prairie east of the Canadian Rockies, Canada's largest cities are located very close to the United States border.

In terms of area, Canada is the second largest country in the world; Russia is the largest, the United States is the third largest. In terms of population, the United States is the third largest country in the world with 310 million people. Canada is the thirty-fifth largest country with only 34 million people.

Canada extends from the border with the United States to the Arctic Ocean. So much of Canada's population is concentrated in and around a few major cities close to the United States that population density as a whole is very low. Most of Canada is still very much a wilderness.

Conclusion

There probably are a large number of parks, forests, and recreation areas within 50 miles (80 km) of your home. You should be able to find everything from one-hour walks to weekend backpacking trips within an hour's drive. Check with your local park and recreation department to find out what's nearby.

CHAPTER 15

 **National Trails**

In This Chapter

➤ Scenic trails

➤ Historic trails

➤ Recreation trails

In the United States, hiking trails vary in length from 1 mile (1.6 km) to thousands of miles. Someone has to build and maintain those trails. That "someone" is usually a local, state, or federal governmental agency, but sometimes trails are built and maintained by nonprofit organizations. This chapter is about trails that have regional or national significance and thus are called national trails.

The National Trails System Act of 1968 established a national trails system comprised of National Scenic Trails, National Historic Trails, and National Recreation Trails (see Part Four for more on National Recreation Trails). New trails are added to the registry every year. Adding a trail to the registry of national trails requires approval by the Secretary of Interior or the Secretary of Agriculture. Let's take a look at the National Scenic and Historic Trails.

National Scenic Trails

National Scenic Trails are long-distance trails that traverse several states and can be found in every region of the United States. They may be hundreds, or even thousands, of miles long, with some running in a north-south direction; others running west-east. The establishment of a National Scenic Trail requires an act of Congress. The ten major trails in the system represent continuous routes through protected corridors.

Hikers may spend an entire lifetime hiking a particular trail, covering perhaps a few hundred miles each year, or hiking their favorite sections over and over again. There are also the thru-hikers, those people with the time, stamina, and financial resources to hike a long-distance trail from one end to the other in a single season. Some of the national trails have enough access points that a person can begin almost anywhere and end almost anywhere. Many access points also serve as good trailheads for day hikes.

Here is a list of the major National Scenic Trails:

➤ Appalachian Trail (AT)

➤ Continental Divide Trail (CDT)

➤ Pacific Crest Trail (PCT)

➤ Florida Trail (FT)

➤ Long Trail (LT)

➤ Ice Age Trail (IAT)

➤ North Country Trail (NCT)

➤ The Pacific Northwest Trail (PNT)

➤ Colorado Trail (CT)

➤ Potomac Heritage Trail (PHT)

What follows are brief descriptions of the major trails.

The Appalachian Trail

The Appalachian Trail is the longest national trail in the United States, if not the longest trail of its kind in the world. The AT had its beginnings in the vision of Benton MacKaye, who began development of the trail in the early 1920s. MacKaye's dream was to have a trail that began at the highest mountain peak in the southeastern United States and ended at the highest mountain peak in the northeastern United States. That made Mount Mitchell in North Carolina the southern terminus of the AT and Mount Washington in New Hampshire the northern terminus. Today, the AT stretches farther in both directions. With a total length of 2,100 miles (3,3780 km), the AT begins at the summit of Mount Oglethorpe in the Blue Ridge Mountains of Georgia and ends at the top of Mount Katahdin in Baxter State Park in Maine.

Including Georgia and Maine, the AT passes through thirteen states. Hikers who wish to thru-hike the entire trail in a single season usually start in Georgia in April and work their way north. A physically fit hiker who can maintain a consistent pace of 15 miles (24 km) a day can complete the trail in about four-and-a-half months. A hiker who maintains a slower, but steady, pace of 10 miles (16 km) a day needs seven months to finish the trail. Either way, a hiker who begins in Georgia in April can expect to reach Mount Katahdin between Labor Day and Thanksgiving.

In 1968, President Lyndon Johnson signed the legislation that created the national trails system and established the AT as the first National Scenic Trail. Today, the land through which the AT passes is protected by the federal government. Oversight of the AT, however, lies with private citizen advocates—the Appalachian Trail Conference (ATC).

For people who don't have the time or inclination to backpack, the AT offers a large number of day hikes in every state through which it passes. Trails range from 1 to 2 miles (1.6 to 3 km) in length, to 10 miles (16 km) or more and are rated from easy to strenuous. If you live in one of the states through which the AT passes, you can probably find access to trailheads close to home.

In the mid-1990s, work began to extend the AT northward from Maine to the Canadian border and beyond. Called the International Appalachian Trail (IAT), the extension travels through the provinces of New Brunswick and Quebec, ending on the Gaspe Peninsula of Quebec. The IAT extension adds 435 miles (700 km) to the AT. The IAT thus merges two nations, two languages (English and French), and two cultures. In Quebec, the official name of the IAT is the Sentier International des Appalaches (SIA). In Canada, all trail signs are in both English and French, and all distances are given using the metric system (as is also true of highway signs in Canada).

Extending the AT into New Brunswick and Quebec was a natural thing to do biogeographically. The Appalachian Mountains do not end in Maine (as I'm sure most Americans think). The Appalachians continue through New Brunswick and Quebec and, in fact, do not even end at the shore of the Atlantic Ocean. The Appalachians actually continue as mountains submerged beneath the ocean, only to reappear on the island of Newfoundland. The route of the IAT/SIA was chosen to pass over, or at least very close to, the highest points in New Brunswick and Quebec—Mount Carleton at 2,690 feet (820 m) in English-speaking New Brunswick and Mont Jacques-Cartier at 4,160 feet 1,268 m)

Historical Quote

"The International Appalachian Trail/Sentier International des Appalaches is a symbol of US-Canadian commitment to work together as neighbors, to sustain our common environments, and to celebrate the grandeur of common landscape. It connects mountains, crosses rivers, threads through spruce and fir forests, and connects the people and cultures of the state of Maine and the provinces of Quebec and New Brunswick."

–Two-term governor of Maine, Joseph E. Brennan (1934–)

in French-speaking Quebec. Including the highest points in the two Canadian provinces is very appropriate since Mount Katahdin at 5,268 feet 1,606 m) is the highest point in Maine.

The Continental Divide Trail

The Continental Divide Trail (CDT) is 3,100 miles (4,990 km) long and runs between the Mexican border and the Canadian border. The CDT passes through the states of New Mexico, Colorado, Wyoming, Idaho, and Montana. It is best described as a primitive and challenging trail; along several sections the trail currently suffers from lack of maintenance. In fact, 30 percent of the trail is judged to be unusable.

The CDT passes through a variety of ecosystems. Southern New Mexico is part of the Chihuahuan Desert grasslands. As the trail wends its way north, it passes through mountain wildernesses, canyonlands, and the badlands of the El Malpais National Monument.

Entering Colorado, the trail works its way through high mountain wilderness and stays at altitudes above 11,000 feet (3,350 m) for almost 70 miles 113 km). The highest point on the CDT is found in Colorado on top of Grays Peak at an altitude of 14,270 feet (4,349 m). As of early 2012, however, almost 200 miles (320 km) of the trail in Colorado were still under construction.

In Wyoming, the CDT passes through the Wind River Range and Grand Teton and Yellowstone National Parks. The shortest segment of the CDT at 180 miles (290 km) is found in the southeastern corner of Idaho. In Montana, the CDT traverses such majestic regions as the Bob Marshall Wilderness Area and Glacier National Park. Several hundred miles of the CDT in Idaho and Montana have not been completed.

The Pacific Crest Trail

The Pacific Crest Trail (PCT) runs between the Mexican and Canadian borders and passes through California, Oregon, and Washington. The PCT is 2,650 miles (4,264 km) long. Once the trail crosses the desert in southern California, almost the entire remaining trail traverses mountains. Basically, once you are at high elevation, you stay at high elevation. It is almost anomalous that there is less up and down hiking on the PCT than there is on the AT even though the PCT is mostly at much higher elevations than the AT is.

The PCT passes through seven national parks, three national monuments, twenty-four national forests, and thirty-three designated wilderness areas. It also passes the three deepest lakes in the United States—Lake Tahoe at 1,645 feet (501 m) in California, Crater Lake at 1,932 feet (589 m) in Oregon, and Lake Chelan at 1,149 feet (350 m) in Washington.

Local History

In 2001, Brian Robinson became the first person in history to thru-hike the Pacific Crest Trail, the Appalachian Trail, and the Continental Divide Trail in a single calendar year (he finished on October 27, 2001). Robinson hiked 7,371 miles (11,860 km) through twenty-two states, and did it all in only three hundred days. That's an average of 25 miles (40 km) per day!

John Muir Trail

The John Muir Trail (JMT) is not a separate National Scenic Trail, but it is an extremely popular segment of the Pacific Crest Trail. The JMT is 211 miles (339 km) long. It begins at Happy Isles at the east end of Yosemite Valley at an elevation of 4,035 feet (1,230 m) and climbs rapidly out of the valley past Vernal and Nevada Falls to Tuolumne Meadows. From there, the JMT heads south over Donahue Pass at an elevation of 11,056 feet (3,370 m).

On its way south toward Mount Whitney, the JMT passes through incredibly scenic country in the John Muir Wilderness, the Ansel Adams Wilderness, Devils Postpile National Monument, and Sequoia and Kings Canyon National Parks. Once the trail has climbed out of Yosemite Valley, elevations on the trail are rarely below 8,000 feet (2,440 m). Six of the mountain passes the trail traverses are over 11,000 feet (3,350 m) in elevation.

Forester Pass at 13,153 feet (4,009 m) is the highest point on the Pacific Crest Trail and the second highest point on the John Muir Trail. The southern terminus of the JMT is Mount Whitney, which is the highest point in the lower forty-eight states at 14,505 feet (4,421 m). The JMT splits off from the PCT just before heading toward Mount Whitney. Therefore, Whitney's summit technically is not on the PCT.

I have hiked several segments of the JMT and highly recommend it, especially for hikers who lack sufficient time or resources to tackle longer portions of the PCT.

Florida Trail

The Florida Trail (FT) is the longest trail in the southeast at about 1,400 miles (2,250 km) in length and runs the entire length of the state. The southern terminus is at Big Cypress National Preserve. Much of the southernmost portion of the trail is under water most of the year, even during the so-called dry season. Hikers need to be prepared to hike through water.

After traversing the state, the FT ends at its northern terminus at Gulf Islands National Seashore near Pensacola. The entire trail—as well as the entire state—is essentially at sea level. Sections of the trail are popular for day hikes.

The Long Trail

The Long Trail (LT) runs south-north through the state of Vermont, and supporters lay claim to its being the oldest long-distance trail in the United States. (Supporters of the Appalachian Trail and the Long Trail both claim their trails to be the oldest. From my reading, it seems that the LT has the stronger claim; construction began earlier.)

The LT runs 272 miles (438 km) from the Massachusetts state line near Williamstown, Massachusetts, to the Canadian border near North Troy, Vermont, passing mostly through the Green Mountains. About 100 miles (161 km) coincide with the AT. Over 175 miles (282 km) of side trails connect to the LT, effectively increasing the total miles of trails by two-thirds.

The highest point on the LT is Mount Mansfield at an elevation of 4,395 feet (1,340 m). The trail traverses at least a half dozen of Vermont's other major peaks.

The Ice Age Trail

One of the newest cross-country trails in the United States, the Ice Age Trail (IAT), is 1,200 miles (1,930 km) long and winds its way through the state of Wisconsin. The trail is meant to tell the story of how that part of the country was sculpted by glaciers. Over 600 miles (960 km) of the IAT are signed as such. The remainder of the route consists mostly of connecting trails that include walking the main streets of some cities.

The IAT is definitely a work in progress. Eventually, the plan is to convert all of the paved routes to off-road hiking trails. The creators of the IAT hope that the trail will serve to preserve and protect Wisconsin's cultural and glacial heritage.

The IAT follows the noticeable scouring of the land made during the period of the Wisconsin glaciations, which advanced to its southernmost limit, or terminus, about 15,000 years ago and began retreating about 10,000 years ago.

The North Country Trail

The North Country Trail (NCT) passes through seven states—North Dakota and the Great Lakes states of Minnesota, Wisconsin, Michigan, Ohio, Pennsylvania, and New York. The NCT is still under construction but when finished will exceed the Appalachian Trail as the longest continuous trail in the United States. As of early 2012, about 2,000 miles (3,200 km) of the trail had been finished. When the entire trail is completed, it is estimated that the total length will be about 4,600 miles (7,400 km).

The Missouri River and Lake Sakakawea State Park in central North Dakota mark the western terminus of the NCT. The NCT heads east for 475 miles (764 km) across North Dakota, looping south around Fargo and through the Shawnee National Grasslands. In Minnesota, the trail heads through Chippewa National Forest and the headwaters of the Mississippi River (where a person can actually step across the Mississippi), and then splits near Grand Rapids, Minnesota. A northern loop passes through the Boundary Waters Canoe Area Wilderness before joining with the Superior Hiking Trail on the northwest shore of Lake Superior and heading to Duluth. The southern portion after the split goes directly to Duluth. Altogether, 775 miles (1,247 km) of the trail are in Minnesota.

Before reaching the Michigan state line, 200 miles (322 km) of the NCT cut across northern Wisconsin through state parks, state forests, and national forests. The longest section of the trail—1,150 miles (1,850 km)—is in Michigan and traverses both the Upper and Lower Peninsulas. The route through Michigan heads due east through the boreal forest of Ottawa National Forest to the southern shore of Lake Superior. The trail then follows the shoreline to Pictured Rocks National Lakeshore before turning south at Tahquamenon Falls State Park. A shuttle is required to cross the Mackinac Bridge. Once on the Lower Peninsula, hikers may choose to make a side trip for a day or more to Mackinac Island.

Trail Wisdom

Normally, walking across the 5-mile-long (8-km-long) Mackinac Bridge is not allowed. An exception is made once a year on the morning of Labor Day, when hiking enthusiasts gather for the annual Bridge Walk.

The NCT continues down western Michigan through Manistee National Forest. In the southern part of the state, the trail begins to head east and crosses into Ohio at about the center of the Michigan-Ohio state line west of Toledo.

In Ohio, the NCT hugs the perimeter of the state going south parallel to the Ohio-Indiana state line close to Cincinnati, then east across southern Ohio just north of Kentucky, and finally north on the eastern side of the state before entering Pennsylvania. Altogether, there are 1,050 miles (1,690 km) of the NCT in Ohio.

The northwest corner of Pennsylvania hosts 265 miles (426 km) of the NCT. The primary attraction of the trail in Pennsylvania is the Allegheny National Forest with its valleys, streams, and rolling hills.

The NCT enters the state of New York at Allegheny State Park in southwestern New York. Passing 625 miles (1,006 km) through central New York to the Adirondack Mountains, the trail finally arrives at its eastern terminus at Crown Point State Historic Site on the shores of Lake Champlain, which marks the New York-Vermont state line.

Pacific Northwest Trail

The Pacific Northwest Trail (PNT) is the country's newest long-distance trail. The PNT crosses three states—Washington, Idaho, and Montana. It starts at Cape Alava near the northwest tip of the Olympic Peninsula, goes to Port Townsend, crosses by ferry to the Bellingham area, and then runs parallel to the Canadian border; its eastern terminus is the Continental Divide near Polebridge, Montana.

The PNT is 1,200 miles (1,930 km) in length. The trail crosses four mountain ranges—the Rockies, the Selkirks, the North Cascades, and the Olympics. It traverses three national parks—Glacier, North Cascades, and Olympic—and seven national forests.

The Colorado Trail

The Colorado Trail is a 500-mile-long (800-km-long) trail that winds its way through Colorado from Durango to Denver. The trail passes through eight mountain ranges and six wildernesses; its average elevation is over 10,000 feet (3,050 m). The highest elevation reached is just below Coney Summit at 13,271 feet (4,045 m). Hikers share portions of the trail with bicyclists. Some of Colorado's most spectacular mountain terrain is traversed by the Colorado Trail.

Potomac Heritage Trail

The Potomac Heritage Trail is a series of trails that follow the Potomac River rather than a single continuous corridor. Still a work in progress, the completed trail will be 830 miles (1,335 km) in length. The trail begins at the river's mouth on Chesapeake Bay and ends in the Alleghenies in Seward, Pennsylvania.

The trail is divided into sixty segments with lengths ranging from a few miles to more than 20 (32 km), all of which can be accomplished as day hikes.

National Historic Trails

National Historic Trails have been established as efforts to preserve our nation's past. There are a total of nineteen such trails in the United States. Their names should be seared into our memories from the study of US history. There is a considerable amount of romance, adventure, and sorrow associated with them; your own ancestors may have traveled these trails. Perhaps the most-traveled trails were the ones to California, Oregon, and Utah. During the 1800s, an estimated 0.5 million people began the trip.

Hundreds, if not thousands, of lives, were lost by pioneers who left the eastern United States and died en route to the promised land. These trails are the story of manifest destiny, of nineteenth-century America's conviction that America was meant to populate the North American continent "from sea to shining sea."

Like National Scenic Trails, the establishment of a National Historic Trails requires an act of Congress.

In general, the trails do not pass continuously through contiguous corridors. In most cases, only segments of the trails are available as hiking trails. In between segments, hikers most likely have to drive to get to another accessible segment. In a few cases the trail may be a river as the historic means of transport was by boat, not by foot or by horseback. Nevertheless, there are still thousands of miles of trails open to hiking, bicycling, and equestrian use.

Here is a list of the major National Historic Trails:

> ➤ California Trail
>
> ➤ Iditarod Trail
>
> ➤ Lewis and Clark Trail
>
> ➤ Oregon Trail
>
> ➤ Pony Express Trail
>
> ➤ Santa Fe Trail
>
> ➤ Trail of Tears

The California Trail

The California Trail includes a total of 5,665 miles (9,115 km), although that includes the multiple number of routes that different travelers would take. On average, the actual distance traveled was about 2,000 miles (3,200 km). Travelers could begin at Independence, Missouri or Omaha, Nebraska, and finish at San Francisco, California, or possibly other destinations along the coast, the Central Valley of California, or the gold fields of the Sierra foothills. A wagon train would have taken four-and-a-half to five months to make the trip. To put the trip in perspective, the opening of the transcontinental railroad in 1869 reduced the time required to about eight days. Today's interstate highways have reduced the distance to 1,817 miles (2,924 km), and the trip can be made fairly easily in three days.

The California Trail begins at Independence, Missouri, and continues through Iowa, Kansas, Nebraska, Wyoming, Utah, Nevada, and California, with spurs going through Idaho and Oregon. The first part of the trail coincides with the Oregon Trail and the Mormon Trail, which lead to Salt Lake City, Utah. There are 350 historic sites along the trail.

At least 30,000 persons traveled the trail in 1849 to the California gold fields. Perhaps the most famous tragedy in trail history involved the Donner Party in 1846, the members of which became snowbound in the Sierras west of present-day Reno and perished.

The Iditarod Trail

The Iditarod Trail was a winter trail traversed by dog sled teams between Seward and Nome, Alaska. There are a total of 2,450 miles (3,942 km) of trails, although the main route is 938 miles (1,509 km).

The Iditarod Trail is commemorated each year by the world famous Iditarod dog sled race that begins in March at Anchorage and runs to Nome. The trail crosses rivers and mountain passes and runs through tundra and spruce forests. Only small portions of the trail can be hiked in summer, since the trail passes through wetlands and marshes that make the trail impassable.

The Lewis and Clark Trail

I admit it: I'm a Lewis and Clark buff. Anywhere I travel along the route of their 1804–1806 Corps of Discovery Expedition and am in the vicinity of one of their historic sites, I have to check it out. What an incredible trip that must have been! According to all accounts of the expedition, Meriwether Lewis and William Clark were outstanding leaders—certainly the best men President Thomas Jefferson could have chosen to lead the expedition.

Altogether, the Lewis and Clark National Historic Trail includes 3,700 miles (5,950 km) of trails and passes through Illinois, Missouri, Kansas, Nebraska, Idaho, South Dakota, North Dakota, Montana, Idaho, Washington, and Oregon. There is not a continuous corridor to follow, and some of the trail is actually river, such as the Missouri River, up which they paddled for the first segment of their journey. However, there are state parks, recreation areas, historic sites, and wilderness areas along the way that provide access to significant portions of the trail.

The Oregon Trail

The Oregon Trail is approximately 2,170 miles (3,490 km) in length. It begins in Missouri and passes through the states of Kansas, Nebraska, Wyoming, Idaho, Oregon, and Washington. In Kansas, the trail follows the Platte River.

One of the most accessible portions of the trail is the South Pass segment, which runs 125 miles (201 km) from Independence Rock to Farson, Wyoming. In Oregon, the trail crosses the Pacific Crest Trail. Several historic sites are located along the length of the trail.

The Pony Express Trail

The Pony Express Trail is 1,966 miles (3,164 km) long. Like the Oregon and California Trails, it begins in Missouri and traverses Kansas and Nebraska. The Pony Express Trail goes through Colorado, Wyoming, Utah, and Nevada before ending at Sacramento, California. Although the Pony Express was in existence for only eighteen months, it represents a romantic episode of American history.

This National Historic Trail is more of a route than an actual trail. In places it can be followed on foot or horseback, whereas in others it's more of a vehicle route.

Historical Quote

Being a Pony Express rider was not for the fainthearted. The help wanted advertisement read, "Wanted: Young, skinny, wiry fellows not over eighteen. Must be expert riders, willing to risk death daily. Orphans preferred." Buffalo Bill Cody was perhaps the most famous Pony Express rider.

The Santa Fe Trail

The Santa Fe Trail is approximately 1,203 miles (1,936 km) in length. Like the other trails, it starts in Independence, Missouri, but unlike the other trails, its destination is the Southwest, not California or the Northwest. The Santa Fe Trail runs through Missouri, Kansas, Oklahoma, Colorado, and New Mexico.

Historically, the trail diverged at Dodge City, Kansas. The mountain route went through southeastern Colorado and entered New Mexico at the present site of Raton Pass. The Cimarron route continued from Dodge City to the southwestern corner of Kansas, crossed the Oklahoma panhandle, and entered New Mexico in the northeast corner of the state. Both routes converged at Watrous, New Mexico, before finishing at Santa Fe.

Today, sections of the Santa Fe Trail are well marked. In Cimarron National Grassland in southeastern Kansas, there is a hiking and equestrian trail. Forts and historic sites exist along the route.

Trail of Tears

The Trail of Tears was established in 1987. Consisting of approximately 2,200 miles (3,500 km) of trails through federal, state, and local land in nine states, the Trail of Tears follows the routes that were used to relocate Cherokee Indians from their historic lands in North Carolina and Georgia to Oklahoma.

Conclusion

There are people with the time and resources to thru-hike one of the national trails. Don't feel, however, that thru-hiking is the only way to go. Day hikes or other short backpacking trips along any of these trails can be extremely enjoyable and memorable.

PART FOUR

Destinations

CHAPTER 16

Pacific Northwest

Alaska, Washington, and Oregon are all premier hiking destinations—from the temperate rain forests of Alaska and Washington to the Cascade mountain range of Oregon and Washington. There are a dozen major national parks in the Pacific Coast states—half a dozen in Alaska, three in Washington, and one in Oregon. And that doesn't begin to count numerous national monuments, national forests, and wilderness areas.

The Pacific Northwest can boast three major National Scenic Trails—the Pacific Crest Trail and the Pacific Northwest Trail in Washington and Oregon, and the Iditarod in Alaska. The Lewis and Clark and Oregon National Historic Trails also run through these states.

Volcanoes

Almost all of America's volcanoes outside Hawaii are located in national parks in the Pacific Northwest. The Cascade Mountains in western Washington and Oregon are all of volcanic origin, but none of them is currently erupting. There are several volcanoes, however, that erupted during the twentieth century and could erupt again—Mount St. Helens in Washington; Aniakchak, Katmai, Iliamna (Lake Clark National Park), and Wrangell in Alaska.

Mount Rainier in Washington and Mazama (Crater Lake) in Oregon are among the dormant volcanoes in the western United States that are still geologically active and that could erupt again in the near future. The likelihood is so high that Mount Rainier could erupt at any time that certain traffic corridors in the nearby community of Puyallup have been marked as evacuation routes.

There are hiking trails to the tops of most of America's volcanoes. In some cases, you can even hike into the caldera of a dormant or extinct volcano.

Alaska

Most of Alaska is roadless, which means that getting to many of the forty-ninth state's natural areas requires boats or bush planes. Where there are no landing strips, floatplanes provide service. Alaska's ruggedness means that unless you are traveling with an organized tour group, you may be completely on your own in the backcountry with no established trails and more grizzly bears than people. Put simply, Alaska's backcountry is not for the fainthearted or the inexperienced.

Flying by floatplane is an adventure in itself. For one thing, there is no first-class seating; you may be sitting with the baggage. Speaking of baggage, your pilot will probably weigh your baggage (yourself included) to ensure the plane is balanced once it's loaded.

Hiking Vocab

To the Athabascans, Mount McKinley was Denali, the High One. When the national park was established in 1917, both the park and the mountain were named after the late President McKinley. In 1980, the park was enlarged and renamed Denali. Some people call both the park and the mountain Denali. The National Park Service calls the park Denali and the mountain McKinley. Either way, people know what you're referring to.

Speaking of the pilots—no wings on their shoulders. Expect a pilot who is wearing a T-shirt, shorts, and flip-flops, and who may not have shaved for a few days. When I good-naturedly asked one of my pilots where he had received his flight training, he said at one of the local FBOs (fixed-base operation, also known as the local airport). But, you can also expect your pilot to know his (or her) plane and how to fly it.

Alaska has lots of good hiking for folks who prefer not to venture too far into the unknown. Anchorage, Fairbanks, Juneau, Sitka, and the Kenai Peninsula offer miles of well-traveled trails.

The highest point in Alaska— and also in North America — is Mount McKinley, located in Denali National Park, with a summit topping out at 20,320 ft (6,194 m). Because McKinley is so close to the Arctic Circle, only experienced mountaineers in exceptionally good physical condition should consider attempting to conquer it.

Recommended Places to Hike in Alaska

Location	Features
Denali National Park	6 million acres (24,300 sq km) Open for day hiking and backpacking Many ranger-led hikes Shuttle buses drop off hikers anywhere along the main road through the park Mount McKinley is highest point in Alaska and North America at 20,320 feet (6,194 m) 14.6-mile (23.5-km) Mount Eielson loop is a good introductory backpacking trek Wildlife viewing is exceptional—grizzly bears, caribou, bighorn sheep, mountain goats, golden eagles, willow ptarmigans, and gyrfalcons
Gates of the Arctic National Park and Preserve	Access to the park is primarily by floatplane No established trails or campsites Rivers, bogs, Brooks Range
Arctic National Wildlife Refuge	The size of South Carolina Alpine and tundra ecosystems Musk oxen, grizzlies, 0.5 million caribou Cross-country hiking
Katmai National Park and Preserve	Located on the Alaska Peninsula Access is primarily by floatplane Day hiking around Brooks Camp (known for its salmon runs and superb brown bear viewing); Brooks Camp has an established campground Backpacking in the Valley of Ten Thousand Smokes
Kobuk Valley National Park	25 square miles (65 sq km) of sand dunes 40 miles (64 km) north of the Arctic Circle No developed facilities; access is by plane or boat Hiking, backpacking, camping, fishing, wildlife viewing
Wrangell-St. Elias National Park and Preserve	Largest national park in the United States—13 million acres (52,600 sq km) Numerous trails for both day hiking and backpacking
Arctic National Wildlife Refuge	Day hiking in Atigun Gorge Access to backcountry mostly by aircraft Backcountry hiking and camping allowed
Kenai Peninsula	Kenai Fjords National Park Easy walk to Exit Glacier Harding Icefield Trail is a 17.4-mile (28-km) round trip Very few designated trails in the backcountry

Location	Features
Lake Clark National Park and Preserve	Located southwest of Anchorage on the Cook Inlet Access is by plane or boat Remote and primitive hiking and camping; no established trails Numerous day hiking opportunities
Tongass National Forest	Largest national forest in the United States—17 million acres (69,000 sq km) cover a large portion of southeast Alaska Best described as a temperate rain forest Over 150 rustic cabins can be rented in the backcountry Spectacular scenery and wildlife viewing
Chugach National Forest	Second largest national forest in the United States—6 million acres (24,000 sq km) 22.6-mile (36.5-km) Crow Pass Trail Glaciers, meadows, wildflowers Wildlife viewing, including moose, bears, wolves, and Dall sheep
Anchorage and Vicinity	Hundreds of miles of hiking trails Chugach State Park is the third largest state park in the United States 26-mile (42-km) Crow Pass trail is a portion of the Iditarod sled race trail Over 100 miles (160 km) of trails in the park
Juneau and Vicinity	The backcountry is part of the Tongass National Forest Mount Roberts at 3,819 feet (1,164 m) is a favorite destination that takes hikers into alpine tundra; hike up the mountain or take a tram Popular hikes go to Mendenhall and Herbert Glaciers In the mountains behind Juneau, the Perseverance Trail takes hikers into the mountains
Fairbanks and Vicinity	Fairbanks historic trails Backpacking in the Tors Trails in Chena River State Recreational Park
Sitka and Vicinity	Roads go only a short distance in any direction from Sitka, but they all provide access to hiking trails in the Tongass National Forest.

Washington

The Puget Sound region of the state of Washington is famed for its beauty. On the west side of the sound, the Olympic Peninsula, which is home to Olympic National Park, represents an ecosystem that is unique to the lower forty-eight states—a temperate rain forest.

Probably the number one destination for hikers and backpackers in Washington is the Cascades on the east side of Puget Sound. The Cascades begin on the northeast side of Puget Sound and continue south through Oregon and into northern California.

Persons in good physical condition can reach the summit of Mount Rainier as long as they are part of a guided group. In addition, Mount Rainier National Park has over 300 miles

(480 km) of trails. A spectacular trail is the Wonderland Trail, which is 93 miles (150 km) long and encircles the entire park.

Recommended Places to Hike in Washington

Nature Note

The Cascades are part of the Ring of Fire that encircles the Pacific Ocean and includes volcanoes—some extinct, but mostly ones that are either active or dormant—from Indonesia north to Japan and Alaska, and south all the way to Mounts Shasta and Lassen in California. In Washington, the best-known peaks are Mount Rainier and Mount St. Helens, the latter of which erupted violently in 1980.

Location	Features
Mount Rainier National Park	50 trails; glaciers; Mount Rainier, highest point in Washington at 14,410 feet (4,392 m); includes a portion of the Pacific Crest Trail; Wonderland Trail completely circles the park
Olympic National Park	Terrain ranges from 60 miles (96.5 km) of coastal trails to the temperate rainforest; gets the most annual rainfall in the continental United States
North Cascades National Park	Over 360 miles (579 km) of trails; includes 14 miles (22.5 km) of the Pacific Crest Trail (PCT); alpine scenery; glaciers; trails at higher elevations are not open until mid-July; a patchwork of trails together comprise the Ptarmigan Traverse
Mount Saint Helens National Volcanic Monument	The 8,363-foot (2,549-m) summit permits views into the crater; views of Mount Rainier to the north and Mount Hood to the south (in Oregon)
Pacific Crest Trail (PCT)	500 miles (804.5 km) of the PCT runs through Washington from Oregon to Canada; passes through two national parks and eight wilderness areas; because of snow, generally only passable from mid-July to mid-October
San Juan Islands	Over 170 named islands (and many unnamed ones) in Puget Sound; most access is by ferries; some can be accessed by kayak, canoe, or boat; limited plane service; many private and public campgrounds; lots of short trails; lighthouses; whale watching, seabirds

Location	Features
Mount Adams Wilderness Area	At 12,276 feet (3,741.5 m), Mount Adams is the second highest peak in Washington; glaciers, forests, subalpine meadows; twenty-five routes to the summit, some requiring technical climbing; 21 miles (34 km) of the PCT go through the area; another 50 miles (80.5 km) of trails
Alpine Lakes Wilderness	Allows only twenty permits a day; steep terrain; large elevation changes; best hiking months are August and September; spectacular scenery; wildlife viewing
Mount Baker National Recreation Area	Over 1,400 miles (2,253 km) of trails; Mount Baker at 10,778 feet (3,285 m) is highest peak; mountains, alpine meadows, lakes, streams, glaciers, and snowfields; wildlife viewing
Pasayten Wilderness Area	Adjoins Canadian border in the vicinity of Mount Baker; the PCT passes through here
Salmo-Priest Wilderness Area	On the Canadian border; Salmo Mountain peaks at 6,828 feet (2,081 m); wildlife viewing, including woodland caribou, grizzlies, wolves, deer, black bears, bighorn sheep, moose, and lynx
Wenatchee National Forest	Located in central Washington; area with the third most miles of trails in the state—over 2,500 miles (4,023.5 km); highest point is Glacier Peak at (10,541 feet (3,213 m)
Olympic National Forest	Surrounding Olympic National Park on the Olympic Peninsula; over 250 miles (402.5 km) of hiking trails for both day hiking and backpacking; low-elevation trails are accessible year-round
Lewis and Clark Trail	Follows the Columbia River from the Idaho state line to the Pacific Ocean; route was followed by the Lewis and Clark Corps of Discovery; part of the trail is in Washington, part in Oregon
Pacific Northwest Trail	Follows the Canadian border from the Pacific Ocean to the Idaho state line

Oregon

Oregon's highest point is Mount Hood at 11,239 feet (3,425.5 m), with several good trails in the area. A number of mountains continue in a chain running north-south and parallel to the Willamette Valley. Altogether, Oregon has over one hundred peaks with elevations in excess of 7,500 feet (2,286 m), with several peaks higher than 10,000 feet (3,048 m).

Oregon's coast has some of the most spectacular scenery anywhere in the United States and can be hiked or bicycled. Oregon residents are proud of the beauty of their state. Cities like Portland have many miles of hiking trails. Not to be outdone is Crater Lake National Park, with its system of trails encircling the lake.

Recommended Places to Hike in Oregon

Location	Features
Mount Hood Wilderness	Mount Hood is the highest point in Oregon; 36-mile (58-km) Mount Hood Timberline Trail
Lewis and Clark Trail	Follows the Columbia River; part is in Oregon, part in Washington
Crater Lake National Park	Crater Lake is the deepest lake at 2,000 feet (609.5 m) in the United States; trails encircle the lake
Pacific Crest Trail	430 miles (692 km) of the PCT run from the California state line to the Washington state line; passes through the Cascade Mountains; fairly gentle trail compared to the PCT in California and Washington
Kalmiopsis Wilderness	Located in southwestern Oregon; part of the Rogue River-Siskiyou National Forest; over 150 miles (241.5 km) of established hiking trails
Oregon Coast Trail	382 miles (615 km) of exceptionally scenic hiking along the coast; portions of the trail are accessible only during low tides; camping is permitted at many, sometimes isolated, beaches
Rogue River-Siskiyou National Forest	40 miles (64 km) long and follows the Rogue River
North Umpqua Trail	About 80 miles (128.5 km) of trails in the Cascades; accessible from a dozen different trailheads; campgrounds are located at most trailheads; primitive camping is permitted
Willamette National Forest	About 1,700 miles (2,736 km) of hiking trails; eight wilderness areas; several mountain peaks; lower-elevation trails are accessible year-round; numerous backpacking and day hiking opportunities
Deschutes National Forest	About 1,600 miles (2,575 km) of trails; wild and scenic rivers; Crooked River National Grassland has trails; numerous backpacking and day hiking opportunities
Fremont-Winema National Forests	Numerous hiking trails; wildlife viewing; migratory birds
Portland and Vicinity	Forest Park, at 5,000 acres (20 sq km), is the largest urban wilderness park in the United States; Riverside Park; other parks and trail systems
The Sisters	South Sister is the third highest peak in Oregon at 10,358 feet (3,157 m); North Sister is 10,085 feet (3,074 m); Middle Sister is 10,047 ft (3,062 m); all three peaks can be summited; South Sister is the steepest hike, but is the most popular of the three
Aspen Butte/Lake Harriette	Two-day loop trail in Mountain Lakes Wilderness northwest of Klamath Falls; 16 miles (26 km); elevations range from 5,720 feet (1,743.5 m) to 8,208 feet (2,502 m); spectacular views all the way to Mount Shasta in northern California
Sky Lakes Wilderness	Southern Oregon; Sky Lakes loop trail; 25.5 miles (41 km); elevations range from 5,800 feet (1,768 m) to 7,582 feet (2,311 m) at the summit of Devil's Peak
North Fork John Day Wilderness	Northeastern Oregon; 27.4-miles (44-km) round trip; great fishing

Location	Features
Hells Canyon Wilderness and Hells Canyon National Recreation Area	Northeastern Oregon; McGraw Creek Loop is 14 miles (22.5 km) of moderate to steep hiking; elevations range from 1,760 to 3,360 feet (536.5 to 1,024 m); Hells Canyon Loop is about 30 miles (48 km); Hells Canyon is the deepest gorge in North America (maximum depth of the gorge is 7,900 feet (2,408 m)
Black Canyon Wilderness	Located in north-central Oregon east of Prineville; 11.6-mile (18.5-km) trail follows Black Canyon Creek
Diamond Peak Wilderness	West-central Oregon; 23-mile (37-km) loop trail; trailhead is at Odell Lake campground; Diamond Peak's summit is at 8,744 feet (2,665 m)

Conclusion

I've listed a lot of choices of trails in this chapter. You can't go wrong on any of them. Enjoy!

CHAPTER 17

Pacific Southwest

In This Chapter

➤ California trails

➤ Nevada trails

➤ Hawaii trails

Like the Pacific Northwest, the Pacific Southwest offers a wide diversity of trails. California has something for everyone—the Pacific Ocean, mountains, valleys, deserts, and the highest and lowest points in the lower forty-eight states.

Nevada's landscape is more uniform; it is almost entirely desert. Although the desert doesn't offer well-traveled trails, the state does have some mountains along its western state line, in the east almost to Utah, and around Las Vegas.

Nature Note

Mount Whitney, just west of Lone Pine, California, is the highest point in the lower forty-eight states; Badwater, in Death Valley National Park, is the lowest point. Whitney has an elevation of 14,505 feet (4,421 m); Badwater has an elevation of 282 feet (86 m) below sea level. What's remarkable is that the two places are only 76 miles (122 km) apart.

Hiking in California

As a native Californian, I'm partial to California. California boasts one of the crown jewels of the national park system—Yosemite. My parents began taking me to Yosemite when I was a toddler, and I've been hiking Yosemite most of my adult life. I took my family there on many vacations while the kids were growing up.

Yosemite

Yosemite is located in the Sierra Nevada Mountains in eastern California. Nestled into some of the most beautiful country in North America, Yosemite lies 200 miles (322 km) from San Francisco and 400 miles (643.5 km) miles from Los Angeles. Access is usually by private vehicle or bus.

Yosemite has two general regions that are quite distinct from each other:

1. Yosemite Valley, which lies at an elevation of 4,000 feet (1,220 m)

2. The High Country, which ranges in elevation from 7,000 feet (2,130 m) to mountain peaks that top out at over 13,000 feet (3,960 m).

The park is bisected by the Tioga Road (Highway 120), which runs roughly west-east; it crosses the Sierras at Tioga Pass at an elevation of 9,945 feet (3,031 m) before descending into the Mono Lake basin on the east side of the mountains. Numerous day hikes begin from trailheads in Yosemite Valley and along the Tioga and Wawona Roads, the latter running north-south and exiting the park in the direction of Fresno, California.

Hikes can be as short as the 1-mile (1.6-km) loop to the base of Lower Yosemite Falls or as long as hiking over 200 miles (322 km) on the John Muir Trail south from Yosemite to the summit of Mount Whitney, located in Sequoia National Park. There are day hikes and backcountry overnighters of all lengths and degrees of difficulty in-between. The John Muir Trail represents just a portion of the Pacific Crest Trail that runs from Mexico to Canada.

The Pacific Crest Trail begins on the Mexican border at Campo, California. Anyone who thru-hikes the trail probably travels south to north, and begins at Campo in spring before the desert gets too hot. The trail enters Oregon near Interstate 5. There are 1,723 miles (2,773 km) of the trail in California. Most of this section of the trail goes through the Sierra Nevadas.

Day hikes out of Yosemite Valley involve steep climbs, typically of 2,000 feet (610 m) or more. Probably the most popular hike in the Valley begins east of Yosemite Village at Happy Isles and takes hikers to Vernal and Nevada Falls. Except to provide access for physically handicapped visitors, private vehicles are not allowed on the loop road to Happy Isles. Free shuttle buses provide transportation and keep regular schedules from early morning until well after dark.

The first segment of the hike is a short—0.8 miles (1.3 km)—but it is a steep climb to the Vernal Falls bridge spanning the Merced River. Many day hikers only hike as far as the bridge, but it is well worth the trip. The falls are usually full all spring and early summer and are a spectacular sight. Hardier hikers continue to the top of Nevada Falls, which is a bit more than another 2.0 miles (3.2 km), and an even more strenuous climb.

The Vernal-Nevada Falls trailhead is the beginning of hikes to several other destinations. Another popular day hike for the exceptionally fit hiker is to go to the top of Half Dome, a solid granite monolith that is one of the defining geological formations of Yosemite Valley. The hike from Happy Isles to Half Dome and back is a round trip distance of 16.4 miles (26.4 km), with an ascent of roughly 4,700 feet (1,433 m). I have done the hike once. It was pretty exhausting, but I was younger then; I would consider doing it again someday.

The Vernal-Nevada Falls trail also takes backpackers to Little Yosemite Valley and Merced Lake, which is about 14 miles (22.5 km) one way, depending upon which trail is followed. From Merced Lake you have a choice of several directions to go. Trails can take you to either Tenaya Lake or Tuolumne Meadows, both of which are along the Tioga Road. You can also continue on the John Muir Trail heading south.

From the top of Nevada Falls, you can also continue on a clockwise loop to Glacier Point, a popular lookout over Yosemite Valley. Most people, however, drive or take a bus to Glacier Point and then hike in a counterclockwise direction back down to Happy Isles, a distance of 9.1 miles (14.6 km). That is the way my family did it several years ago. We shuttled one car to do so, although taking a bus to Glacier Point works well, too.

A popular hike begins near Yosemite Lodge and ascends a steep trail that skirts Upper and Lower Yosemite Falls and levels out at the top of Upper Yosemite Falls. The round trip is 6.6 miles (10.6 km), with spectacular views overlooking the valley floor as well as the falls themselves.

Most people think of Yosemite as overflowing with visitors during the summer months, which is probably true in the valley. However, venture more than a mile from the Tioga Road in the high country, and the number of people you encounter drops dramatically. A stroll along the banks of the Tuolumne River is so beautiful and so relaxing, you probably won't even notice if other people are there.

Along the Tioga Road, there are several trails out of White Wolf Campground that are suitable for children.

Nature Quote

"Climb the mountains and get their good tidings. Nature's peace will flow into you as sunshine flows into trees... Cares will drop away from you like the leaves of Autumn"

–naturalist John Muir

A trek I highly recommend for someone new to Yosemite is the system of High Sierra Camps—half a dozen backcountry camps offering the choice of staying in cabins or adjacent campgrounds. Because of lingering snow at higher elevations, this loop is best accomplished in July or August. All of the camps can be visited on a 50-mile (80-km) loop trip for which at least a week should be allowed.

Starting in Tuolumne Meadows, each camp is roughly one day's distance from the previous camp. Hikers have a choice. The priciest option is to stay in the cabins and eat in the dining halls. There are advantages that offset the price: you only have to carry your clothes for the trip and food and water for the day (you can purchase sack lunches at the dining halls); in the event of inclement weather, you can sleep indoors warm and dry.

For those of us who are on a tight budget, the campgrounds are a good option, especially since they're free. The only drawback I've experienced is outhouses that often reek. But piped, potable water is available at the campgrounds, alleviating the need to purify your water.

Unless you carry a water purification system, be sure to carry enough water to get you from one camp to the next. You can hike throughout Yosemite's high country and not stay at the High Sierra Camps. In that case, you definitely need to carry a means for purifying water.

A third option is also available—a compromise between the full cost of the camps and the no cost of the campgrounds. You can stay in the cabins, but bring your own food and do your own cooking.

While there is always the possibility of getting a same-day reservation at one of the camps, it is best to make reservations and to do so reasonably well in advance. Backcountry camping requires a permit, for which there is no cost.

If you know you're only going to be in Yosemite for a short window of time and have a specific trail you want to hike, reserving a permit in advance is probably wise (for which there is a token reservation fee). The permit is not for specific places to camp each night. The permit just designates from which trailhead you are departing, and there is a limit to the number of backpackers who can depart from a given trailhead each day. If you're flexible, though, you can always get a permit for the same or the next day. Spaces are not reserved at any of the campgrounds adjoining the High Sierra camps, but getting a campsite shouldn't be a problem.

Because Yosemite's high country is black bear country, persons camping overnight are required to carry their food at all times in bear-proof canisters. Canisters can be purchased or rented at several locations in Yosemite.

Nature Note

In the early years of tourism to the national parks, feeding the bears was part of the fun; Yogi and Boo Boo were popular characters in Saturday morning cartoons. Eventually, park service personnel understood that feeding bears (or any other wild animals) is harmful to both bears and humans for several reasons:

➤ Human food is generally unhealthy for bears

➤ Bears become dependent on humans for food

➤ Bears lose their fear of humans and become aggressive, increasing the number of injuries to visitors

➤ Nuisance bears have to be euthanized

Today, it is against the law to feed wild animals in national parks. In parks like Yosemite, all food carried into the backcountry must be kept secure in locking bear canisters.

Some of the High Sierra camps are close enough to the Tioga Road that they can also be done as day hikes. It can be a long day, but in July or August there are enough hours of daylight that a person in good condition who maintains a reasonable pace can put in 15 to 16 miles (24 to 26 km) in a day.

Several of Yosemite peaks can be summited as day hikes. Others require mountaineering skills. Probably the most popular peak in the park is Half Dome, which was discussed above. The highest peak in Yosemite is Mount Lyell at 13,144 feet (4,006 m), which requires mountaineering skills because of snow and steepness. Mount Dana is almost as high at13,083 feet (3,988 m) but can be summited as a day hike.

Located at the geographic center of the park, you can easily climb Mount Hoffmann at 10,850 feet (3,307 m) as a day hike. Mount Hoffmann rises above May Lake, the location of one of the High Sierra camps. Besides making the climb as a day hike, you also have the option of staying at the camp or camping at the campground near the lake.

Yosemite is only the beginning of adventure in California. Kings Canyon National Park lies just south of Yosemite, and Sequoia National Park adjoins Kings Canyon. Both are beautiful parks with miles and miles of trails.

Lake Tahoe

Lake Tahoe is the largest mountain lake in the United States. The 165-mile (266-km) Tahoe Rim Trail goes completely around the lake. Part of the trail goes through Desolation Wilderness. There are several towns in which to replenish food supplies—Incline Village and Zephyr Village in Nevada, and Tahoe City in California. Because snow can linger in the Sierras until mid-July, promising mosquitoes and black flies, the trail is most popular in August and September.

Elevations range from about 6,500 feet to 10,000 feet (1,980 to 3,050 m). The entire loop typically takes two weeks. For hikers who only have three to four days, the section on the southwest side of the lake is a favorite. It runs from Echo Lake trailhead to Barker Pass trailhead and is a little over 30 miles (48 km) in length.

The shore of Lake Tahoe itself is almost all private property, so the trail does not actually go along the lakeshore itself. With only a couple of exceptions, the trail does not come even close to the lake itself. This poses a problem for obtaining fresh water. Fortunately, there are a few smaller lakes along the trail that make good places to camp. Otherwise, it is necessary to carry a two- to three-day supply of water with you.

Recommended Places to Hike in California

Location	Features
Yosemite National Park	Over 800 miles (1,290 km) of trails Rivers, subalpine and alpine meadows, summer wildflowers, mountain peaks, glaciers, forests, sequoia groves, wildlife viewing High Sierra camps and John Muir Trail are particularly enjoyable high-country routes
Sequoia and Kings Canyon National Parks	Over 800 miles (1,290 km) of hiking trails In Sequoia, Mount Whitney is highest point in California and lower forty-eight states (14,494 feet; 4,418 m), and the southern terminus of the John Muir Trail In Kings Canyon, North Palisade is highest peak at 14,248 feet (4,343 m) Sequoia trees, mountains, rivers, valleys, alpine hiking, wildlife viewing
Lassen Volcanic National Park	Over 150 miles (240 km)of trails Short nature walks, day hikes, and backpacking trails Mount Lassen is 10,457 feet (3,187 m) and is readily accessible on a 2.5-mile (4-km) trail
Redwood National Park	Over 135 miles (220 km) of hiking trails Redwood trees Also several state parks in the area
Death Valley National Park	Lowest point in the United States—282 feet (86 m) below sea level at Badwater Basin

Location	Features
Pacific Crest Trail (PCT)	A total of 1,723 miles (2,773 km) of the PCT are in California
John Muir Trail	211 miles (340 km)from Yosemite Valley to Mount Whitney A portion coincides with the PCT and passes through Devil's Postpile National Monument
Ansel Adams Wilderness	349 miles (562 km) of trails through some of the most beautiful mountains in the United States
Point Reyes National Seashore	150 miles (240 km) of trails in rugged coastal environment Backcountry camping Wildlife viewing
Tahoe Rim Trail	165-mile-long (266-km-long) trail encircling the highest alpine lake in the United States
Lost Coast Trail	50 miles (80 km) of coastal hiking in northern California Gray whale sightings possible during winter and spring migrations
Big Sur	Coastal mountain range and the Pacific Ocean Pfeiffer Big Sur State Park has several trails that connect to other trails in the region
San Francisco Bay Area	Trails throughout the Golden Gate Recreation Area 330 miles (531 km) of the Bay Area Ridge Trail have been completed When finished, the trail will go around the entire San Francisco Bay and will be over 550 miles (885 km) long Hikers have been able to walk across the Golden Gate Bridge for years to get from San Francisco to Marin County
Backbone Trail System	A 68-mile-long (109-km-long) trail in the Santa Monica Mountains of southern California Portions are shared with bicyclists and equestrians
Anza-Borrego Desert State Park	California's largest state park—nearly the size of the state of Rhode Island 110 miles (177 km) of trails Sightings of bighorn sheep possible
Bigfoot Trail	A strenuous trail in northern California that ends in Redwood National Park Approximately 400 miles (640 km) long Built to celebrate the biodiversity of northern California's temperate coniferous forest, with thirty-two species of conifers Trail is still under construction
Mount Shasta	A beautiful mountain that rises high above its surroundings Summit is 14,162 feet (4,317 m); numerous trails in the area

Hiking in Nevada

Most of Nevada is not densely populated and is characterized by the Great Basin Desert. Hiking mainly occurs in mountains that rise out of the desert—Great Basin National Park near the Utah state line, Mount Charleston, the Humboldt-Toiyabe National Forest, the Ruby Mountains, and the eastern slope of the Sierras between Lake Tahoe and the Reno/Carson City area.

Nevada has twenty-four state parks, recreation areas, and historic sites. Its highest point is Boundary Peak at 13,143 feet (4,006 m), located very close to the California state line.

Recommended Places to Hike in Nevada

Location	Features
Great Basin National Park	Over 60 miles (96 km) of hiking trails Trail access limited to summer months because most trails are at elevations above 9,000 feet (2,740 m) Highest point is Wheeler Peak at 13,065 feet (3,982 m)
Mount Charleston Wilderness Area	20-mile (32-km) Mount Charleston National Recreation Trail Large colony of bristlecone pines Three peaks exceeding 11,000 feet (3,350 km)—Mount Mummy, Mount Charleston, and Mount Griffith
Humboldt-Toiyabe National Forest	Largest national forest in lower forty-eight states Boundary Peak is highest point in Nevada at 13,143 feet (4,006 m) Not a contiguous national forest but divided into ten separate ranger districts
Ruby Mountains	Referred to as Nevada's Swiss Alps Highest peak is Ruby Dome at 11,387 feet (3,471 m) Actually named for the red garnets found in the area Two dozen lakes Wildlife viewing Numerous backpacking trails
Jarbridge Wilderness Area	Eight peaks over 10,000 feet (3,050 m) Over 125 miles (200 km) of trails Remote and mountainous terrain
Tahoe Rim Trail	The trail goes completely around Lake Tahoe A 23-mile-long (37-km-long) segment is in Nevada
Valley of the Fire State Park	Popular because of its proximity to Las Vegas Some trails are easy family hikes Other trails require canyoneering skills

Hiking in Hawaii

With Hawaii, travelers have to consider each island separately. The Big Island of Hawaii has Hawaii Volcanoes National Park. Two of the world's most active volcanoes are found in the park—Mauna Loa and Kilauea.

Mauna Loa is the state's highest peak at 13,677 feet (4,169 m). There are at least a dozen trails in the park. Mauna Loa can be summited, and a complete loop trail encircles the Kilauea caldera. Cabins may be reserved on the Mauna Loa trails for hikers who which to spend more than a single day completing the hike.

Haleakala National Park is situated on the island of Maui. Geologists classify Haleakala as an active volcano, although its last eruption was in 1790. The park has at least ten hiking trails. Most of them are quite short and can be completed in a half day or less.

In addition to Maui, Oahu, and the Big Island, a favorite destination for hikers is the island of Kauai.

Hiking Vocab

A caldera is a crater in a volcano that is much larger than the volcano's vent. It is formed by violent explosions or the collapse of the central part of the volcano.

Recommended Places to Hike in Hawaii

Location	Features
Hawaii Volcanoes National Park	Over 150 miles (240 km) of trails Mauna Kea is the highest point in Hawaii at 13,796 feet (4,205 m) 11-mile (17.5-km) rim trail around Kilauea caldera 38-mile (61-km) trail to summit of Mauna Loa (stay at a backcountry cabin overnight) Backpacking opportunities in wilderness areas
Haleakala National Park	13 miles (21 km) of trails Day hikes and backpacking available both in the mountains and along the coast
Akaka Falls State Park	Short loop trail through lush tropical landscape
Ha'ena State Park	On the island of Kauai 11-mile (17.5-km) Kalalau Trail

Location	Features
Kokee State Park	On the island of Kauai Several short trails through forests Waterfalls
Palaau State Park	On the island of Molokai Very short trails
Papakolea Beach Trail	4-mile-long (6.4-km-long) trail on the Big Island
Maui State Park	Several short day hikes
Island of Oahu	Several short trails, including hikes to summit of Diamond Head, the Makapu'u Point Lighthouse, and Wa'ahila Ridge

Conclusion

I hope I have convinced you of the incredibly large number of great trails there are in the Pacific states. If you already have a lot of experience on the more popular trails, consider trails that you haven't hiked before. I think you'll find there are some real gems out there.

CHAPTER 18

Interior Southwest

The Southwest offers trails to hike year-round. If winter snow limits access to trails in the mountains, you can hike in the desert. In summer, hikers can at least be on the trail during the first few hours after sunrise and again during the hours just before sunset. But if summer temperatures make desert hiking unbearable, you can head to the mountains.

I have done all my Grand Canyon backpacking during the more pleasant months of September through May. When the temperature at the bottom of the canyon reaches 120°F (49°C) during June, July, and August, I head for the mountains. Throughout the Southwest, when the deserts are baking in summer's heat, Texas, New Mexico, and Arizona have mountain ranges that beckon to hikers.

Metropolitan areas—Oklahoma City, Tulsa, Austin, Dallas/Fort Worth, San Antonio, Houston, Albuquerque, Santa Fe, Phoenix, Flagstaff, and Tucson—have numerous parks and forests with hiking trails. Many of these trails are accessible year-round.

The Southwest offers spectacular scenery, which is why it has so many national parks; forests; wilderness and recreation areas; and state, county, and city parks.

Hiking in Oklahoma and Texas

Oklahoma is one of the plains states. As such, you might think its terrain is relatively flat, so it may come as a surprise that Oklahoma's highest mountain, Black Mesa, has an elevation of 4,973 feet (1,516 m). Black Mesa is located in the very northwest corner of Oklahoma, but eastern Oklahoma has the Ouachita Mountains that reach elevations of 2,600 feet (790 m). The Ouachitas are the highest peaks between the Rockies and the Appalachians.

The Ouachita National Recreation Trail begins in Oklahoma and continues into Arkansas. It is Oklahoma's longest trail and has a total length of 192 miles (309 km), including the portion in Arkansas.

A jewel in north-central Oklahoma, just south of the Kansas state line, is Salt Plains National Wildlife Refuge. Very attractive nature trails wind through woods and riparian habitats. Salt Plains State Park is adjacent to the refuge and offers camping facilities.

Nature Note

Salt Plains National Wildlife Refuge attracts birders from throughout the southwest. The refuge boasts nesting least terns and an impressive heronry with several species of breeding herons and egrets, including little blue egrets. What was particularly fun for me when I visited the refuge was my first sighting of badgers in the wild.

Texas

Texas is a big state—it was the biggest state until Alaska was admitted to the union. It's natural that a state that big has very different regions. East and West Texas are as different as apples and oranges. East Texas has rolling hills and a wetter climate; West Texas is drier because it is part of the Chihuahuan Desert. The Texas panhandle is part of the Great Plains.

West Texas has Texas's two national parks—Guadalupe and Big Bend. Guadalupe adjoins the New Mexico state line. Its mountains are part of the range that runs to Carlsbad Caverns National Park in the southeastern corner of New Mexico. Originally a section of the ocean floor during the Permian Era, the Guadalupe Mountains consist of layers of limestone rich with fossils.

Guadalupe National Park headquarters are on the south side of the park. A northern section of the park can be reached from New Mexico. I've done several day hikes in the park, including the ascent of Guadalupe Peak, Texas's highest mountain at 8,749 feet (2,667 m). It's an easy day hike, but there is also a backcountry campground just below the peak for hikers who wish to make it an overnight trip.

The next three highest peaks in Texas are also in Guadalupe. I highly recommend hiking McKittrick Canyon, a wooded riparian habitat teeming with wildlife. If you hike into the backcountry, there's very little water, so carry your own.

The Rio Grande River enters Texas between Las Cruces, New Mexico, and El Paso, Texas, and forms the border between the United States and Mexico.

Big Bend gets its name from the big bend the Rio Grande River makes on its way to the Gulf of Mexico. The Big Bend area contains both Big Bend State Park and Big Bend National Park.

West Texas is predominately Chihuahuan Desert at or just above the elevation of the Rio Grande. In the center of the park, however, are the Chisos Mountains at a significantly higher, cooler elevation.

There are numerous short hiking trails in the desert area of the national park. People hike them almost exclusively from about November through April; it's too hot in the summer to hike or tent camp. In summer, rafting trips down the Rio Grande through Santa Eleña, Colorado, Mariscal, and Boquillas Canyons are more popular.

Trails in the Chisos can be hiked year-round. The most popular trails in the Chisos are the 5-mile (8-km) round-trip to the Window—an easy hike for children—and the 12.6-mile (20.3-km) round-trip via the Pinnacles and Boot Canyon Trails to the South Rim of the Chisos Mountains.

A spur trail off the Pinnacles leads to an ascent of Emory Peak at 7,825 feet (2,385 m). Emory is the highest peak in Big Bend National Park and the most prominent geographic feature of West Texas. On a clear day you can see 200 miles (320 km) in any direction from Emory. I found the hike to Emory and back to be a moderately easy and scenic day hike. Older children were on the trail and seemed to be handling it well.

There is no water in Big Bend's backcountry, either in the desert or in the mountains, so be sure to carry your own.

San Antonio, Austin, Dallas, Fort Worth, and Houston all have natural areas with hiking trails. Texas also has a regional system of ten heritage trails located throughout the state that commemorate Texas history; the Hill Country Trail, for example, runs from San Antonio to Austin.

An added bonus of traveling in Texas is the local cuisine. Be sure to sample Mexican and Tex-Mex dishes when you're there. I recommend enchiladas smothered with green chili.

Recommended Places to Hike in Oklahoma and Texas

Location	Features
Black Mesa (OK)	The highest point in Oklahoma at 4,973 feet (1,516 m)
Ouachita National Recreation Trail (OK)	192 miles (309 km) in total length, including a portion in Arkansas Elevations from 600 to 2,600 feet (183 to 792.5 m)
Oklahoma City (OK)	Several parks and lakes in and around the city with hiking trails
Chickasaw National Recreation Area (OK)	Almost 10,000 acres (40 sq km) Over 20 miles (32 km) of trails
Salt Plains National Wildlife Refuge and State Park (OK)	Short nature trails; wildlife viewing
Big Bend National Park (TX)	Thirty-two hiking trails totaling more than 150 miles (240 km) Desert, grassland, and mountain hiking Southern boundary of the park is the Rio Grande River
Guadalupe National Park (TX)	Over half the park is designated wilderness area 80 miles (128.5 km) of hiking trails Guadalupe Peak is the highest point in Texas, with a 9.0-mile-long (14.5-km-long) trail to the top; a backcountry campsite is near the summit A 25-mile-long (40-km-long) trail goes through McKittrick Canyon
Big Bend Ranch State Park (TX)	Adjacent to the west side of Big Bend National Park; hiking trails; wetter habitat than in the national park
Hill Country Trail (TX)	868-mile-long (1,397-km-long) trail that runs between San Antonio and Austin

Hiking in New Mexico

New Mexico's motto is Land of Enchantment. And it really is—enchanting. The state has beautiful geography, a rich Native American and Hispanic heritage, and (in my opinion anyway) a capital city—Santa Fe—with which no other city in the United States can compare for atmosphere.

Hiking opportunities abound in the mountains surrounding Santa Fe, Taos, and Albuquerque. Pristine mountain vistas call hikers to the Gila Wilderness in southwestern New Mexico.

Local History

The noted forester and environmentalist Aldo Leopold (1887–1948) is best known for his classic book *Sand County Almanac*, and for his career as professor of game management at the University of Wisconsin. Leopold began his career as a young forester at Gila National Forest. What Leopold experienced there inspired the development of his environmental ethics. Leopold was instrumental in the creation of the wilderness system. It is not a coincidence that the first nationally designated wilderness was the Gila Wilderness.

Recommended Places to Hike in New Mexico

Location	Features
Carson National Forest	Over 300 miles (480 km) of hiking trails that include four wilderness areas Wheeler Peak is the highest point in New Mexico at 13,161 feet (4,011 m).
Carlsbad Caverns National Park	Over 50 miles (80 km) of trails through desert landscape and pinyon-juniper woodland
Bandelier National Monument	Over 70 miles (113 km) of trails The monument is known for its prehistoric ruins
Gila National Forest	Over 1,400 miles (2,250 km) of trails One of the largest national forests in the lower forty-eight states Includes the Gila Wilderness
Santa Fe National Forest	Over 1,000 miles (1,600 km) of trails The highest point is Truchas Peak at 13,103 feet (3,994 m) Several mountain ranges Four wilderness areas
Lincoln National Forest	More than 250 miles (400 km) of trails One section of the national forest connects two national parks—Guadalupe and Carlsbad Caverns
Cibola National Forest	Over 270 miles (434 km) of trails The highest point is Mount Taylor at 11,301 feet (3,444,5 m)
Continental Divide Trail	About 75 percent of the planned 770 miles (1,239 km) in New Mexico has been completed The Chihuahuan Desert is in the south, with mountains in the north
White Mountains Wilderness	44-mile-long (71-km-long) Crest Trail passes through meadows and along streams

Hiking in Arizona

Arizona has the Grand Canyon; probably America's best-known natural feature, the Grand Canyon attracts tourists from all over the world. My rough estimate is that I have hiked something on the order of 800 miles (1,290 km) at the canyon in the past twenty-two years. To hard-core Grand Canyon hikers, that wouldn't seem like a lot, but it's more than 99 percent of the park's visitors have done.

Personal Anecdote

All of my children hiked the Grand Canyon numerous times until they graduated from college. They're all married now and have children of their own. I'm looking forward to the day when my grandchildren are old enough to hike the canyon with me.

Grand Canyon National Park has trails for people of all ages and abilities. You really should be in pretty good physical condition to hike far into the canyon itself. For casual visitors to the South Rim, especially visitors who only have a day or two to spend in the park or who have small children, I recommend the Rim Trails.

There are 15 miles (24 km) of paved trails that hug the rim. Walking these trails provides a constantly changing view into the Canyon and of the Colorado River. Shuttle buses provide visitors with access to several parts of the Rim Trail, so you don't have to hike the entire length. Families with children can hike a mile or two and then hop back on a bus.

Most people, though, want to hike into the canyon. The most popular trail for doing so is the Bright Angel Trail. The Bright Angel is probably the best-known trail in the national park system because it's the one used by visitors to ride the mules to Phantom Ranch.

For visitors in reasonably good condition, a descent of the Bright Angel Trail to Indian Gardens, which is 9 miles (14.5 km) round-trip, is a good day hike. There are two rest houses between the rim and Indian Gardens that have outhouses all year and potable water in spring, summer, and fall. There are a picnic area and campground at Indian Gardens. Both have outhouses and potable water year-round.

For those hikers who wish to see the Colorado River, a side hike from Indian Gardens to Plateau Point adds another 3.0 miles (4.8 km) out and back. From Plateau Point you can gaze straight down at the river.

Backcountry permits are required to camp anywhere in the Grand Canyon below the rims. Applications for permits are available online at the national park's website. On the more popular trails, like the Bright Angel, competition for permits is intense. You can apply for a permit up to four months in advance; for example, for an October permit, you can apply beginning June 1. Almost everyone faxes their applications on the first day they can apply. Wait a day and you probably won't get a permit.

The next most popular trail is the South Kaibab, which is shorter but steeper than the Bright Angel. There is one outhouse on the South Kaibab but no water and little shade; rangers recommend not hiking up the South Kaibab on a hot day. Both trails lead to the Colorado River. The distance is a little farther on the Bright Angel than on the South Kaibab, but most people prefer the scenery along the Bright Angel. There are two suspension bridges across the river—the black bridge and the silver bridge. Both mules and hikers use the black bridge. Only hikers use the silver bridge.

My children and I have often hiked the two trails as a loop. We have descended the South Kaibab to the river and camped at Bright Angel Campground the first night, ascended the Bright Angel to Indian Gardens for the second night, and then hiked out the third day. Two of my children were eleven years old when they did that hike the first time. Time permitting, we have also camped at Bright Angel Campground two or more nights before hiking out.

In addition to camping at Bright Angel Campground, an alternative is to stay at Phantom Ranch. Visitors who ride the mules down to the bottom of the canyon stay in dormitories or cabins at Phantom Ranch, which offers a snack bar, breakfast and dinner at a dining hall, showers, and ranger programs. Many people also choose to hike down and stay at Phantom Ranch rather than camp. Some people bring their own food; some eat at the dining hall. Some people camp at Bright Angel Campground but eat some of their meals at Phantom Ranch. There are several combinations of options.

As a general rule, Phantom Ranch reservations need to be made a year or more in advance. During the winter months, however, there are fewer visitors and cancellations are common. Check at the registration desk at Bright Angel Lodge for availability; getting a dormitory bed or cabin on week days tends to be fairly easy.

Phantom Ranch is rustic, historic, and somewhat pricey. I've never stayed there, but my family and I have enjoyed the ice-cold lemonade and snacks sold there, ranger programs, and the Phantom Ranch T-shirts that can be purchased only at Phantom Ranch.

All of the ranch's supplies come down the trail on the backs of mules, and all the trash goes back out again on the mules. If you mail a postcard or letter, you can stamp on it that it was carried out by mule. I sometimes think of staying at Phantom Ranch just for the experience; maybe I will one of these days.

There are many more trails at the Grand Canyon than just the Bright Angel and the South Kaibab. From Phantom Ranch, the North Kaibab Trail continues for 14 miles (22.5 km) to the North Rim.

Personal Anecdote

One March my younger son, some of his fellow Boy Scouts and leaders, and I did a rim-to-rim-to-rim hike. We hiked down the Bright Angel Trail and stayed at Bright Angel Campground the first night. The second day we hiked 7 miles (11 km) to Cottonwood Campground on the North Kaibab Trail. Leaving our packs at Cottonwood for the day, we spent the third day doing a 14-mile (22.5 km) round-trip hike to the North Rim and back to Cottonwood. On the fourth day we hiked back to Bright Angel Campground, and on the fifth day we hiked back out to the South Rim. The total distance on the trails is 48 miles (77 km). Add a couple more miles for a side hike to Ribbon Falls along the North Kaibab, and we called it an even 50 miles (80 km).

From May to October there is a shuttle service that runs between the South and North Rims of the Grand Canyon. You can ride to the North Rim and hike back, or hike to the North Rim and ride back.

The most popular goal for many Grand Canyon hikers is to hike from the South Rim to the river and back in one day, despite all the signs the park service has put up warning people not to try to do that. Most hikers make it; those who don't get added to the number of people who have to be rescued. I have never hiked to the river and back in one day. I don't want to: the bottom of the Grand Canyon is an exotic place. I so thoroughly enjoy being at the river that I wouldn't want to have to turn around and head right back up the trail again. I prefer to linger, to savor the experience.

Once you have hiked the corridor trails—the Bright Angel and the South Kaibab—you should consider some of the other trails at Grand Canyon; almost all of them lead to the river.

From the South Rim, the next most popular trail is probably the Hermit, followed by the Grandview. The Grand Canyon Field Institute (GCFI) offers guided backpacking trips on all the park trails. I recommend that you consider a GCFI trip, especially if you wish to see some of the less-traveled sections of the park.

Nature Quote

After visiting the Grand Canyon, President Theodore Roosevelt said, "Leave [the Grand Canyon] as it is. You can not improve on it. The ages have been at work on it, and man can only mar it. What you can do is to keep it for your children, your children's children, and for all who come after you, as one of the great sights which every American if he can travel at all should see." In 1908, Roosevelt used his authority under the Antiquities Act to establish Grand Canyon National Monument. In 1919, Congress made it a national park.

If Grand Canyon National Park weren't enough, Arizona offers so much more:

➤ The Havasupai Reservation at the west end of the Grand Canyon with the world-famous beautiful Havasu and Mooney Falls

➤ The San Francisco Peaks near Flagstaff with Arizona's highest peak, Mount Humphrey, at 12,633 feet (3,859.5 m)

➤ Oak Creek Canyon in the red rock country surrounding Sedona

➤ The White Mountains, which also have some of the best fishing in Arizona

➤ The Superstition Wilderness in the central part of the state

➤ The Phoenix and Tucson metropolitan areas

➤ Saguaro National Park near Tucson

➤ The sky islands of southeastern Arizona

I would be remiss not to mention my hometown of Prescott, where I can step out my front door and start hiking.

In addition to several trails in the surrounding national forest, the city is working on a 50-mile-long (80.5-km-long) trail that when finished will completely encircle Prescott.

Recommended Places to Hike in Arizona

Location	Features
Grand Canyon National Park	400 miles (640 km) of trails Most trailheads are on the South Rim The corridor trails are heavily used by day hikers; remote trails get very little use
Havasupai Indian Reservation	Famed for its waterfalls; non-Native Americans need a permit The 8-mile (13-km) Walapai Trail takes visitors to Supai Village; from there it's an additional 2.0 miles (3.2 km) to the campground and falls
Coconino National Forest	Over 300 miles (480 km) of trails in northern Arizona Includes the San Francisco Peaks and Arizona's highest peak, Mount Humphrey 53 miles (85 km) of the 133-mile (214-km) General Crook State Historic Trail run through the national forest In the upper Verde Valley, Sycamore Canyon and Oak Creek Canyon have numerous trails
Oak Creek Canyon	Numerous trails around Sedona are suitable for day hikes; the best first hike is West Fork of Oak Creek Beautiful red rock scenery
Saguaro National Park	Two separate units—east and west 5-mile (8-km) hike up Wasson Peak 5.2-mile (8.4-km) Douglas Spring Trail 27-mile (43-km) backpacking trek in the east unit 6.5-mile (10.5-km) trail ascends Rincon Peak at 8,482 feet (2,585 m) in the east unit Hiking is best from late fall through early spring because of extreme summer heat
Superstition Wilderness	Desert hiking east of Phoenix Loop trails that are easy two- to three-day hikes Both permanent and ephemeral springs
Chiricahua National Monument	Sky islands in the southeastern corner of the state Several short trails are easy day hikes Backcountry camping permitted
Arizona Trail	Longest thru-hike in the Southwest 790 miles (1,271 km) running from Mexico to Utah Passes through six mountain ranges, the Sonoran Desert, and the Grand Canyon
Prescott National Forest	Over 300 miles (480 km) of trails Because of its higher elevation, four-season hiking is possible
Tonto National Forest	Eight wilderness areas Over 800 miles (1,290 km) of trails, including the 51-mile (82-km) Highline National Recreation Trail, the 29-mile (47-km) Mazatzal Divide Trail, and the 28-mile (45-km) Verde River Trail Best seasons are winter and early spring at lower elevations

Location	Features
Coronado National Forest	More than 900 miles (1,450 km) of hiking trails Highest point is Mount Graham at 10,717 feet (3,267 m) Rugged terrain, mountains, canyons, scenic vistas, wildlife viewing
Apache-Sitgreaves National Forest	875 miles (1,408 km) of hiking trails The highest peak is Mount Escudilla at 10,912 feet (3,326 m) 29-mile (47-km) Eagle National Recreation Trail

Conclusion

Choosing a trail in the interior Southwest depends very much on the time of year. Low deserts are too hot for most people in summer but can be ideal between November and May. High elevations may be snowed in during winter, but make for spectacular hiking in summer.

You can see I'm partial to the Grand Canyon because I've spent so much time there. If you have never been to the Grand Canyon, consider it a must-see destination. I recommend fall or spring for hikes below the rim, although backcountry permits can be difficult to get for the corridor trails during the most popular months of October and April. Come in winter and the trails are almost empty; just be prepared for snow and freezing temperatures.

If you're hesitant about hiking the Grand Canyon on your own, consider a group hike led by the Grand Canyon Field Institute. Hike leaders are knowledgeable about Grand Canyon geology, natural history, and human history; participants rave about their experiences.

CHAPTER 19

Northern Rockies

In This Chapter

➤ Idaho

➤ Montana

➤ Wyoming

Every Rocky Mountain state offers exceptional hiking opportunities. People have spent whole lifetimes exploring the trails in these states and have not run out of trails to hike. Several national parks famous for their rugged wilderness, scenic vistas, and wildlife are located in these states, including Yellowstone, Grand Teton, and Glacier.

Idaho Trails

Idaho is a state of rugged wilderness with few highways. Hikers can spend weeks in the backcountry without crossing any roads. The Frank Church-River of No Return Wilderness is one of the state's highlights. Another popular destination is Hell's Canyon National Recreation Area, also popular for river running. Two national trails pass through Idaho—the Lolo and the Lewis and Clark Trails.

Local History

Frank Church (1924–1984) was a native Idahoan who spent thirty-three years in the United States Senate. Church was a strong advocate of wilderness protection and played an important role in the passage of the Wilderness Act in 1964 and in the establishment of the River of No Return Wilderness in 1980. Just weeks before Church's death, the wilderness was renamed the Frank Church-River of No Return Wilderness and is the largest wilderness in the lower forty-eight states.

Recommended Places to Hike in Idaho

Location	Features
Borah Peak	Highest point in Idaho at 12,622 feet (3,847 m)
Hell's Canyon National Recreation Area	Over 900 miles (1,448 km) of trails Rough terrain, old mining buildings Petroglyphs Wildlife viewing
Stanley Basin	165 miles (265 km) of groomed trails also used during the winter for snowmobiling Many miles of ungroomed trails Lakes, meadows, magnificent scenery Surrounded by the Sawtooth Mountains
Frank Church-River of No Return Wilderness	2,446 miles (3,936 km) of hiking trails 400 miles (640 km) are in primitive condition Many trails are along rivers and lead to lake basins Over one hundred bridges allow means to cross rivers 10,000 acres (40.5 sq km) of trail-less wilderness
Lolo Trail	One of the most remote sections of the Lewis and Clark Trail Best for experienced backpackers Crosses into Montana over Lolo Pass
Pacific Northwest Trail	Crosses the Idaho Panhandle parallel to the Canadian border

Montana Trails

The state of Montana is blessed with two major national parks—Glacier and the northwest corner of Yellowstone—and numerous national forests and wilderness areas.

Glacier National Park and Alberta's Waterton Lakes National Park share the international border between the United States and Canada. Together, the two parks are designated the Waterton-Glacier International Peace Park. The border is freely crossed by both four-footed animals and humans.

Glacier has one major highway running east-west that bisects the park; from numerous trailheads along Going-to-the-Sun Road, hikers can head off into the wilderness for day hikes, overnight treks, and encounters with wildlife that include moose, grizzly bears, and mountain goats. The continental divide bisects the park as it runs north-south; it is actually a triple divide—rivers flow to the Pacific Ocean, the Gulf of Mexico, and Hudson Bay.

Six peaks in Glacier are over 10,000 feet (3,050 m) in elevation. Mount Cleveland, at 10,466 feet (3,190 m), is the tallest. Don't wait too long if you want to see the glaciers for which the park is famous —global warming is taking such an awful toll on them that within a few decades the glaciers may all be gone.

Local History

Bob Marshall had a long career with the United States Forest Service. Marshall was known for exceptionally long solo day hikes. A day hike of 35 miles (56 km) was not unusual for him, and he was even known to cover 70 miles (113 km) in one day. (That's a pace of 3 mph (5 kph) for twenty-four hours.) Marshall campaigned for the preservation of wilderness. He died in 1939, but his untiring efforts ultimately bore fruit with the passage of the Wilderness Act in 1964.

Just south of Glacier National Park, and covering over 1 million acres (4,045 sq km) is Bob Marshall Country, which includes Bob Marshall Wilderness, a mountainous terrain with at least eighty-five named trails.

Yellowstone is the most famous national park in the Rocky Mountains. Only a small portion of the park is in Montana, however; most of the park is in Wyoming.

Personal Anecdote

My one and only sighting of a wild mountain goat was at Glacier—it was a beautiful animal.

Recommended Places to Hike in Montana

Location	Features
Glacier National Park	Known as a hiker's park, it has more trails than roads There are more than 700 miles (1,130 km) of trails The highest point is Mount Cleveland at 10,466 feet (3,190 m) Glaciers, rivers, scenic vistas Wildlife viewing includes grizzlies, bighorn sheep, mountain goats, pine martins, and lynx Very few backcountry campers, so a good park in which to find solitude
Bob Marshall Wilderness Area	Called "the Bob" by locals The Big Salmon Lake Trail is a 57-mile (92-km) loop Over eighty other trails offer wilderness backpacking unparalleled in the lower forty-eight states Some trails are day hikes; other trails are described as moderately strenuous to strenuous multiday treks
Continental Divide Trail (CDT)	800 miles (1,290 km) of the CDT are in Montana The southern section hugs the Idaho-Montana state line The northern section goes through Glacier National Park

Location	Features
Mount Granite	Highest point in Montana at 12,799 feet (3,901 m)
Pacific Northwest Trail	Enters the state from Idaho, parallels the Canadian border, and ends at the Continental Divide
Great Falls and Vicinity	A great location to find Lewis and Clark historic sites Connected by hiking trails
Missoula and Vicinity	Several interconnecting riverside trails Rattlesnake National Recreation Area and Wilderness Pattee Canyon Recreation Area Blue Mountain Recreation Area

Wyoming Trails

Tucked away in the northwest corner of the state are two of America's premier national parks—Yellowstone and Grand Teton. Yellowstone has the distinction of being the world's first national park; it was founded in 1872, over two decades before anyone envisioned a national park system, and forty-six years before the National Park Service was established.

Local History

When early European Americans explored the Yellowstone region, they first considered ways to exploit Yellowstone for commercial gain. Around a campfire one night, though, it was decided that Yellowstone belonged to all Americans. Returning to Washington with reports, photographs, and paintings of the region's scenery, the men convinced Congress to set aside Yellowstone as the world's first national park. In 1872, President Ulysses S. Grant signed into law the bill that created the park.

Before Alaska was admitted to the union, Yellowstone was the largest national park in the United States. One of the attractions of Yellowstone is its isolation; it isn't close to any major cities. One of its distractions, though, is its size; if you don't plan your days carefully, you can spend more time in the park driving its roads than hiking its trails. It's best to choose one of the major sections of Yellowstone—the geyser basins, Yellowstone Lake, or Yellowstone Falls, for example—and focus on thoroughly exploring a small area as opposed to exploring a little bit here and a little bit there.

One of my favorite Yellowstone hikes is the trail to Cascade Lake. The trailhead is along the highway between Old Faithful and Yellowstone Lake. Few people know about it, so the trail is uncrowded. The terrain makes for relatively easy hiking, the scenery is pretty, and there are good opportunities for wildlife encounters.

Hiking through the geyser basins is best described as nature walks. Interpretative brochures are sold at the trailheads, and interpretative signs are posted at several of the geysers. A trip to Yellowstone would not be complete without spending at least a little time at the geysers. Besides Old Faithful, Norris Geyser Basin is a popular destination. Because of the fascination of geysers, they're great places to take children. Just be sure they don't wander too close to the pools; the water is scalding.

Personal Anecdote

Moose are my favorite large mammal, probably because they're such icons of the wilderness. My all-time best, up close, in-your-face encounter with a moose was at a marsh at Yellowstone.

Words cannot do justice to the Tetons; they're spectacular, magnificent, inspiring, and more. See them for yourself and you'll think of your own superlatives. The Tetons are America's Alps; the peaks are an awesome sight, and viewed from the shores of Grand Teton National Park's pristine lakes, they're breathtaking.

Once you've seen Jenny Lake, you'll spend the rest of your life comparing all other lakes to Jenny. Outside of the park itself, Jackson Hole is an incredible place to hike and sightsee.

Recommended Places to Hike in Wyoming

Location	Features
Yellowstone National Park	Over 1,000 miles (1,609.5 km) of trails spread throughout a wilderness that encompasses 2 million acres (8,100 sq km) Numerous 2- to 5-mile (3- to 8-km) short hikes Several 10- to 20-mile (16- to 32-km) day hikes Longer trails are 20 to 100 miles (32 to 160 km) one way Mountain scenery, geyser basins, waterfalls, forests Wildlife include bison, elk, deer, grizzly bears, black bears, and wolves
Grand Teton National Park	Incredible mountain scenery The loop trail from Death Canyon trailhead through southern Tetons is a 30.5-mile (49-km) round-trip Popular climbs include Mount Moran at 12,605 feet (3,842 m) and Grand Teton at 13,775 feet (4,198.5 m), the second highest peak in Wyoming Miles of other trails for day hiking include trails around Colter Bay, Two Ocean Lake, and Jenny Lake Backpacking trails include Cascade Canyon Trail and Paintbrush Trail and travel through rugged mountain wilderness
Devils Tower National Monument	A very pretty park in the northeast corner of the state, just west of the Black Hills 8 miles (13 km) of hiking trails, with a loop that goes completely around Devils Tower Scaling Devils Tower requires technical climbing gear
Bighorn Mountains	Over 200 miles (320 km) of trails through mountains with scenic views Two hundred lakes Wildlife viewing includes moose, elk, and deer Excellent trout fishing
Wind River Range	Gannett Peak is the highest point in Wyoming at 13,804 feet (4,207 m) 80-mile (129-km) Highline Trail
Flaming Gorge	National Recreation Area Most of the recreation centers are on the reservoir with boating and fishing Several miles of hiking trails go through meadows and to peaks above timberline
Continental Divide Trail	550 miles (885 km) of the CDT pass through Wyoming, including Yellowstone, the Teton and Bridger Wildernesses, and the Absaroka and Wind River Mountain Ranges
Mount Washburn	6.2-mile (10-km) round-trip to the top of Mount Washburn, which rises 10,243 feet (3,122 km)
Absaroka Wilderness	On the Wyoming-Montana state line Its highest point is Francs Peak at 13,153 feet (4,009 m) Part of the Greater Yellowstone Ecosystem 700 miles (1,130 km) of trails Hundreds of lakes

Conclusion

The population density of the Rocky Mountains is the lowest in the continental United States. Large sections of these states are under federal jurisdiction and have been set aside as national parks, national recreation areas, and wilderness areas. If your goal is solitude plus gorgeous scenery, then the Rockies are the place for you.

CHAPTER 20

 # Southern Rockies

In This Chapter

➤ Utah

➤ Colorado

The Southern Rockies have some of the most beautiful scenery in the United States. Southern Utah is known for its red rock country; Colorado is known for its fourteeners—mountain peaks that peak at altitudes greater than 14,000 feet (4,270 m). Several national parks famous for their rugged wilderness, scenic vistas, and wildlife are located in these states, including Rocky Mountain, Canyonlands, Capitol Reef, Bryce, and Zion.

Utah

Utah is blessed with gorgeous scenery, from the Wasatch Mountains of the north-central part of the state to Zion National Park in the southwestern corner; from Capitol Reef and Bryce National Parks and the Grand Staircase-Escalante National Monument in south-central Utah to Arches and Canyonlands National Parks in the southeastern corner. Southern Utah, especially Paria Canyon, is known for its slot canyons, where canyon walls can be so close together that you can reach out and touch both walls at the same time. As if Utah's large number of federal lands were not enough, the state also boasts numerous state parks.

Nature Quote

"You can talk about the Grand Canyon, you can talk about Yellowstone, Yosemite, I'm biased, I'm not sure they compare with the Canyonlands"

–The late Stewart Udall, Secretary of the Interior under Presidents Kennedy and Johnson

Colorado may be known for its fourteeners, but Utah is equally well known for its thirteeners. The Wasatch Mountains alone are known for their peaks of 11,000 feet (3,350 m) or higher.

The number of national park units in Utah is amazing. When trails in high-elevation parks are snowbound in winter, trails in the deserts are open. In summer, when the desert is too hot for most people, the high-country parks beckon.

My favorite Utah national park is Bryce Canyon. Technically, Bryce Canyon is not actually a canyon because it only has one wall; to the south and east the landscape just falls away to the Paria and Colorado Rivers.

Bryce Canyon is famous for its hoodoos—towers of limestone that have been left standing as the sandstone around them eroded away. Many of the hoodoos resemble people or familiar objects, and fanciful names have been assigned to several of them, such as Queen Victoria, Mary and Joseph, the Three Wise Men, Alley Oop, Thor's Hammer.

Bryce's rim is at an elevation of 9,000 feet (2,740 m). In the summer, that means cool nights and mild days that are ideal for hiking. Several trails start at the rim, descend a brief distance into the canyon, and branch out in various directions along the canyon floor before ascending back to the rim. A day hike can be 2 to 3 miles (3 to 5 km) in length, or 10 miles (16 km) or more. Backpacking has never seemed to be very common there—probably because there's little water below the rim—but it's a great place for day hiking . Because the changes in elevation on the trails are small for mountain hiking, children do well on the trails.

Several towns in Utah are well known as gateways to the national parks. The best known is probably Moab in southeastern Utah. In addition to being the gateway to Arches and Canyonlands National Parks, Moab is famous for rafting trips, single-track biking, and jeep trails.

Recommended Places to Hike in Utah

Location	Features
Bryce Canyon National Park	65 miles (104.5 km) of trails Elevations range from 7,000 to 9,000 feet (2,130 to 2,740 m), making summer hiking very pleasant Considerable snow in winter Known for sculptured limestone features (hoodoos)
Zion National Park	140 miles (225 km) of trails Steep-walled canyons, high cliffs up to 3,000 feet (914 m) Northern section of park is at higher elevations 47-mile (76-km) trail from East Rim trailheads to Lee Pass Solitude, scenery Best hiked in spring and fall due to extreme summer temperatures
Dixie National Forest	Sections border Bryce Canyon and Zion Its highest point is Mount Bluebell at 11,322 feet (3,451 m) 640 miles (1,030 km) of trails Canyons, mesas, colorful rocks, lakes, meadows, forests, sagebrush Wildlife viewing
Capitol Reef National Park	Beautiful and isolated little park with 75 miles (120 km) of trails Wildlife viewing Spring and fall are best hiking seasons
Canyonlands National Park	Over 80 miles (128 km) of trails Arid, high desert landscape Spectacular views Spring and fall are best hiking seasons
Arches National Park	Several short trails to the various arches Most popular is the 3-mile (5-km) round-trip trail to Delicate Arch Spring and fall are best hiking seasons
Dinosaur National Monument	Several very short trails near the Quarry Visitor Center Off-trail backcountry hiking permitted in remote areas of the park
Great Western Trail	Section of a 2,400-mile (3,860-km) trail running north-south from Mexico to Canada Utah's section of the trail runs through five national forests
Grand Staircase-Escalante National Monument	Administered by BLM instead of the National Park Service Three distinct regions called Grand Staircase, Escalante Canyons, and Kaiparowits Plateau Majestic canyon country; most hiking is on rugged, remote, unmarked routes Always carry plenty of water
Paria Canyon	38 miles (61 km) along the Paria River from southern Utah to Lees Ferry in Arizona Narrow canyon, side hikes, springs, dramatic landscape
High Uintas Wilderness Area	Contains Kings Peak, the highest point in Utah at 13,528 feet (4,123 m)

Location	Features
Unita National Forest	Mountains include Mount Nebo at 11,877 feet (3,620 m) and Mount Timpanogos at 11,750 feet (3,581 m) 500 miles (800 km) of trails Lakes, rivers, waterfalls, meadows, tundra, forests Wildlife viewing
Wasatch-Cache National Forest	Located in northern Utah, parts near Salt Lake City Highest point is Gilbert Peak at 13,442 feet (4,097 m) 1,050 miles (1,690 km) of trails Substantial wilderness areas
Manti-Lasal National Forest	Over 200 miles (320 km) of trails Narrow canyons Red rock cliffs Peaks over 12,000 feet (3,660 m) in elevation Wildlife viewing

Colorado

Colorado has the Rocky Mountains; the state is well known for its fourteeners. Colorado alone has fifty-four of the sixty-one mountains in the continental United States that are over 14,000 feet (4,267 m) in elevation. To put Colorado's mountains in perspective, none of them are very much lower than Mount Whitney in California, the highest mountain in the lower forty-eight states with a summit at 14,505 feet (4,421 m). Running north-south through Colorado is Interstate 25 (I-25), which is the demarcation between the Rocky Mountains to the west and the Great Plains to the east. All fifty-four fourteeners are located west of I-25.

The hiking season begins whenever the winter snow has finally melted (usually by mid-June) and lasts well into the fall. Summer flowers are most likely to peak between late July and mid-August. Fall is a beautiful season in which to hike because of the fall colors and mild temperatures. Hikers in good physical condition can reach the top of most of the peaks and descend in one day.

Grays Peak, at 14,270 feet (4,349 m), is a popular first fourteener to hike. The peak is located west of Denver just south of Interstate 70, which runs east-west through northern Colorado. Connected by a short ridge to Grays Peak is Torreys Peak at 14,267 feet (4,349 m). The two peaks can be bagged in one day.

The two tallest mountains in Colorado are Mount Elbert at 14,433 feet (4,399 m) and Mount Massive at 14,421 feet (4,396 m). Both are located in central Colorado southwest of Leadville—a community which itself boasts one of the highest elevations of any town in the lower forty-eight states at 10,152 feet (3,094 m). Elbert and Massive are both rated as easy to moderate climbs. In winter, cross-country skiers often make the trip to Mount Elbert's summit.

Mount Evans at 14,264 feet (4,348 m) is a popular peak located west of Denver. Both a trail and a highway lead to the top. Pike's Peak at 14,110 feet (4,301 m) rises above the west side of the city of Colorado Springs. The summit of Pike's Peak, named for explorer Zebulon Pike (1779–1813) and probably Colorado's most famous fourteener, also can be reached by highway or by cog railway.

Historical Quote

Pike's Peak only ranks number thirty-one in height but was made famous by singer Katherine Lee Bates. In 1893, Ms. Bates traveled to Pike's Peak and was so overwhelmed by the view of the mountains to the west and the plains to the east that she was inspired to compose the lyrics to America the Beautiful. I have been to the summit of Pike's Peak, and admittedly, it's hard not to burst out into:

"O beautiful for spacious skies,
For amber waves of grain,
For purple mountain majesties
Above the fruited plain!"

Central Colorado does not have a monopoly on 14,000-plus foot (4,267-plus m) summits. The sixth highest peak in the state is Uncompahgre Peak at 14,309 feet (4,361 m), located in southwest Colorado near the community of Ouray. At number sixteen, Mount Wilson at 14,246 feet (4,342 m) lies just southwest of Telluride. Altogether, southwestern Colorado boasts thirteen of the fifty-four fourteeners.

Nine of the fourteeners are found in south-central Colorado, mostly north of Highway 160, connecting Alamosa and Walsenburg. Ranking number four in height is Blanca Peak at 14,345 feet (4,372 m), just off Highway 160.

And those are just the fourteeners. There are over six hundred thirteeners—mountains that peak above between 13,000 and 14,000 feet (3,962 and 4,267 m).

My parents took me to Rocky Mountain National Park for the first time when I was eleven years old, and it has remained one of my favorite national parks. One reason is that there are no concessioners in the park—no restaurants, no lodging, no gift shops, not even an ice cream stand. The only way to eat in the park is to bring your own food. The only way to sleep in the park is to camp. You can buy your souvenirs, books, and maps at one of several park visitors' centers, but you can only have ice cream if your RV has a freezer. Not having concessions creates a different atmosphere. It means less pavement, fewer parking lots, fewer manufactured structures blocking the scenery, and a greater feeling of wilderness.

For visitors not camping in the park, the town of Estes Park, adjacent to the park on its east side, does offer all the amenities. That's where the restaurants, motels, lodges, gift shops, and ice cream stands are. There are also additional campgrounds in Este Parks if the campgrounds inside the park are full. Visitors entering Rocky Mountain National Park from the west side find similar accommodations at Grand Lake. Trail Ridge Road (closed in winter) winds through alpine terrain to take travelers from the west side to the east side of the park.

For day hikers, a popular, and highly recommended, destination is Bear Lake, which during summer is best reached by shuttle bus due to limited parking at the lake. Shuttle bus stops occur all along the main park road beginning at Moraine Park. You can leave your car at the Moraine Park campground or visitors' center, or at other bus stops along the road.

A 1-mile (1.6-km) trail loops around Bear Lake, is completely level, and is easily hiked by small children. I've taken my children, and even some of my grandchildren, on it. Additional trails lead from Bear Lake to other lakes in the region—Dream, Nymph, and Emerald Lakes are as beautiful and romantic as their names suggest. Trailheads connecting to two longer trails loop back to Moraine Park. Both trails are mostly downhill and lead through backcountry where you're likely to encounter more wildlife than people. Trailheads from Bear Lake also take multiday hikers into the backcountry. Backcountry trails and campsites are lightly traveled; always be on the lookout for wildlife.

Longs Peak at 14,255 feet (4,345 m) is the highest peak in Rocky Mountain National Park and a popular day hike, although it has the reputation of being one of the most difficult of the fourteeners to climb. The trailhead begins at 9,400 feet (2,865 m) and ascends 4,855 feet (1,480 m) in a distance of 7.5 miles (12 km). One problem is that only one approach to the summit allows hikers to reach the top without requiring roped climbing. Another problem is weather. It's too dangerous to try to reach the summit during a thunderstorm, when lightning is frequent, and afternoon storms are common all summer.

If your heart is set on climbing Longs Peak, you should plan to be at the park for several days just in case you have to sit out a day or two of foul weather before conditions permit your attempt. Even then, many hikers begin their climb before dawn with the objective of reaching the summit by late morning. That way they have already descended a distance back down the trail before a mid-afternoon thunderstorm strikes.

A major trail in Colorado is the 469-mile (755-km) Colorado Trail, which begins southwest of Denver, winds through the mountains, and ends in Durango in southwestern Colorado. In places, hikers share the trail with mountain bikers and equestrians. The trail is accessible at several locations and can be traveled in segments.

Recommended Places to Hike in Colorado

Location	Features
Rocky Mountain National Park	Over 355 miles (571 km) of well-marked trails ranging from easy to strenuous Includes a portion of the Continental Divide National Scenic Trail Numerous backcountry camping locations One-third of the park is above timberline Wildflowers, wildlife viewing, gorgeous scenery
Mesa Verde National Park	To protect archaeological sites, hiking is permitted only on designated trails 20 miles (32 km) of permitted trails
Black Canyon of the Gunnison National Park	18 miles (29 km) of rim trails Hiking into the inner canyon is permitted, but there are no established trails
Great Sand Dunes National Park	150,000 (607 sq km) of grasslands, wetlands, forests, and sand dunes in central Colorado No designated trails through the dunes Several trails through forested and alpine areas
Continental Divide Trail	A portion of the 3,100-mile (4,989-km) trail goes through Colorado
Colorado Trail	469 miles (755 km) of trail from Denver to Durango Magnificent mountain scenery in six national forests and five wilderness areas The trail is shared by hikers, mountain bikers (with the exception of wilderness areas), and equestrians
Colorado's Fourteeners	Fifty-four peaks over 14,000 feet (4,267 m) in elevation The highest is Mount Elbert at 14,433 feet (4,399 m)
Colorado's Thirteeners	An impressive six hundred-plus peaks in Colorado that range between 13,000 and 14,000 feet (3,962 and 4,267 m) in elevation
Arapaho and Roosevelt National Forests	Contains the Indian Peaks Wilderness Area 900 miles (1,448 km) of trails
White River National Forest	Near Glenwood Springs in west-central part of state Over 1,400 miles (2,250 km) of trails Over one-third is wilderness
Rio Grande National Forest	Includes a portion of the Weminuche Wilderness Area 1,300 miles (2,090 km) of trails Forests, alpine meadows, tundra, wildlife viewing

Location	Features
San Juan National Forest	Includes another portion of the Weminuche Wilderness 1,100 miles (1,770 km) of trails Wildlife viewing
Eagles Nest Wilderness Area	Over 200 miles (320 km) of hiking trails Accessible only in summer months
Denver and Vicinity	One hundred hiking trails in the Denver-Boulder-Greeley area My favorite trails within metropolitan Denver are along the South Platte River, Bear Creek, and Cherry Creek
Colorado Springs and Vicinity	Pikes Peak at 14,110 feet (4,301 m) stands out as the premier hike in the area The Barr Trail goes to the top and is 13 miles (21 km) one way Other trails are found in Garden of the Gods, Palmer Park, Seven Bridges, Manitou Springs, and Red Rock Canyon
Weminuche Wilderness and San Juan Mountains	In the southwestern corner of the state near Durango Colorado's largest designated wilderness Elevations range from 8,000 to 14,083 feet (2,438 to 4,292 m) Bisected by the Continental Divide Beautiful backpacking trails

Conclusion

It almost isn't fair that Utah has such a high density of national parks and recreational areas. They're all beautiful. After you've done justice to Zion and Bryce, head for Moab and the Canyonlands of southeastern Utah. Moab seems to attract a culture of desert enthusiasts probably unmatched anywhere else in the United States.

The demographics of Denver and Colorado Springs are weighted heavily with younger people. Part of the reason is the amount of four-season outdoor recreation that's available in the Rockies. Spend time in Colorado and you may not want to leave; I know I find it hard to leave.

CHAPTER 21

 Central States

In This Chapter

➤ Hiking in North Dakota

➤ South Dakota trails

➤ Hiking trails in Nebraska and Kansas

➤ Trekking through Arkansas

When I think of the northern Great Plains, I think of Meriwether Lewis, William Clark, and their famous expedition of the early nineteenth century. Wouldn't it be great if today we could travel as freely across prairies that were as virgin as they were two hundred years ago with plains still teeming with bison and elk, great rivers still flowing free and undammed? Although it's true that much of the prairie has been plowed under to become the nation's breadbasket, it's also true there are remnants that look much like they did when the Corps of Discovery went through.

There are not many national parks in the central states. However, there are numerous

Hiking Vocab

The Corps of Discovery Expedition is a name given to what you more familiarly know as the Lewis and Clark Expedition. This transcontinental expedition, the first of its kind for the United States, was undertaken from 1804 to 1806 to study the natural region and come up with ways it could be used to help the US economy.

national wildlife refuges, national recreation areas, national trails, and state and local parklands. For mountain hiking and camping, the Black Hills of South Dakota are a popular destination. Altogether, the central states have much to offer hikers.

North Dakota

Western North Dakota is home to Theodore Roosevelt National Park. The park is known for hiking and nature trails that bring travelers close to a diversity of wildlife—pronghorns, free-ranging herds of bison, elk, and deer.

The North Country Trail has its western terminus in North Dakota. From there, the trail heads east through most of the Great Lakes states.

The Rocky Mountains end in eastern Montana before reaching North Dakota. Although North Dakota is not known for high mountains, it can be described as having rolling hills of grasslands.

Local History

The reason there is a national park named after President Teddy Roosevelt is because Roosevelt camped and hunted in the area. Roosevelt suffered poor health and stamina as a young man. To toughen himself, Roosevelt engaged in vigorous outdoor activities, which in addition to time spent in North Dakota, included trips to Africa and South America.

Recommended Places to Hike in North Dakota

Location	Features
Theodore Roosevelt National Park	96-mile-long (154-km-long) Maah Daah Hey Trail
North Country Trail (NCT)	When finished, the NCT will pass through seven states and total 4,540 miles (7,305 km) As of 2012, 222 miles (357 km) of an eventual 475 miles (764 km) in North Dakota have been completed
Lewis and Clark State Park	Rugged scenery Nature trail
Dakota Prairie National Grasslands	35 miles (56 km) of trails through grasslands filled with native plants Migrating waterfowl Prairie chickens, sharp-tailed grouse, raptors, sparrows, and longspurs are endemic to prairie environments
White Butte	The highest point in North Dakota at 3,506 feet (1,068.5 m)

South Dakota

The Black Hills rise above the plains in western South Dakota. They were sacred to Native Americans, and the gold in the Black Hills was coveted by white Americans, which led, at least in part, to some of the clash between the two cultures. Today, the Black Hills are best known for Mount Rushmore, on which bas-relief images of Presidents Washington, Jefferson, Lincoln, and Theodore Roosevelt have been carved.

The best Black Hills destination for hikers is Custer State Park, known for its free-ranging herd of bison and other wildlife. At 7,242 feet (2,207 m), Harney Peak is the highest point in South Dakota and the highest point in the United States east of the Rockies.

South Dakota's largest national park is Badlands, which is known for its geology. Short trails lead to scenic overlooks.

Local History

Not to be outdone by the carvings at Mount Rushmore, Native Americans in South Dakota have been carving a likeness of Chief Crazy Horse into a mountain south of Rushmore.

Recommended Places to Hike in South Dakota

Location	Features
Badlands National Park	20-mile (32-km) loop through Sage Creek Unit 5-mile (8-km) Castle Trail Deer, pronghorn, bison Striking geological landscape Cross-country backpacking and camping allowed
Black Hills: Wind Cave National Park	30 miles (48 km) of trails Mostly prairie; some forest and riparian habitats 6-mile (9.6-km) section of the Centennial Trail Limited backcountry camping
Black Hills: Custer State Park	71,000 acres (287 sq km) 61 miles (98 km) of trails At 7,242 feet (2,207 m), Harney Peak is the highest point in South Dakota Wildlife viewing, especially bison Excellent fishing
Black Hills: Bear Butte State Park	4.3 miles (6.9 km) of trails Northern terminus of the 111-mile (179-km) Centennial Trail Sacred to Native Americans
Black Hills: George S. Mickelson Trail	South Dakota's first rails-to-trails conversion 109 miles (175 km) in length Forests and mountains characteristic of the Black Hills
Yankton Area	30 miles (48 km) of trails throughout the city Lewis and Clark Recreation Area has 7 miles (11 km) of multiple-use trails Scenic and historic Lewis and Clark sites
Big Sioux River Recreation Trail (Sioux Falls)	19 miles (31 km) of trails through tallgrass prairie
Sica Hollow State Park (Sisseton)	16 miles (26 km) of trails Wooded terrain, bridges, waterfalls, and wildflowers
Centennial Trail	Marked the hundredth anniversary of statehood (1989) 111 miles (179 km) from Bear Butte State Park to Wind Cave National Forest
Fort Pierre National Grassland (Pierre)	116,000 acres (467 sq km) of prairie

Nebraska and Kansas

There's a good reason the University of Nebraska's football team is called the Cornhuskers. Drive Interstate 80 from Wyoming to Iowa and about all you'll see is corn. However, I-80 hugs the Platte River, which was the route followed by settlers moving west along the Oregon and California Trails. Remnants of those trails are open to hiking.

The northern section of Nebraska is too hilly for farming; ranches are more common there. But the northern section also contains several state parks and national wildlife refuges.

West and east Kansas seem to me like they're two different states. The big cities are in the eastern half; by comparison the western half seems almost deserted. The major trail in Kansas is the Santa Fe Trail, which passes through the state on its way to New Mexico.

Recommended Places to Hike in Nebraska and Kansas

Location	Features
Steamboat Trace (NE)	21-mile (34-km) rails-to-trails conversion The trailhead is at Brownville Part of route followed by Lewis and Clark
Pine Ridge National Recreation Area (NE)	Ponderosa pine forests 80 miles (129 km) of marked trails shared with mountain bikers and equestrians
Fort Niobara Wilderness and National Wildlife Refuge (NE)	Short nature trail in the refuge leading to a picturesque waterfall Backpacking opportunities in the wilderness area
California National Historic Trail (NE)	450 miles (724 km) along the route known as the Great Platte River Road
Oglala National Grassland (NE)	6-mile (9.6-km) round-trip Bison Trail through grasslands
Lewis & Clark National Historic Trail (NE)	The trail follows the Missouri River along the Nebraska-Iowa state line
Johnson Township, Kimball County (NE)	The highest point in Nebraska at 5,424 feet (1,653 m)
Elk River National Recreation Trail (KS)	15-mile-long (24-km-long) trail along the shore of Elk City Lake and then through forest terrain
Mount Sunflower (KS)	The highest point in Kansas at 4,039 feet (1,231 m)
Santa Fe Trail (KS)	500 miles (804.5 km) of the trail are in Kansas
Cimarron National Grassland (KS)	23 miles (37 km) of the Santa Fe Trail Wagon ruts are visible

Arkansas

Arkansas doesn't seem to receive the attention it deserves. First of all, the Ozarks are beautiful. Secondly, how many people know that there are 133 waterfalls in Arkansas? Woodlands, mountains, streams, and waterfalls beckon hikers, backpackers, and other outdoor enthusiasts.

There are two completely separate geographic regions to Arkansas. In the southeast there is the Mississippi River Delta. The northwestern part of the state, however, is dominated by two sets of mountains—the Ozarks and the Ouachitas. The Ouachitas are home to Arkansas' only national park—Hot Springs—located in the west-central part of the state (southwest of the capital city of Little Rock). Although primarily known for its hot springs, the park also has hiking trails.

Recommended Places to Hike in Arkansas

Location	Features
Hot Springs National Park	26 miles (42 km) of hiking trails are accessible year-round
Ozark Highland Trail	165 miles (265 km) Rated the best hiking trail in Arkansas, and one of the top ten hiking trails in the United States Excellent swimming Numerous waterfalls Seventeen campgrounds
Buffalo River Trail	24 miles (39 km) Follows an historic farm road
Devil's Den State Park	14.5-mile (23-km) Butterfield Loop Trail Three primitive campsites
Magazine Mountain	The highest point in Arkansas at 2,753 feet (839 m) 14-mile (22.5-km) trail Camping along, but out of sight, of the trail
Pinnacle Mountain State Park	30 miles (48 km) of the Ouachita National Recreation Trail
Ouachita National Recreation Trail	223-mile-long (359-km-long) trail that begins in Oklahoma Lots of good access for day hikes
Ouachita National Forest	39.5-mile (63.5-km) Womble Trail, third longest trail in Arkansas Eagle Rock Loop Trail, a 26.8-mile (43-km) loop hike Little Blakely Loops, an 18.6-mile (30-km) combination of five smaller loops Scenic 15.5-mile (25-km) Little Missouri Trail
Mississippi Delta region	73.5-mile (118-km) Delta Heritage Trail Under development as of 2012
Ozarks	180-mile (290-km) Ozark Highlands Trail through remote and scenic mountain areas; numerous trails good for short day hikes

Conclusion

The grasslands of the central United States may not have the high elevations of the western United States, and snow and ice can cover them all winter, but in spring and summer the prairie comes alive with wildflowers. The remnants of prairie that have been restored throughout these states are well worth visiting when the flowers are blossoming.

CHAPTER 22

 # The Midwest

---

In This Chapter

➤ The upper Midwest: Michigan, Minnesota, Wisconsin

➤ Ohio and Indiana

➤ Illinois and Kentucky

➤ Iowa and Missouri

The Midwest is dotted with many lakes. Thousands of years ago, glaciers scoured the landscape and covered the region of the Great Lakes; as the glaciers retreated, melting ice filled the lakes. There are five Great Lakes:

1. Superior

2. Michigan

3. Huron

4. Erie

5. Ontario

Only Lake Michigan lies entirely within the borders of the United States; the other four lakes mark the border between the United States and Ontario, Canada.

The Great Lakes contain a large percentage of the world's fresh water that isn't locked away in the ice of Greenland or Antarctica. In addition to the Great Lakes themselves, the Great

Lakes states have innumerable smaller lakes. All that fresh water is great for long-distance hikers, who should be able to count on having water at every campsite.

West of the Mississippi River, the Midwest is best described as deciduous forest to the south, boreal forest to the north, and prairie to the west. The Great Lakes border six of the Midwestern states:

1. Minnesota borders Lake Superior

2. Wisconsin borders Lake Michigan

3. Illinois borders Lake Michigan

4. Indiana borders Lake Michigan

5. Michigan borders Lakes Michigan, Superior, Huron, and Erie

6. Ohio borders Lake Erie

Additionally, Michigan, Minnesota, and Wisconsin have a large number of lakes. All of these lakes—both large and small—are relicts of the last Ice Age. As a consequence, many of the hiking trails in this part of the country connect lakes or run along the shores of lakes.

The lakes are teeming with fish. If your fishing skills are good, you don't even have to carry food with you; you can eat fish three times a day.

Several national and state trails wind their way through the Great Lakes region:

➤ The North Country Trail

➤ The Ice Age Trail

➤ The Lake Superior Trail

➤ The Buckeye Trail

Hiking Trails in Michigan

Michigan's motto is the Water Wonderland. Lakes are found throughout the state and lend themselves to several forms of outdoor recreation:

➤ Hiking

➤ Boating

➤ Waterskiing

➤ Fishing

I spent most of my childhood growing up in a suburb of Detroit, Michigan, so most of my hiking as a youth was done in Michigan. Almost five decades later, I still have fond memories of Boy Scout hikes at Pinckney State Recreation Area northwest of Ann Arbor. I earned medals for hiking the Wilderness and Pontiac Trails north of Detroit. Other state and local parks and recreation areas abound throughout the state.

Michigan is divided into the Upper and Lower Peninsulas, which are separated by the Straits of Mackinac and connected by the Mackinac Bridge. Most of Michigan's population is found in the Lower Peninsula. Much of the Upper Peninsula is still wilderness and a hiker's paradise. The Superior and Michigan lakeshores are just simply breathtaking. You might find yourself so taken by the scenery that you forget you're supposed to be hiking.

Isle Royale National Park is known for its wilderness backpacking, moose, and wolves. The 31,800-square-mile (82,330-sq-km) island is located at the western end of Lake Superior. Access to the island is by seaplane or ferry from Minnesota or the Upper Peninsula of Michigan.

There are two national lakeshores in Michigan. Sleeping Bear Dunes lies along the shore of Lake Michigan, and Pictured Rocks lies along Lake Superior.

Nature Note

Isle Royale didn't always have moose and wolves. Some winters Lake Superior freezes over. Isle Royale is close enough to Ontario that during one particularly cold winter in the mid-1900s, a few moose crossed the lake to the island and established a population. Wolves later crossed over. Today, wolves keep the moose population in check; ecologists use the Isle Royale's moose and wolves as a classic example of a predator-prey relationship.

Mackinac Island is located in Lake Huron just east of the Mackinac Straits. Visitors access the island via ferry or aircraft from either St. Ignace on the southern tip of the Upper Peninsula or Mackinaw City on the northern tip of the Lower Peninsula. (The different spellings of Mackinac and Mackinaw reflect Ojibwa Indian words that were picked up by early French settlers.)

Mackinac Island is unique in several respects. First of all, no cars are allowed on the island. That makes it nice for hikers; just keep an eye out for horse-drawn carriages. Unfortunately, the small size of the island precludes camping, so most visitors find overnight lodging or tour the island as a day trip from the mainland.

The North Country Trail passes through the entire length of Michigan along the western side of the Lower Peninsula and the northern part of the Upper Peninsula. In the Upper Peninsula, part of the trail coincides with Michigan's Lakeshore Trail.

Recommended Places to Hike in Michigan

Location	Features
Isle Royale National Park	170-mile (274-km) network of trails Arrangements can be made for boat shuttles to trailheads 15-mile (24-km) trail from McCargoe Cove to Rock Harbor 37.3-mile (60-km) trail from McCargoe Cove to Windigo Moose, wolves, otters, waterfowl
Tahquamenon Falls State Park	25 miles (40 km) of hiking trails Beautiful waterfalls
Sleeping Bear Dunes National Lakeshore	Thirteen trails totaling 100 miles (160 km) along the shore of Lake Michigan Great lake swimming after a day's hike
Upper Peninsula	Over eight hundred trails in Michigan's Upper Peninsula
Mackinac Island	The perimeter of the island can easily be done as a day hike; other trails crisscross the island
Pictured Rocks National Lakeshore	The Lake Superior Trail passes through
Porcupine Mountains Wilderness State Park	Twenty-two trails totaling 90 miles (145 km) The longest trail in the park is the 16-mile-long (26-km-long) Lake Superior Trail The locals call the mountains the porkies
North Country Trail (NCT)	758 miles (1,220 km) of an eventual 1,150 miles (1,8515 km) in Michigan have been completed as of 2012 The NCT enters Michigan from Ohio, traverses the western side of the Lower Peninsula, crosses the Mackinac Bridge, and continues across the Upper Peninsula to Wisconsin
Mount Arvon	Highest point in the state at 1,979 feet (603 m)

Minnesota Trails

Minnesota is the land of 10,000 lakes. Minneapolis is the city of lakes. Like other Great Lakes states, Minnesota has lots and lots of lakes, and where there are lakes there's boating, fishing, and hiking.

Minnesota has sixty-six state parks, fifty-eight state forests, and six state recreation areas. Altogether, there are 1,255 miles (2,020 km) of hiking trails in the parks. Some of the twenty-two trails designed as state trails are paved and also used for bicycling.

Minneapolis has a wonderful system of walking paths that encircle the city's lakes, wind along creeks, and hug the edge of the Mississippi River. My favorite walks are around Lakes Harriett and Calhoun and along the Minnehaha Parkway and Mississippi River.

Recommended Places to Hike in Minnesota

Location	Features
Voyageurs National Park	Mostly a canoeing and kayaking park but also has a number of hiking trails Kab-Ash Trail is the longest at 28 miles (45 km) and is rated as strenuous
Lake Superior Trail	277-mile-long (446-km-long) trail beginning in Duluth and running along the north shore of Lake Superior to the Canadian border
North Country Trail	As of 2012, 486 miles (782 km) of an eventual 775 miles (1,247 km) in Minnesota have been completed Follows the Lake Superior Trail before heading westward Wildlife viewing includes possible sightings of moose, deer, lynx, and black bears
C. J. Ramstad/North Shore State Trail	146-mile-long (235-km-long) natural surface trail from Duluth to Grand Marais
Taconite State Trail	Extends 165 miles (266 km) from Grand Rapids to Ely Traversed on foot, bicycle, or horseback Used by snowmobilers in winter
Paul Bunyan State Trail	120 miles (193 km) long The longest continuously paved trail in Minnesota
Minneapolis, St. Paul, and Vicinity	Miles and miles of footpaths around the lakes and along the rivers Bicyclists and in-line skaters have parallel paths
Eagle Mountain	Highest point in state at 2,301 feet (701 m)

Hiking in Wisconsin

There are two national scenic trails in Wisconsin:

1. The North Country Trail: Passes through Wisconsin

2. The Ice Age Trail: Contained entirely within the state

Both trails are still works in progress.

Wisconsin has 15,000 miles (24,140 km) of snowmobile trails, all of which serve as hiking trails when there's no snow on them. It also has over 8,500 lakes, 7,446 rivers and streams,

Nature Note

There are so many loons in the city of Mercer, Wisconsin, that Mercer is known as the loon capital of the world.

41 state trails (including the 2 national trails) totaling 1,700 miles (2,740 km), 47 state parks, 6 state recreation areas, and 12 state forests.

Wisconsin is definitely a state that enjoys four-season outdoor recreation—hiking, canoeing, kayaking, waterskiing, and bicycling in summer; downhill and cross-country skiing in winter; hunting in season; and fishing year-round.

Recommended Places to Hike in Wisconsin

Location	Features
Door County	A charming part of the state on the peninsula between Green Bay and Lake Michigan Five state parks and 250 miles (400 km) of shoreline pleasant summer weather
North Country Trail (NCT)	122 miles (196 km) of an eventual 200 miles (322 km) in Wisconsin have been completed as of 2012 Camping is available in several state parks and wilderness areas Waterfalls, wildlife viewing, fall colors
Madison and Vicinity	200 miles (322 km) of scenic trails in and around the capital city of Madison
Ice Age Trail	About 1,000 miles (1,610 km) in length Highlights the geological history of the last Ice Age
Kettle Moraine State Forest	32-mile-long (51.5-km-long) section of the Ice Age Trail
Wausau and Vicinity	Several parks, including Rib Mountain State Park, are found in and around Wausau in central Wisconsin Many miles of trails; Rib Mountain is 1,940 feet (591 m) high
Timms Hill	Highest point in Wisconsin at 1,951 feet (595 m)

The Trails of Ohio and Indiana

Ohio is bounded by Lake Erie on the north and the Ohio River on the south. Both areas offer hiking opportunities along aquatic environments. Shawnee State Forest, named for the Shawnee Indians who once lived in the state, borders the Ohio River and is the largest contiguous wilderness in the state of Ohio. Often referred to as Ohio's Little Smokies, this 63,000-acre (255 sq km) state forest features mountains, woodlands, meadows, lakes, and streams.

Ohio has eighty-three state parks, twenty state forests, twenty-eight state wildlife areas, two state natural areas, and one national forest. Indiana has twenty-five state parks, and sixteen state forests and recreation areas.

Recommended Places to Hike in Ohio and Indiana

Location	Features
Shawnee State Forest (OH)	More than 130 miles (209 km) of roads provide access to more than 70 miles (113 km) of hiking trails
Zaleski State Forest (OH)	29-mile-long (47-km-long) Backpack Trail goes through a hardwood forest
Campbell Hill (OH)	Highest point in Ohio at 1,550 feet (472 m)
North Country Trail (OH)	When finished, the NCT will pass through seven states and total 4,540 miles (7,306 km) As of 2012, 432 miles (695 km) of an eventual 1,050 miles (1,690 km) in Ohio have been completed; the NCT enters the state from Pennsylvania and exits in Michigan; 800 miles (1,290 km) follow part of the Buckeye Trail and part of the Wabash Cannonball Trail
Buckeye Trail (OH)	The country's largest circular trail; 1,445 miles (2,325 km) long It goes roughly around the perimeter of the state
Wabash Cannonball Trail (OH)	Multiuse trail located in northwestern Ohio 63 miles (101 km) long A rails-to-trails conversion that crosses thirteen bridges Indiana Dunes National
Lakeshore (IN)	On the southernmost shore of Lake Michigan Sand dunes 15 miles (24 km) of beach Over 27 miles (43 km) of hiking trails
Brown County State Park (IN)	Indiana's largest state park; 20 miles (32 km) of hiking trails
Indiana Dunes State Park (IN)	8-mile (13-km) loop along Lake Michigan
Hoosier Hill (IN)	Highest point in Indiana at 1,257 feet (383 m)

Hiking in Illinois and Kentucky

Illinois and Kentucky were both characterized by tallgrass prairie before it was cultivated by settlers. It's said the grass was so tall that riders on horseback could barely see over it. Remnants of those prairies exist today.

Shawnee National Forest is Illinois' largest public forested area and the state's major outdoor recreation attraction. Hiking is through deciduous forests filled with oaks, maples, mulberries, sycamores, pawpaws, elms, willows, hickories, and beeches.

Illinois has one hundred forty state parks, six state forests, twelve state recreation areas, and four state natural areas.

Kentucky has several national park units—Mammoth Cave is the largest and best known.

Recommended Places to Hike in Illinois and Kentucky

Location	Features
Shawnee National Forest (IL)	280,000 acres (1,130 sq km) Hiking trails
Charles Mound (IL)	Highest point in Illinois at 1,235 feet (376 m)
The Sheltowee Trace (KY)	257-mile-long (414-km-long) national recreation trail Easy access for day hikers
Mammoth Cave National Park (KY)	Hike 12-plus miles (19-plus km) of underground trails in the world's longest known cave More than 60 miles (96 km) of aboveground trails
Cumberland Gap National Historic Park (KY)	Hike the trail Daniel Boone followed into Kentucky 85 miles (137 km) of hiking trails
Daniel Boone National Forest (KY)	More than 600 miles (960 km) of trails Some trails are shared with mountain bikers and equestrians Birds, wildlife viewing, scenic views
Buckley Wildlife Sanctuary (KY)	374-acre (1.5-sq km) facility with nature trails
Black Mountain (KY)	Highest point in Kentucky at 4,145 feet (1,263 m)

Iowa and Missouri Hiking

In recent years I have spent increasingly more time in Iowa during my trips. Considerable effort has been expended to restore Iowa's large segments of tallgrass prairie. To see prairie wildflowers, I highly recommend the Neal Smith National Wildlife Refuge east of Des Moines. There are no camping facilities on the refuge itself, but there are state parks nearby.

My favorite region of Missouri is the Ozarks. Ozark National Scenic Riverways was established to protect the Current and Jacks Fork Rivers. The watershed covers 80,000 acres (325 sq km) of the Ozarks.

Recommended Places to Hike in Iowa and Missouri

Location	Features
Hawkeye Point	Highest point in Iowa at 1,670 feet (509 m)
Neal Smith National Wildlife Refuge (IA)	An excellent example of restored tallgrass prairie Beautiful fields of wildflowers Several short hiking trails
Backpack Trail (IA)	25-mile-long (40-km-long) trail along bluffs, creeks, and marshes
Katy Trail (MO)	185-mile (298-km) multiuse trail that parallels the Missouri River in eastern Missouri Part of the route was followed by Lewis and Clark The trail crosses Katy Trail State Park Commercial shuttle services are available Pastoral scenery; fall colors
Lake of the Ozarks State Park (MO)	Twelve trails wind through forested areas
Ozark National Scenic Riverways (MO)	Several short trails Fall colors
Mark Twain National Forest (MO)	The Big Piney Trail is a 16.5-mile (26.5-km) loop Forests, springs, waterfalls
Taum Sauk (MO)	Highest point in Missouri at 1,772 feet (540 m)

Conclusion

All of the Midwestern states are known for their recreational opportunities. A diversity of habitats ranges from the boreal forests of northern Minnesota, Wisconsin, and Michigan to the prairie of Iowa and Illinois, to the hardwood forests of Ohio, Indiana, Kentucky, and Missouri. Lakes and rivers abound. Autumn colors are truly spectacular in all of these states.

CHAPTER 23

New England

In This Chapter

➤ Maine's trails

➤ Hiking around Vermont and New Hampshire

➤ Massachusetts, Connecticut, and Rhode Island hikes

I love New England. There is so much diversity—mountains, forests, coast, historical sites, fall colors, and great seafood.

The northern Appalachians consist of three separate mountain ranges:

1. The Green Mountains in Vermont and northern Massachusetts

2. The White Mountains in New Hampshire

3. The Longfellow Mountains in Maine

The stretch of the Appalachian Trail through these states is the most rugged portion of the trail and is heavily traveled during summer and early fall.

Weather-wise, September and October are ideal hiking months.

Winter brings snow, lots of it in some years and avalanches are possible . Although winter hiking is possible, keep on eye out for trails that are closed because of avalanches or the threat of avalanches. The most dangerous location for avalanches is Tuckerman Ravine on the east side of Mount Washington in northern New Hampshire. Snow begins to melt in April and can usually be counted on to be gone by mid-May.

Higher elevations consist of boreal forest—balsam fir and black spruce—with hardwood forest—beech, maple, and birch—predominating at lower elevations. Peaks in New Hampshire and Maine are high enough for alpine tundra, the only real tundra in the eastern United States. Climate in the tundra is characterized as subarctic or even arctic. Jet stream winds are squeezed between ridges producing some of the highest winds in the United States; in the case of Mount Washington, some of the highest winds in the world.

Maine

Maine is easily my favorite state east of the Mississippi River. Unfortunately, Maine is also the eastern state farthest from where I live in Arizona. Although I've been to New England half a dozen times in my life, it's not enough. There is so much to do and enjoy there.

Located on the coast of Maine immediately adjacent to the town of Bar Harbor, Acadia National Park is my favorite eastern national park. Bar Harbor and the park are situated on Mount Desert Island (pronounced like "dessert" by the locals). Altogether there are about sixty trails in Acadia, and most of them are easy day hikes. The shortest trails are only 1 to 2 miles (1.6 to 3.2 km) long and are well suited for younger children. Several trails are 3 to 5 miles (5 to 8 km) in length and are suitable for older children. The longest trails are about 7 to 9 miles (11 to 14.5 km) in length.

Many of the trails run along the shore, which means their elevation is at or close to sea level. The highest peak on Mount Desert Island is Cadillac Mountain at an elevation of 1,532 feet (467 m). The trail begins at 406 feet (124 m) and climbs 1,126 feet (343 m) in 2.2 miles (3.5 km) to reach the summit. On a clear day the views from the top are spectacular. I was particularly impressed on one visit to see Mount Katahdin at 5,267 feet (1,605 m) in the distance, the northern terminus of the Appalachian Trail.

Acadia National Park receives a lot of rain in the summer, so you should be prepared for changes in weather. Mosquitoes come hand in hand with the rain, so use insect repellent. Although it is cloudy much of the time, do not be fooled into thinking that sunscreen is not necessary.

When hiking along the seashore, be aware of tides. It is easy at low tide to venture out from shore and then be caught or trapped by the incoming tide. This is especially of concern when hiking with children.

Mount Desert Island has campgrounds both in Acadia and on private land, so there are several choices of where to camp. Some of the natural areas that visitors should be sure to visit include the following:

➤ Schoodic Peninsula

➤ Otter Cliffs

➤ Wonderland

➤ Jordan Pond

➤ Seawall

➤ Bubble Rock

There are also several attractions to visit, including these:

➤ Bass Harbor Lighthouse

➤ Asticou Azalea Gardens

➤ Thuya Gardens

➤ Jordan Pond House

➤ Sieur de Monts Spring

In wet areas, trails consist of boardwalks. Bar Harbor is the main town on the island, but visitors should also check out Northeast Harbor, Southwest Harbor, and Bass Harbor.

Baxter State Park is Maine's last true wilderness, encompassing 200,000 acres (809 sq km) of forest and mountains in north-central Maine. Baxter is an incredibly wild state park that has undergone little change since Thoreau's time in the nineteenth century. The park is renowned for its hiking trails, campgrounds, fishing, solitude, and wildlife viewing (especially moose).

Local History

We are indebted to the late Percival Baxter, governor of Maine in the early 1920s, for painstakingly buying up parcels of land around Maine's highest peak, Mount Katahdin, and donating them to the people of Maine. That land is now Baxter State Park.

Recommended Places to Hike in Maine

Location	Features
Acadia National Park	7.5-mile (12-km) trail from Door Mountain to Cadillac Mountain, highest peak in the park at 1,530 feet (466 m) Views of the ocean and harbors and of Mount Katahdin on clear days
Baxter State Park	10-mile (17-km) strenuous, round-trip hike up Mount Katahdin, highest point in Maine (5,267 feet; 1,605 m) and northern terminus of the Appalachian Trail Several shorter and easier trails
Appalachian Trail (AT)	281 miles (452 km) of the AT are in Maine and are considered to be the most rugged portion of the AT Crosses several mountains Fifteen locations provide access for day hikers
100–Mile Wilderness	Very popular section of the AT that no paved or public roads cross Mountains, streams, fishing
Grafton Loop Trail	21-mile (34-km) trail beginning in Grafton Notch State Park Climbs East Baldpate (3,812 feet; 1,162 m), Lightning Ledge (2,644 feet; 806 m), Long Mountain (3,021 feet; 921 m), and Puzzle Mountain (3,080 feet; 939 m).

Local History

You may remember the Green Mountains from your high school US history class. Ethan Allen originally organized the Green Mountain Boys to protest a ruling in New York that their Vermont holdings actually belonged to the state of New York and needed to be purchased from New York. When the Revolutionary War broke out in 1775, Allen and the Green Mountain Boys—aided by Benedict Arnold—captured Fort Ticonderoga from the British army.

Vermont and New Hampshire

Vermont differs from its New England neighbors in several ways. For one thing, Vermont is the most rural state in the United States, as measured by how few people live in big cities. The population of Vermont is the smallest state east of the Mississippi River. In addition, Vermont is the only New England state that does not have a coast. On the other hand, a good portion of the Appalachian Trail runs through the Green Mountains, which make up much of the state. On the west side of the state, Vermont shares Lake Champlain with New York. Lake Champlain is the largest freshwater lake in the United States after the Great Lakes.

Highly recommended is the Long Trail that runs north-south along the length of Vermont. Part of the trail overlaps the Appalachian Trail (AT). Some people claim the Long Trail is the oldest long-distance trail in the United States, preceding the AT by several years. Both trails took several years from conception to completion; because the time periods overlap, it's difficult to assign seniority with complete certainty.

Hikers in New Hampshire focus on the White Mountains in the northern half of the state. The Presidential Range is there, with several mountain peaks named for presidents of the United States. A popular section of the AT goes through the White Mountains.

The center for AT hiking in New Hampshire is Pinkham Notch at the base of Mount Washington, which at 6,288 feet (1,916 m) is the highest point in the Northeast. Lodging is available at Pinkham Notch, as well as a restaurant, laundry facilities, and an outfitting store. When I visited Pinkham Notch, I was very impressed with the facilities. Restaurant prices seemed a bit high, but a veteran AT friend of mine assures me that the meals are worth the price after you have been living solely on trail food for days or weeks.

There are three ways to reach the top of Mount Washington. You can ride a cog rail train to the top, drive—or ride a bus—over a toll road, or hike to the top. Shuttle buses leave regularly from Pinkham Notch and drive the perimeter of the mountain, stopping at various places for passengers to board or disembark. The charge for the shuttle depends on the distance you ride. An option is to leave your car at Pinkham Notch, ride one bus to the base of the toll road, change buses, ride to the summit, and then hike back down to Pinkham Notch. There are camp sites along the mountain, so it is not necessary to do a complete hike in a single day.

The drawback of hiking Mount Washington is harsh weather. The highest non-tornado related wind speeds in the world have been recorded there. A wind speed of 231 mph (372 kph) occurred in April 1934, and held the world record until January 1996, when a wind speed of 253 mph (407 kph) was recorded at Barrow Island, Australia. Mount Washington's combination of high winds, snow, freezing temperatures, and fog has earned it the reputation as home of the world's worst weather. It certainly seems true for a place frequented by numerous visitors. All that being said, I'm willing to bet that I've whetted your appetite to go there and test your mettle as an outdoor person.

Personal Anecdote

If you are in New Hampshire's White Mountains and looking for a place to stay, just across the state line from Gorham, NH, is a really nice hostel in Bethel, Maine. I have stayed at several hostels around the country, and I give Bethel's hostel a 10 for being a relaxing, quiet place to stay—during the summer and fall anyway. During the winter, Bethel is the Lake Placid of Maine's ski resorts. I imagine the hostel is packed then.

Recommended Places to Hike in Vermont and New Hampshire

Location	Features
Appalachian Trail	146 miles (235 km) of AT in Vermont Coincides with the Long Trail for 98 miles (158 km) 161 miles (259 km) of AT in New Hampshire Six-day hikes in Vermont and twelve in New Hampshire cover short sections of the trail
The Long Trail (VT)	270-mile-long (435-km-long) trail running the length of Vermont from the Massachusetts state line to the Canadian border Cabins are maintained by Green Mountain Club 175 miles (282 km) of side trails Considered by many to be Vermont's best hiking
Mount Mansfield State Forest (VT)	Over thirty different trails Mount Mansfield is the highest point in Vermont at 4,393 feet (1,339 km)) Outstanding views Forests Wildlife viewing
Taconic Mountains (VT)	Southwest corner of state along New York state line on the west and Massachusetts state line on the south Several trails in the area
Rutland (VT)	Several hiking trails in the area: North Peak Trail, Castle Peak Trail, Bald Mountain Hiking Trail
State Parks (VT)	State parks throughout the Green Mountains; all have hiking trails
Mount Washington (NH)	Highest point in New Hampshire at 6,288 feet (1,917 m) The AT passes by its base
White Mountains (NH)	Presidential Peaks—Washington, Jefferson, Adams, and Madison (all over 5,000 feet; 1,524 m) King Ravine Trail, 10.2 miles (16.4 km) Mountain huts maintained by the Appalachian Mountain Club

Massachusetts, Connecticut, and Rhode Island

Massachusetts has Cape Cod and Martha's Vineyard (an island off the coast). Cape Cod is a scenic peninsula jutting out into the Atlantic Ocean and is well worth the trip.

Sections of the Appalachian Trail traverse Massachusetts and Connecticut. Short sections are easily accessible and make good day hikes.

Nicknamed the Ocean State, what Rhode Island lacks in size it more than makes up for in coastline. Delaware is smaller in total area, but Rhode Island is smaller in land area. It is only 42 miles (68 km) from the southwestern corner of the state (next to Connecticut) to the southeastern corner (next to Massachusetts), but Rhode Island has one of the most miles of shoreline of any state bordering the Atlantic or Pacific Oceans.

Narragansett Bay is the East Coast's second largest estuary (only Chesapeake Bay is larger). What is not coast is interior, and the interior has an abundance of lakes, reservoirs, state wildlife management areas, state parks, state forests, and hiking trails. Just remember that the highest elevation in the state is only 812 feet (247 m), so most of the trails are going to seem relatively level and as though they are not much above sea level.

Local History

Elizabeth Dickens taught natural history and ornithology on Block Island. The Elizabeth Dickens Trail is named in her memory and traverses high bluffs overlooking the ocean.

Recommended Places to Hike in Massachusetts, Connecticut, and Rhode Island

Location	Features
Appalachian Trail	Fourteen day-hikes in Massachusetts and eight in Connecticut cover short sections of the trail 90 miles (145 km) of AT in Massachusetts, 52 miles (84 km) in Connecticut
Mount Greylock (MA)	Highest point in Massachusetts at 3,487 feet (1,063 m)
Bay Circuit Trail (MA)	Still under construction; when finished, there will be a 200 miles (320 km) of trails from south of Boston to north of Boston Passes through nature sanctuaries, national historic parks, state parks, beaches, salt marshes, lakes, rivers, swamps, and bogs
Cape Cod (MA)	Over 43,000 acres (174 sq km) of shoreline, and uplands comprise Cape Cod National Seashore Twenty-one nature trails throughout Cape Cod
Martha's Vineyard (MA)	Access is by boat or plane Seven nature trails
Mount Frissell (CT)	Highest point in Connecticut at 2,380 feet (725 m)
Devil's Hopyard State Park (CT)	Over 15 miles (24 km) of trails through hemlock forest and marshlands
Housatonic Valley River Trail (CT)	Bird-watching sanctuaries, nature trails, and historic spots Wildlife viewing
White Memorial Conservation Center (CT)	Connecticut's largest nature center 35 miles (56 km) of old carriage roads now used for hiking, horseback riding, and cross-country skiing
Metacomet Trail (CT)	51-mile (82-km) portion of the New England National Scenic Trail Revolutionary War sites

Location	Features
Connecticut River Jerimoth Hill (RI)	Highest point in Rhode Island at 812 feet (247 m)
Beach Pond State Forest (RI)	West of Providence Several marked short trails
North South Trail (RI)	72 miles (116 km) in length, running from the Massachusetts state line on the north to the southern coast
Hope Valley (RI)	Short trails around Blue, Long, and Ell Ponds
Block Island (RI)	Located about 15 miles (24 km) off the coast in the Atlantic Ocean More than 30 miles (48 km) of trails Lighthouses Fall colors Breathtaking scenery The entire perimeter of the island can be walked along the beaches in about eight hours

Conclusion

In my opinion, hiking in New England is comparable in experience to hiking in the Pacific Northwest. It's a different ocean and the mountains aren't as high, but New England is every bit as scenic.

CHAPTER 24

 **Mid-Atlantic States**

The central Appalachian Mountains are the highlight of the Mid-Atlantic states. The central Appalachians are considered to be a series of ranges encompassing the Alleghenies and Poconos in Pennsylvania and the Catskills and Adirondacks in New York.

Boreal forest with balsam fir and black spruce characterizes the highest mountains. Hardwood forests containing beeches, maples, and birches predominate at lower elevations. In the Mid-Atlantic states, only the summit of Adirondack's Mount Marcy at 5,344 feet (1,629 m) is high enough for alpine tundra to be present.

Despite their relative proximity to the Atlantic Ocean, the Appalachians' climate is continental, not coastal. That means the temperature in the Appalachians tends to be cool most of the year. Rain in summer and snow in winter are frequent.

When the snow has finally melted and summer has arrived, black flies become a major problem for hikers, so carry insect repellent. The melting snowpack also tends to leave many trails boggy.

Autumn brings cooler, drier weather, far fewer bugs, and fall colors. Until snow begins to fall again, autumn hiking can be ideal.

Hiking through the Mountains of New York

Most people have heard of the *Last of the Mohicans*, but probably few people know that James Fennimore Cooper set his book in the mountains of New York. A person can spend a lifetime exploring the Adirondack Mountains, which cover a huge area, and still not see them all. For a change of pace, there are also the Hudson River Valley and the Catskills, which were made famous by Washington Irving through his characters Rip Van Winkle and Ichabod Crane.

New York has about 150 state parks—all with trails, albeit many are short. Additional recreational opportunities are offered by sixty forest areas. The gem of New York's state park system is Watkins Glen State Park.

Recommended Places to Hike in New York

Location	Features
Appalachian Trail (AT)	88 miles (142 km) of the AT are in New York, mostly in the Hudson River Valley north of New York City Short sections are popular day hikes
Catskills Mountains	Catskill Mountains Escarpment, 23 miles (37 km) one-way Mountain peaks The tallest peak is Slide Mountain at 4,204 feet (1,281 m) Scenic views of the Hudson River Valley
Adirondacks	Mount Marcy (5,344 feet; 1,629 m) is the highest point in New York Phelps Trail, featuring 5,114-foot (1,559-m) Mount Algonquin 50-mile (80-km) loop through Five Ponds Wilderness Numerous other trails throughout the region
Watkins Glen State Park	Considered by many to be New York's most beautiful state park The North Country Trail passes through the park

The Trails of Pennsylvania

A western extension of the Appalachians, the Allegheny Mountains run through southwestern Pennsylvania and West Virginia. Forming the eastern continental divide, streams on the east side of the Alleghenies run to the Atlantic Ocean, and streams on the west side drain to the Gulf of Mexico. Between the two states, the Alleghenies range in elevation from 2,000 feet (610 m) to more than 4,800 feet (1,460 m).

Pennsylvania has just one national forest—Allegheny National Forest—but boasts 113 state parks. Valley Forge National Historic Park and Gettysburg National Military Park are also located in Pennsylvania. Short hiking trails are available in all of these.

A fairly long, scenic section of the Appalachian Trail passes through Pennsylvania and is probably the most popular trail in the state for long-distance hikers.

Recommended Places to Hike in Pennsylvania

Location	Features
Potomac Heritage Trail	Begins in Conemaugh Gorge near Johnstown, runs south to Maryland, and continues through Maryland
Appalachian Trail	232 miles (373 km) of the AT runs through Pennsylvania
Forbes State Forest	At 3,213 feet (979 m), Mount Davis is the highest point in Pennsylvania Several very short trails in the area
Pine Creek Rail Trail	50-long (80-km-long) loop through Pine Creek Gorge, known as Pennsylvania's Grand Canyon

New Jersey Hiking

New Jersey is one of the most industrialized states in the United States, but the population tends to be concentrated in just a few major cities. That leaves quite a bit of room for the rest of us to roam around in.

Hiking opportunities exist along the Hudson River, which forms the state line between New Jersey and New York, and several state parks and forests. Northwestern New Jersey contains a portion of the Appalachian range known as the Kittatinny Mountains.

The entire lower half of the state is described as coastal plain. Cape May has a diversity of coastal habits with several short hiking trails. Unfortunately, New Jersey's Atlantic coast is a very popular vacation area, so it may be best to avoid the coast itself during the summer.

Nature Note

On the southernmost tip of New Jersey, Cape May Bird Observatory is the premier East Coast destination for birders. In spring, birders gather to witness the courtship flights of American Woodcock. In autumn, birders gather to observe the southbound migration of songbirds and hawks.

Recommended Places to Hike in New Jersey

Location	Features
High Point State Park	At 1,803 feet (550 m), High Point Peak is the highest point in New Jersey 50 miles (80 km) of trails within park
Appalachian Trail	74 miles (119 km) of the AT pass through New Jersey 27-mile (43-km) section between Delaware Water Gap and Culvers Gap is especially popular
Hoeferlin Memorial Trail	13 miles (21 km) in length; 700-foot (213-m) elevation change Moderately strenuous
Norvin Green State Forest	7.5-mile-long (12-km-long) Wyanokie Circular Trail 1,100-foot (335-m) elevation change Moderate difficulty
Abraham S. Hewitt State Forest	8-mile-long (13-km-long) Bearfort Ridge Trail 1,000-foot (305-m) elevation change Moderately strenuous
Hudson River	7-mile-long (11-km-long) Palisades Hike 400-foot (122-m) elevation change—an easy hike
South Mountain Reservation	19 miles (31 km) of hiking trails Cascades and waterfall Moderate difficulty
Great Swamp National Wildlife Refuge	5–6 miles (8–9.6 km) of easy hiking Wildlife viewing
Round Valley Recreation Area	10-mile-long (16-km-long) loop around Round Valley Reservoir 400-foot (122-m) elevation change Moderate difficulty
Lebanon State Forest	8.5-mile-long (13.7-km-long) hike, including a portion of Batona Trail Moderately strenuous
Morristown National Historical Park	15-mile-long (24-km-long) loop where George Washington and his troops spent a winter Wetlands, woodlands, Speedwell Lake

Maryland and Delaware Trails

Maryland and Delaware are both very small states in terms of area. Maryland, however, has its share of mountains and gets a small share of the Appalachian Trail. Delaware doesn't really have mountains; its highest elevation is less than 450 feet (137 m). Both states have a large amount of coastline—most of Maryland's coastline is along the Chesapeake Bay, although some is along the Atlantic Ocean. Delaware's coastline is along Delaware Bay or the Atlantic Ocean and tends to be pretty marshy.

Recommended Places to Hike in Maryland and Delaware

Location	Features
Blackbone Mountain (MD)	Highest point in Maryland at 3,360 feet (1,024 m)
Chesapeake and Ohio Canal (MD)	15-mile-long (24-km-long) trail through the Green Ridge State Forest
Potomac Heritage Trail (MD)	185-mile-long (298–km-long) trail Follows the Potomac River on the Maryland side
Appalachian Trail (MD)	41 miles (66 km) of the AT pass through Maryland
Cape Henlopen State Park (DE)	Delaware's largest state park; 6 miles (9.6 km) of hiking along the ocean shoreline
Elbright Road (Delaware—Pennsylvania state line)	Highest point in Delaware at 448 feet (137 m)

Virginia and West Virginia Hiking

Virginia has the Blue Ridge Parkway and the Shenandoah Mountains, which together offer travelers some of the best scenery east of the Mississippi River. Virginia's highest peaks are found in the Blue Ridge—Mount Rogers at 5,729 feet (1,746 m) and Whitetop Mountain at 5,520 feet (1,682 m).

The birthplace of eight presidents, Virginia is rich in history, from England's first settlement at Jamestown to colonial Williamsburg to the British surrender at Yorktown, which ended the Revolutionary War, to General Robert E. Lee's surrender at Appomattox, which ended the Civil War.

Because of its proximity to the District of Columbia, Shenandoah National Park is heavily visited. The main attraction for most tourists is the 105-mile (169-km) Skyline Drive. Motorists tend not to travel far from the roadways, leaving the trails for hikers.

The Appalachian Trail passes through Virginia and the southeastern corner of West Virginia. This is a heavily traveled portion of the trail, again because of proximity to cities on the east coast.

Nature Note

Most all of West Virginia is covered by the Appalachian Mountains, hence its nickname, the Mountain State.

Virginia has twenty-five state parks, six state forests, and several recreation areas. The Appalachian Mountains encompass virtually all of West Virginia, making it one of the most rugged states in the United States.

West Virginia's highest peak is Spruce Knob at 4,862 feet (1,482 m) (most of the high peaks in the state are called knobs). The Monongahela National Forest covers a significant region in the eastern part of the state along the Virginia state line. Most of West Virginia's population is in the southwestern part of the state around the state capital of Charlestown, and in the north around Wheeling and Morgantown. The central and eastern parts of the state are mountainous enough that population density is very low.

Recommended Places to Hike in Virginia and West Virginia

Location	Features
Shenandoah National Park (VA)	Over 500 miles (800 km) of trails shared by hikers and equestrians Backcountry campgrounds and cabins, including about 100 miles (160 km) of the AT Highest point in park is Hawksbill Mountain at 4,409 feet (1,344 m) Forests, meadows, and wildlife viewing One hundred-plus species of trees and nine hundred-plus species of wildflowers Sixteen waterfalls Scenic mountain views Spectacular fall colors
Jefferson National Forest (VA)	Over 550 miles (885 km) of hiking trails, including 300 miles (480 km) of the AT Encompasses Mount Rogers National Recreation Area Mount Rogers, highest point in Virginia at 5,729 feet (1,746 m) 200,000 acres (809 sq km) of hiking and backpacking
Big Blue Trail (VA and WV)	Trail runs from Maryland to Shenandoah National Park 112 miles (180 km) in Virginia, 31 miles (50 km) in West Virginia Mountain scenery
George Washington National Forest (VA)	Over 950 miles (1,530 km) of hiking trails, including 70 miles (113 km) of the AT Highest point is Elliott Knob at 4,472 feet (1,363 m)
Appalachian Trail (VA)	Five hundred forty-four miles (875 km) of the AT pass through Virginia 4 miles (6.4 km) touch West Virginia
Blue Ridge Parkway and Skyline Drive (VA)	More than one hundred hiking trails totaling almost 500 miles (800 km), including 95 miles (153 km) of the AT Thousands of trails branch off the main trails Waterfalls Fall colors
Cumberland Gap National Historic Park (VA)	21-mile-long (34-km-long) historical Ridge Trail that was used by Daniel Boone to get to Kentucky
Allegheny Trail (WV)	In eastern West Virginia; still under construction as of 2012 When completed, the trail will be the longest trail in West Virginia—with a planned length of 330 miles (531 km)

Location	Features
American Discovery Trail (WV)	A section of the American Discovery Trail (ADT) passes through northern West Virginia A 72-mile (116-km) section goes through North Bend State Park Hike through thirteen old railroad tunnels
Dolly Sods Wilderness (WV)	24-mile-long (395-km-long) loop that includes mountaintops, scenic vistas, wildflowers, and waterfalls
Spruce Knob (WV)	Highest point in West Virginia at 4,862 feet (1,482 m)
Morgantown (WV)	52 miles (84 km) of the West Virginia Rail Trail follow the Monongahela River through Morgantown

Conclusion

Because so many Americans live along the eastern seaboard, it's possible that you live close to one or more of the parks or trails described in this chapter. Start with those and then expand to other trails in your area. If you live in other parts of the United States or Canada, based on my own experience, I highly recommend the Adirondacks, Watkins Glen State Park, Shenandoah National Park, and any sections of the Appalachian Trail.

CHAPTER 25

The Southeastern States

> ## In This Chapter
>
> ➤ Hiking in Tennessee
> ➤ Trekking through the Carolinas
> ➤ Florida trails
> ➤ Gulf states hiking

The southern Appalachians run through eastern Tennessee, the western half of North Carolina, the northwest corner of South Carolina, northern Georgia, and the northeastern corner of Alabama.

The southern Appalachians differ from the northern Appalachians in that glaciers never advanced south of Pennsylvania. Advancing glaciers pushed plant species ahead of them. The glaciers retreated thousands of years ago, but most of the plants stayed. Since those species are now mingled with the species that were indigenous to the southern Appalachians before the last Ice Age, the south has a much richer diversity of plant species than the north. This diversity is best seen at Great Smoky Mountains National Park in eastern Tennessee and western North Carolina.

Unlike the northern Appalachians, the southern Appalachians have no true timberline, thus no alpine tundra. There are grassy, treeless mountaintops called balds, but they aren't considered tundra.

Hiking Vocab

Balds are areas near the top of mountains that don't have a climate cold enough to provide a timberline or be considered tundra. Nevertheless, trees don't grow on balds, leaving the land open for grass and shrub growth.

As a general rule there is less snow in the southeast than in the northeast. Certainly along the Gulf of Mexico and in Florida, snow would be unusual. When trails in the Northeast are closed for winter, trails in the Southeast may be open.

The Appalachian Trail (AT) runs through three southeastern state:

1. North Carolina

2. Tennessee

3. Georgia

The AT's southern terminus is at Springer Mountain, which rises 3,780 feet (1,152 m), in Georgia. Persons who thru-hike the AT usually start at Springer Mountain in spring and hike north.

Florida is completely different from any of the other southeastern states. South Florida is subtropical; there are plants and animals at Everglades National Park that are found nowhere else in the United States.

Tennessee

Great Smoky Mountains National Park is one of the crown jewels of the national park system. It covers 800 square miles (2,070 sq km) and is the largest federally protected mountainous area in the eastern United States.

Bisected by the North Carolina Tennessee state line, Great Smoky Mountains National Park has the greatest biodiversity of any area of equal size located in a temperate climate—17,000 species of plants and animals and still counting.

Elevations in Great Smoky Mountains National Park range from 875 to 6,643 feet (267 to 2,025 m). The variation in altitude leads to diversity in plant and animal life similar to what you would find if you traveled from Georgia to Maine. Species at the park's lower elevations are characteristic of the Southeast in general, whereas species at the park's higher elevations are representative of those normally found in New England.

The Great Smoky Mountains are one of the wettest regions in the United States—second only to the Olympic Peninsula in the state of Washington. More species of native trees (about one hundred) are found in the Smokies, which is more than in any other national park in the United States.

The climate in the Smokies is mild enough that hiking and backpacking take place twelve months a year. With the Appalachian Trail passing through the park, an abundance of hikers make the Great Smoky Mountains one of their destinations.

Recommended Places to Hike in Tennessee

Location	Features
Great Smoky Mountains National Park	Crown jewel of the eastern national parks Clingmans Dome, highest point in Tennessee at 6,643 feet (2,025 m), straddles Tennessee-North Carolina state line Huge diversity of plant and animal life
Appalachian Trail	371 miles (597 km) of the AT passes along the Tennessee-North Carolina state line, mostly in Great Smoky Mountains National Park
Natchez Trace National Scenic Trail	24-mile-long (39-km-long) Leipers Fork Trail
Roan Highlands	14.4-mile (23.2-km) section of the AT
Sheltowee Trace	59-mile-long (95-km-long) trail that runs from Pickett, Tennessee, to Cumberland Falls State Resort Park, Kentucky Cumberland River Seventy-five waterfalls

North Carolina

Since North Carolina shares the Smokies with Tennessee, the section of Great Smoky Mountain National Park in North Carolina is a popular destination. A portion of the Appalachian Trail runs through the North Carolina side of the park.

The highest peak in the United States east of the Mississippi River is Mount Mitchell in the Appalachian Mountains near Asheville, North Carolina. The peak itself is at an elevation of 6,684 feet (2,037 m). There are several trails that can be taken to reach the summit, but the trail that is recommended for first-timers on the mountain is the 12.5-mile-long (20-km-long) Black Mountain Crest Trail. Water sources are infrequent, so carry at least one day's supply of water with you.

Local History

The Bartram Trail, which goes from North Carolina to Georgia, is named after the naturalist William Bartram (1739–1832), who spent the years 1773–1777 traveling through the Southeast, cataloging the plants and animals (and native Americans) he encountered. His book detailed his journey and was one of the first real books on the natural history of the American colonies.

Recommended Places to Hike in North Carolina

Location	Features
Great Smoky Mountains National Park	Within the park are one hundred fifty official trails, covering more than 800 miles (1,290 km); mountain hiking, waterfalls, spectacular fall colors, wildlife viewing A portion of the AT passes through the park Big Creek Trail is a 16.4-mile (26.4-km) loop through the park
Cape Hatteras National Seashore	30 miles (48 km) of hiking along the ocean shoreline Historic lighthouses Excellent birding
Appalachian Trail	371 miles (597 km) of the AT pass along the North Carolina-Tennessee state line Clingmans Dome (6,643 feet, or 2,025 m) straddles the Tennessee-North Carolina state line
Mt. Mitchell	Highest point in North Carolina and in the Appalachians at 6,684 feet (2,037 m)
Bartram Trail	115-mile-long (186-km-long) trail from Georgia to North Carolina 78 miles (126 km) of the trail are in North Carolina
Pisgah National Forest	36-mile-long (58-km-long) Art Loeb Trail

South Carolina

South Carolina has a variety of habitats that range from the Atlantic coast to the inland Appalachian foothills. With over 500 miles (800 km) of hiking trails, South Carolina has something for everyone. Hiking trails are found in national parks and forests; wildlife refuges; state parks, forests, and wildlife management areas; and county and municipal trails.

Home of the Swamp Fox of Revolutionary War fame Francis Marion, South Carolina indeed has swamps. I have found that hiking through such areas has the added attraction of always being on the lookout for alligators sunning themselves on the trails! I am disappointed that I've never encountered an alligator while hiking, although admittedly I'm not exactly sure what I would do if I did run into one.

Nature Note

South Carolina has two national forests named after Revolutionary War heroes:

1. Sumter, named after Brigadier General Thomas Sumter (1734–1832)

2. Francis Marion, named after Brigadier General Francis Marion (1732–1795)

Following the war, Sumter served in Congress for many years. Fort Sumter in Charleston Harbor is also named after him. Marion became famous for his guerilla warfare against the British army, a legacy that was commemorated in the 1950s Disney television series "The Swamp Fox." Following the war, Marion served in the South Carolina state senate.

Recommended Places to Hike in South Carolina

Location	Features
Congaree National Park	10.4-mile-long (16.7-km-long) River Trail through mossy wetlands
Sassafras Mountain	14.1-mile-long (22.7-km-long) log trail from Table Rock State Park to Laurel Valley Ascend the mountain, which is the highest point in South Carolina at 3,554 feet (1,083 m)
Kings Mountain State Park and vicinity	15-mile-long (24-km-long) Kings Mountain National Recreation Trail Camping is permitted in the state park
Caesars Head State Park	4.6-mile-long (7.4-km-long) Raven Cliff Falls Trail Mountain scenery, waterfalls, cascades 10.6-mile-long (17-km-long) Jones Gap Trail and connecting trails
Oconee State Park	6.65 miles (10.6 km) of hiking trails in the Appalachian Mountains
Paris Mountain State Park	7.3 miles (11.7 km) of hiking trails
Table Rock State Park	6.8-mile-long (10.9-km-long) long Table Rock Trail 7.2-mile-long (11.5-km-long) Pinnacle Mountain Trail Both trails are rated as strenuous
Santee Coastal Reserve	11.4 miles (18.2 km) of easy nature trails

Georgia

Among backpackers, Georgia's main claim to fame is that it contains the southern terminus of the AT at Springer Mountain. Many hikers head for Springer Mountain in April or May and begin the trek northward toward Maine. Most hikers do not thru-hike the entire AT in a single year, but there are significant numbers who do. Also, there are hikers who begin at Mount Katahdin in Maine in April or May and head south, arriving at Springer Mountain in October or November. The advantage of starting in the south and heading north is weather. Hiking in April anywhere in the Appalachians could mean snow, but the likelihood of snow is much greater if you begin your hike in New England.

Scattered throughout the state are dozens and dozens of other trails in state parks, recreation areas, and other public lands. Many trails are fairly short and are suitable for relaxing day hikes.

East of Atlanta, the state capital, is Stone Mountain, which is similar to Mount Rushmore in having large bas-relief carvings on it. The Civil War Confederate figures depicted on it are President of the Confederacy Jefferson Davis and Generals Stonewall Jackson and Robert E. Lee. A trail takes hikers to the top of the mountain.

The Georgia coast runs from South Carolina on the north to the Okefenokee Swamp, shared with Florida, on the south. The coast is characterized by swamps, estuaries, sounds, and barrier islands. Several major rivers, including the Altamaha, the Suwannee, and the Savannah empty into the Atlantic Ocean. Loggerhead sea turtles nest on Georgia's shores. Hiking trails are available at national wildlife refuges, national seashores, and state parks.

Recommended Places to Hike in Georgia

Location	Features
Brasstown Bald	Highest point in Georgia at 4,784 feet (1,458 m)
Benton MacKaye Trail	78.5 miles (126 km) in Georgia, continuing in Tennessee Mountain hiking One of the more remote trails in the eastern United States
Appalachian Trail	75 miles (121 km) of the AT pass through Georgia, beginning with the southern terminus of the AT at Springer Mountain, which is 3,780 feet (1,152 m)
Stone Mountain State Park	10 miles (16 km) of trails, including a trail that goes to the top of Stone Mountain; elevation 1,686 feet (514 m)
Black Rock Mountain State Park	Georgia's state park with the state's highest elevation on Brasstown Bald at 4,784 feet (1,458 m) The eastern Continental Divide goes through the park 10 miles (16 km) of hiking trails Wildflowers, streams, forests
Chattahoochee National Forest	Nicknamed the Chat 430 miles (692 km) of trails shared by hikers, bicyclists, and equestrians Camp on summit of Springer Mountain, which is 3,782 feet (1,153 m)
Bartram Trail	115-mile-long (185-km-long) trail from Georgia to North Carolina 38 miles (61 km) of the trail are in Georgia
Tallulah Gorge State Park	11-mile-long (18-km-long) trail that includes steep climbing and breathtaking scenic views
Kennesaw Mountain National Park	5 mile (8 km), challenging uphill hike; the scenery is worth it
Cumberland Island National Seashore	50 miles (80.5 km) of hiking trails through forests, wetlands, marshes, and beaches

Florida

Florida is a very flat state. Its highest point, Britton Hill, tops out at only 345 feet (105 m), which is shorter than a forty-story building. That does not mean, however, that Florida lacks good hiking trails. Besides the trails available at Everglades National Park, there is the Florida Trail, which runs 1,000 miles (1,600 km) from one end of the state to the other.

What makes Florida unique is that the southern part of the state is the only region of the continental United States that has a tropical climate. The result is a mix of trees and other flora found nowhere else in the United States. Birders from all over flock to see birds found nowhere else in the United States. Wildlife refuges offer trails for hikers and access for birders into habitat favored by waterfowl and wading birds.

Recommended Place to Hike in Florida

Location	Features
Everglades National Park	60 miles (97 km) of paved and primitive trails, often shared with bicyclists Short walks include the Anhinga and Gumbo Limbo Trails at the Royal Psalm Visitor Center The Slash Pine Trail at Lone Pine Key is one of the longer trails at 7 miles (11 km) Six trails in the Flamingo Area, with some trails being 4–5 miles (6.4–8 km) in length Alligators, water snakes, large numbers of wading birds Lots of mosquitoes
Britton Hill, Walton County	Highest point in Florida at 345 feet (105 m)
Florida Trail	Over 1,000 miles (1,600 km) from the western tip of the Florida panhandle to the Everglades Best hiked during the winter when temperatures are cool, rain is light, and insects are scarce
Cocoa Beach	Hiking along Canaveral National Seashore Wooded trail along the Little Econ River Wildflowers, wildlife viewing

Alabama

Alabama may be mostly lowlands near the Gulf of Mexico, but it has mountains in the north. Northern Alabama marks the southern end of the Blue Ridge Mountains. Alabama's highest peak, Cheaha Mountain, reaches 2,405 feet (733 m) above sea level.

There are twenty-four state parks and reserves in Alabama. Fishing and aquatic sports are popular, but there's lots of hiking, too. In central Alabama, Oak Mountain State Park has 51 miles (82 km) of trails, the most in the state.

Recommended Places to Hike in Alabama

Location	Features
Cheaha Mountain	Highest point in Alabama at 2,405 feet (733 m)
Pinhoti Trail	A National Recreation Trail 335 miles (539 km) total length; 171 miles (275 km) run through Alabama and Georgia
Talladega National Forest	A section of the Pinhoti Trail More than 100 miles (161 km) of hiking trails through pine and hardwood forests and along mountain streams
Sipsey Wilderness	Third largest wilderness area east of the Mississippi River Also called land of a thousand waterfalls 52 miles (84 km) of trails
Conecuh National Forest	20-mile-long (32-km-long) Conecuh Trail, links between Alabama and the Florida Trail Flat hiking through forests of cypress trees and natural ponds Wildlife viewing
Oak Mountain State Park	Alabama's largest state park 51-plus miles (82-plus km) of trails 6.4-mile (10.3-km) Shackleford Point Trail leads to Shackleford Point, highest elevation in the park at 1,260 feet (384 m)
Birmingham	Ruffner Mountain Nature Center has 12 miles (19 km) of trails
Tuskegee National Forest	14 miles (22.5 km) of trails

Mississippi

Mississippi is a pretty flat state. Its highest point, Woodall Mountain, ranks 47th among state peaks in the United States at 806 feet (246 m). Among long-distance hikers and cyclists, Mississippi is best known for the Natchez Trace National Scenic Trail, which begins in the southwest corner of the state, runs diagonally the entire length of the state in a northeastern direction, and passes through a corner of Alabama before ending just south of Nashville, Tennessee.

Mississippi has twenty-four state parks. Two of the parks closed because of damage inflicted by Hurricane Katrina.

Recommended Places to Hike in Mississippi

Location	Features
Black Creek National Recreation Trail	41 miles (66 km) of trail, running through forests and the sand bluffs along Black Creek
Natchez Trace National Scenic Trail	In segments, 65 miles (105 km) of the original 500 mile (805 km) trail that connected Natchez, Mississippi, to Nashville, Tennessee
Woodall Mountain	Highest point in Mississippi at 806 feet (246 m); located in the extreme northeastern corner of state
Bienville National Forest	23 miles (37 km) of hiking trails Camping, fishing, hunting, swimming
De Soto National Forest	Southeastern part of the state; 500,487 acres (2,025 sq km) 41-mile-long (66-km-long) trail runs parallel to Black Creek
Hattiesburg	41-mile-long (66-km-long) Longleaf Trace Trail The trail is shared with bicyclists and in-line skaters

Louisiana

Louisiana is known for its swamps and bayous. Travel is often by airboat. Still, Louisiana has one large national forest, the Kisatchie, national wildlife refuges, and twenty-two state parks. Cities like New Orleans have parks with walking paths.

The highest point above sea level in Louisiana is only 535 feet (163 m) on Driskill Mountain.

Local History

New Orleans is the birthplace of jazz. I recommend a visit to the Jazz National Historic Site—the smallest unit of the national park system. And while you're at it, take in an evening of music at Preservation Hall in the French Quarter.

Recommended Places to Hike in Louisiana

Location	Features
Driskill Mountain	Highest point in Louisiana at 535 feet (163 m) 2.3-mile (3.7-km) trail to summit
New Orleans Area	27-mile-long (43-km-long) Tammany Trace on north side of Lake Pontchartrain Short sections of walkways are open along the Mississippi River levee
Barataria Preserve	South of New Orleans Part of Jean Lafitte National Historical Park and Preserve 9 miles (14.5 km) of boardwalks and trails through cypress swamp and hardwood forest Wildlife viewing includes alligators
Kisatchie National Forest	Spread out over forty recreation areas in central Louisiana 100 miles (161 km) of trails The 31-mile (50-km) Wild Azalea 10-mile (16-km) Big Branch, and 8-mile (13-km) Sugar Cane National Recreation Trails are open year-round
Shreveport	Walter B. Jacobs Memorial Nature Park has five short nature trails
Bayou Sauvage National Wildlife Refuge	23,000 acres (93 sq km) of hardwood forest and wetlands Nature trails

Conclusion

The Southeast has a wide variety of terrain and ecosystems in which to hike and camp. Spend some time in each state; each one has its own features that distinguish it from the other southeastern states.

CHAPTER 26

 **Canada**

In This Chapter

➤ Yukon Territory

➤ Canadian Rockies

➤ Prairie, Eastern, and Maritime Provinces

Canada is a country that offers an outdoors person plenty of recreational opportunities. The Canadian Rockies are so spectacular many people compare them to the Alps; Banff's Lake Louise is nestled in one of the prettiest settings in North America. Moving eastward, the Rocky Mountains give way to prairie. To the north, boreal forest replaces prairie. Hudson Bay and the Arctic Ocean lie even farther north, and the Saint Lawrence Seaway and Atlantic Ocean lie to the east.

It seems unfair to cover Canada in a single chapter, but there is a reason for that: west of the Great Lakes, most of Canada's population lies roughly between the fiftieth and the fifty-fifth parallels and is squeezed into only a few cities—Winnipeg, Regina, Edmonton, and Vancouver—that lie roughly between the fiftieth and the fifty-fifth parallels.

To the east, Canada's largest cities—Toronto, Ottawa, Montreal, and Quebec—and the maritime provinces lie between the forty-fifth and fiftieth parallels. Most of the land mass of Canada lies north of these regions and is just as wild today as it was when French trappers gathered animal pelts in the seventeenth century and English explorers surveyed the land in the eighteenth century.

East of the Rockies, access to interior Canada is almost exclusively by plane or boat. Except for Whitehorse, the capital city of the Yukon Territory, most of Canada north of the fifty-fifth parallel is sparsely inhabited by Canada's First People and the few tourists who venture into those regions.

Nature Note

Churchill, Manitoba, is located on the shore of Hudson Bay north of the fifty-fifth parallel and attracts large numbers of tourists. In June, birders fly to Churchill to observe nesting shorebirds. In November, before winter becomes too harsh, wildlife enthusiasts arrive to view polar bears. Churchill is the southernmost point in North America where polar bears can be found.

Canada has forty-three national parks. The remote parks are reached by plane. People do go backpacking there, but usually there are no designated or maintained trails; it's all cross-country hiking. Only experienced wilderness backpackers who can handle emergencies on their own tend to go there.

Not to be outdone by its neighbor to the south, Canada is in the process of developing two long-distance trails: the Trans-Canada Trail and the National Hiking Trail. When completed, the Trans-Canada Trail will be the world's longest trail—10,000 miles (16,000 km) in length. The trail starts at Saint John's, Newfoundland, and runs to Vancouver, British Columbia. A second leg branches off at Calgary, Alberta, and runs through the Yukon Territory to the Arctic Ocean. Most sections of the trail are multiuse and are shared by hikers, bicyclists, equestrians, and snowmobilers.

When completed, the National Hiking Trail will be 6,200 miles (9,980 km) long. Unlike the Trans-Canada Trail, the National Hiking Trail is strictly a footpath. Located in eastern Canada, there are long sections where the two trails overlap.

Trekking in the Yukon Territory

In 2005, I had the pleasure of driving the Alaska Highway with my younger son. We made the trip during the first week of May, when northern Canada was just beginning to awaken from its winter sleep. We drove past snow-covered mountains and valleys and ice-choked rivers, and we pitched our tent most nights near snow or ice.

Migratory waterfowl and shorebirds were just beginning to arrive. Ospreys and golden eagles were building nests. I added common loons, red-necked grebes, gyrfalcons, and short-eared owls to my birding life-list; wood caribou, grizzlies, mountain sheep, and bison grazed by the side of the road. A wolf ran across the highway and disappeared quickly. Willow catkins were just beginning to appear and tender horsetail shoots were poking through the wet soil.

We crossed from British Columbia to the Yukon and into Whitehorse. We drove through Kluane National Park the morning before we crossed the border into Alaska. The highway hugged the shores of beautiful Kluane Lake; we spotted Dall sheep high on a ledge; trails beckoned, but they were still covered with snow. Someday I'll go back and spend some serious time in the Yukon.

Recommended Places to Hike in the Yukon Territory

Location	Features
Kluane National Park Reserve	Backcountry trails; 60-mile (96-km) Donjek Glacier trail 53-mile (85-km) Cottonwood Trail Dall sheep The highest peak is Mount Logan at 19,850 feet (6,050 m)—almost as high as Mount McKinley in Alaska
Whitehorse and Vicinity	Several trails along the rivers 33-mile (53-km) Chilkoot Trail follows the route used by nineteenth-century prospectors to get to the Klondike gold fields

Canadian Rockies

The Canadian Rockies have more than 1,900 miles (3,050 km) of hiking trails. Although parks like Banff and Jasper are considerably farther north than parks in the lower forty-eight states, their climate is similar to that of Yellowstone. Snow usually melts by June, giving a hiking season that extends from the first week of July through late October. Like Yellowstone, the Canadian Rockies are known for their spectacular scenery and magnificent wildlife, including grizzly bears, mountain goats, bighorn sheep, and wolves.

Several of the national parks share common boundaries. From north to south, Jasper and Banff straddle the mountains between British Columbia and Alberta. Yoho and Kootenay National Parks are in British Columbia west of Banff. Mount Assiniboine Provincial Park is on the south side of Banff. Backpackers can begin their treks in any one of these parks and continue seamlessly into the other parks.

British Columbia

British Columbia includes Vancouver Island and the western Canadian mainland. Besides the national parks in the Rockies, British Columbia has almost 1,000 provincial parks, regional parks, marine parks, recreation areas, and ecological reserves. A ferry ride or plane trip is required to reach Vancouver Island, but the rest of the province is easily accessible by car.

Recommended Places to Hike in British Columbia

Location	Features
Mount Robson Provincial Park	Mount Robson is the highest peak in the Canadian Rockies at 12,972 feet (3,954 m) To reach the summit requires technical climbing Backcountry camping Headwaters of the Fraser River Excellent wildlife viewing
Mount Assiniboine Provincial Park	Mount Assiniboine at 11,870 feet (3,618 m) is the seventh highest peak in the Canadian Rockies Often called the Matterhorn of the Rockies Lake Magog is a focal point for much of the backpacking activity
Kootenay National Park	Over 125 miles (200 km) of trails, ranging from short nature walks to day trips to extended backpacking trips A limited number of permits are available for backcountry camping Yoho National Park 190 miles (306 km) of well-maintained trails Two popular backcountry trails
Waterton Lakes National Park	Over 100 miles (161 km) of the best-constructed trails in the Canadian Rockies Most trails are day hikes, but some backpacking is available Spectacular views Wildlife viewing
Mount Revelstoke National Park	Selkirk Mountains Lakes and alpine meadows
Vancouver Island	47-mile (76-km) West Coast trail 29-mile (47-km) Juan de Fuca Trail Hiking trails in Goldstream Provincial Park

Location	Features
Gwaii Haanas National Park Reserve and Haida Heritage Site	Located on Queen Charlotte Islands off the coast of central British Columbia No designated, maintained hiking trails; all hiking is bushwhacking Hikers need to have excellent backcountry navigation skills and be able to handle themselves in bear country
Vancouver and Vicinity	Over 400 miles (640 km) of hiking trails in and around Vancouver

Alberta

Alberta's jewel is Jasper National Park. Jasper is known for its glaciers, although the glaciers are shrinking rapidly because of global climate change. The most notable ice is the Columbia Ice Field.

Columbia is the source of ice for Athabasca Glacier, which can be accessed along the parkway that connects Jasper National Park on the north to Banff National Park on the south. I first saw the glacier in 1975; the shrinkage of Athabasca Glacier that had occurred in thirty years was sobering. Jasper's peaks often remind visitors of the Matterhorn and other mountains in the Pennine Alps of Switzerland and Italy.

A main attraction of Jasper National Park is Mount Edith Cavell, which peaks at 11,033 feet (3,363 m).

Local History

Mount Edith Cavell was named for Edith Cavell, an English nurse during World War I who was executed by the Germans for helping allied soldiers escape from Belgium to the Netherlands.

Recommended Places to Hike in Alberta

Location	Features
Jasper National Park	The largest national park in the Canadian Rockies; almost 620 miles (1,000 km) of trails Known for long-distance hiking through remote wilderness areas Mount Edith Cavell 11,033 feet (3,363 m) Several 12,000-feet (3,660-m) peaks Athabasca River Valley and Maligne Lake are exceptionally scenic areas Subalpine meadows 27.4-mile-long (44-km-long) Skyline Trail
Waterton Lakes National Park	See table in British Columbia section
Banff National Park	Canada's first national park The second largest national park in Canadian Rockies More than 900 miles (1,450 km) of trails Most day hikes are in the Lake Louise area

The Prairie Provinces: Saskatchewan and Manitoba

North and south Saskatchewan look like two different provinces. Practically all of the cities, roads, and people are in the south; the north is mostly lakes, rivers, and forest. The population density in the province as a whole is only about four persons per square mile (two per sq km). The capital city of Saskatchewan is Regina, which is only about a two-hour drive from the northeast corner of Montana. Most of the population clusters around the cities of Regina, Saskatoon, and Prince Albert. Overall, Saskatchewan is still wilderness.

Manitoba's capital city of Winnipeg has a population of just over 500,000 people. Brandon has just over 35,000 people; the other cities in the province have fewer than 15,000 people. Manitoba also is mostly wilderness.

Summers are short and winters severe. Historically in Canada, rivers were the highways; Canada's recreation still centers around boating and fishing.

The highest elevation in Saskatchewan occurs in the Cypress Hills at 4,567 feet (1,392 m). The highest point in Manitoba is Baldy Mountain at 2,729 feet (832 m).

Southern Saskatchewan and Manitoba are the wheat-growing capital of North America. Saskatchewan has about 40 percent of the farmland in Canada.

The major geological feature of the Prairie Provinces is the Canadian Shield, a vast rocky region that covers half the land mass of Canada from the shore of Hudson Bay to the south and east. The shield covers northern Saskatchewan, half of Manitoba and Ontario, and nine-tenths of Quebec, plus portions of northern Minnesota, Wisconsin, Michigan, and New York. The soil is unsuitable for agriculture but is rich in minerals. The region is one of the world's major sources of nickel, and it supplies copper, gold, uranium, and other metals.

Recommended Places to Hike in Saskatchewan and Manitoba

Location	Features
Prince Albert National Park (SK)	Located in central Saskatchewan north of Prince Albert, where boreal forest and prairie meet Many lakes and rivers
Grasslands National Park (SK)	On the United States border Front country hiking is on well-maintained trails Backcountry wilderness hiking is cross-country Good navigation skills are required Grassland wildlife—bison, prairie dogs, raptors
Wasacana Trails Provincial Recreation Site (SK)	Near the provincial capital city of Regina Short hikes and nature trails
Riding Mountain National Park (MB)	Trails through and around forests, prairie, and lakes

Ontario

In terms of ecosystems, southern Ontario shares much in common with the Great Lakes states of Minnesota, Wisconsin, and Michigan. Summers tend to be mild with frequent rains. Winters tend to be cold; snow is common. Just as glaciers carved out the Great Lakes themselves and the many lakes in Minnesota, Wisconsin, and Michigan, glaciers carved out 400,000 lakes in Ontario. Forest covers much of the province, with mixed hardwoods predominating in the south and spruces, firs, and birches in the boreal forest to the north.

Trail Wisdom

My favorite region of Ontario has always been the north shore of Lake Superior. Few people, crystal-clear waters, cool summers, and lots of wildlife make the region an especially enjoyable destination for outdoor recreation.

Ontario's two longest trails are the Bruce Trail and the Voyageur Trail. The Bruce Trail is located in eastern Ontario and has a length of 500 miles (800 km) of main trail and 125 miles (201 km) of side trails. The Voyageur Trail is 680 miles (1,094 km) long and hugs the shores of Lakes Huron and Superior.

The highest point in Ontario is in the Timiskaming District east of Sault Saint Marie, Michigan, with an elevation of 2,275 feet (693 m).

The eastern portion of Ontario is more urban than the western portion, with big cities like Toronto and Ottawa (the capital city of Canada). As with many urban centers in the United States, cities in Canada—and their surrounding environs—are filled with parks, hiking trails, and boating and fishing opportunities.

Recommended Places to Hike in Ontario

Location	Features
Algonguin Provincial Park	Outstanding wildlife viewing Fourteen trails for day hiking Three backcountry trails Known for its canoeing
Pukaskwa National Park	On the northeastern shore of Lake Superior Several hiking trails The best backpacking trail is the Coastal Hiking Trail—37 miles (60 km) one-way Most trails follow the lake shoreline
Point Pelee National Park	A long, thin peninsula jutting into Lake Erie Hiking trails and beaches, but no camping inside the park
Georgian Bay Islands National Park	Located off Lake Huron on Georgian Bay Beausoleil Island offers a dozen short day hikes
Bruce Peninsula National Park	On Lake Huron The 480-mile-long (772-km-long) Bruce Trail currently is Canada's longest completed trail 93 miles (150 km) of the trail are in the national park and are considered by many to offer the best hiking experience in southern Ontario Shorter day hikes and guided day hikes are also available
Voyageur Trail	680 miles (1,090 km) in length along Lake Huron and Lake Superior
Saint Lawrence Islands National Park	A series of scenic islands on the Saint Lawrence River

Location	Features
Ontario Provincial Parks	There are too many parks to list separately, but all offer hiking trails. Waterfront Trail is a 560-mile-long (901-km-long) trail stretching from Niagara-on-the-Lake to the Quebec border, and running along Lake Ontario and the Saint Lawrence River
Toronto and Vicinity	Dozens of trails within Toronto and dozens more in the surrounding area

Quebec

Parlez vous français? It helps if you do. Canada is a bilingual country, and French is the official language of the province of Quebec.

Among Quebec's most scenic destinations are the Saint Lawrence Seaway, which connects the Atlantic Ocean to Lake Ontario, and the Gaspe Peninsula. Northern Quebec is remote; access is difficult and few visitors go there.

The highest point in Quebec is at an incredibly remote location in the very northernmost part of the province, almost on the Hudson Strait, which connects Hudson Bay and the Labrador Sea. Mont D'Iberville rises to an elevation of 5,400 feet (1,646 m).

Recommended Places to Hike in Quebec

Location	Features
La Mauricie National Park	Trails through forests and past lakes Mingan Archipelago National Park Reserve Forty islands in the Gulf of Saint Lawrence Forty-four campgrounds on six islands 15 miles (24 km) of hiking trails distributed over four islands
Forillon National Park	Located on the Gaspe Peninsula Canada's first national park Very scenic
Véloroute des Cantons	Located just north of border with New York and Vermont 158-mile (254-km) paved multiuse path through the eastern townships and Montérégie regions Two wide lanes Mostly a bicycle path, but shared with hikers
International Appalachian Trail (IAT)	An extension of the Appalachian Trail The section in Quebec is the longest and most rugged section of the IAT in Canada The trail ends at Cape Gaspe

Maritime Provinces

The easternmost provinces of Canada are called the Maritime Provinces because the Atlantic Ocean is the dominant factor in their industry, commerce, and tourism. The Maritime Provinces are New Brunswick, Nova Scotia, Prince Edward Island, and Newfoundland (of which Labrador is part).

Geologically, New Brunswick is an extension of Maine. The Appalachian Mountains and Appalachian Trail do not end at the Canadian border but continue through New Brunswick. New Brunswick is characterized by boreal forest just like northern New England. Nova Scotia is almost an island, but not quite; it connects to New Brunswick by a land bridge.

Prince Edward Island (PEI) is reached by bridge from New Brunswick and ferry from Nova Scotia. PEI is an absolutely charming little island; farms appear to have been manicured.

Local History

Prince Edward Island was the home of Anne of Green Gables. Visitors can tour sites associated with Anne. All summer in the capital city of Charlottetown, superb performances of Anne of Green Gables are performed to packed houses.

Recommended Places to Hike in New Brunswick, Nova Scotia, and Prince Edward Island

Location	Features
Kouchibouguac National Park (NB)	Located on the east coast of New Brunswick Hiking along beaches
Fundy National Park (NB)	Rugged shoreline The highest tides in North America
Cape Breton Highlands National Park (NS)	Several trails The Skyline Trail at 4.3 miles(6.9 km) long is popular Mountains Deep canyons Great views of the Atlantic

Location	Features
Kejimkujik National Park (NS)	Southwest Nova Scotia Forests, islands, and lakes
Prince Edward Island National Park	Beach hiking, dunes, marshes
Confederation Trail	A 290-mile-long (467-km-long) trail that runs from one end of the island to the other Shared with bicyclists

Newfoundland

The province of Newfoundland and Labrador is a single entity. Newfoundland is an island with an area of 43,000 square miles (111,300 sq km). Labrador is on the mainland and has an area of 113,670 square miles (294,400 sq km).

Newfoundland can be reached by ferry or airplane. The island boasts a robust tourist industry and all of its sites are easily accessible. Labrador is more remote with few roads; comparatively speaking, it has few visitors. Newfoundland has a population of just under 500,000 people. Labrador's population is only about 27,000; Labrador is still a wilderness.

Newfoundland has two beautiful national parks: Gros Morne and Terra Nova. Newfoundland is also known for its marine-mammal- and iceberg-viewing cruises.

Recommended Places to Hike in Newfoundland

Location	Features
Gros Morne National Park	Long Range Mountains Coastal trails; waterfalls
Terra Nova National Park	Trails through spruce forest Icebergs can be viewed off the coast in spring

Conclusion

Given how beautiful and lightly populated Canada is, its national and provincial parks and trails are very attractive places to visit. If you live west of the Mississippi River, give the Canadian Rockies a try. If you live east of the Mississippi, give the Maritime Provinces a visit. Either way, you won't be disappointed.

PART FIVE

Connections

CHAPTER 27

The Bigger World of Hiking

In This Chapter

➤ Big names in hiking

➤ Hiking and conservation clubs

➤ Park associations

➤ Giving back

When people find an interest, a hobby, or an activity that they enjoy, they usually want to learn more about it. They want to begin connecting with other people who have similar interests and enjoy the same activities. The same is probably true of you. You stand to learn much by meeting like-minded individuals.

Local clubs, as well as state and national organizations, are a source of information. Local chapters likely offer regular meetings and outings, and you may be able to go places you would not ordinarily go to by yourself. Participation in a group can be both educational and a source of new friends.

Trail Wisdom

Join a hiking club. Find like-minded people to hike with. You can learn a lot from other people.

Famous Hikers

When I think of famous hikers, several names with national or international repute come to mind:

> ➤ Henry David Thoreau (1817–1862): Author of the environmental classic *Walden*.

> ➤ John Muir (1838–1914): The naturalist who tramped hundreds and hundreds of miles throughout the Sierras. Muir wrote more than a dozen books about the Sierras and our national parks, and more than any other person, was responsible for the creation of Yosemite National Park.

> ➤ Bob Marshall (1901–1939): The U.S. Forest Service ranger who was famous for hiking 50 to 70 miles (80 to 110 km) in a day. Marshall helped create the 1964 Wilderness Act; the Bob Marshall Wilderness in Montana is named after him.

> ➤ Colin Fletcher (1922–2007): Nicknamed the man who walked through time, Fletcher hiked alone from Mexico to Canada, floated alone down the Green and Colorado Rivers from Wyoming to Mexico, and authored a series of books titled *The Complete Walker*.

> ➤ Harvey Butchart (1907–2002): a Northern Arizona University mathematics professor who hiked more miles in the Grand Canyon than any other person. Butchart's journals record that he spent 1,024 days in the canyon and walked 12,000 miles (19,312 km).

Of course, there are many other great hikers with local, state, or regional reputations. The author Bill Bryson may not be a great hiker, but his book *A Walk in the Woods* about his experiences hiking the Appalachian Trail, is very fun reading.

Trail Wisdom

Lots of good books have been written about other people's wilderness experiences. Reading those books suggests places you will want to visit.

Begin at the library. Look for books about hiking and backpacking, especially ones by Thoreau, Muir, Marshall, Fletcher, Butchart, and other famous hikers. You may find them not only inspirational, but also suggestive of places you might like to go to hike.

Hiking Organizations

Check in your own hometown. Chances are there is a hiking club. If not, you can start one. Or, you can volunteer your time with a local Boy Scout or Girl Scout troop that hikes and backpacks. In fact, if you have children ages eleven to eighteen, both Boy Scouts and Girl Scouts are great organizations for introducing your children to the enjoyment of the outdoors. (Boys and girls can start in Scouting at younger ages, but hiking, camping, and backpacking are more likely to start when they are around eleven or twelve years old.) You can share in those activities with them, as well as reap the benefits of engaging in outdoor activities with other parents who are probably close to your own age.

There are several state and national hiking organizations, or organizations that go hiking as part of their activities. They include the following:

➤ American Hiking Society

➤ Appalachian Trail Association

➤ Appalachian Mountain Club

➤ Pacific Crest Trail Association

See "Resources" for contact information for these organizations.

Park Associations

Most units of the national park system have member associations that support park activities and sponsor outings and service activities. These units include national parks, monuments, recreation areas, seashores, lakeshores, and historic sites. The larger organizations include the Grand Canyon, Yellowstone National Park Association, Great Smoky Mountains, Acadia National Park, Everglades, and Rocky Mountains National Park Associations, and the Yosemite Foundation.

The larger national parks sponsor hikes and backpacking trips led by professional guides. Although they are probably more expensive than if you were to hike on your own, several benefits accrue from such trips, including the following:

➤ Knowledge learned from the leader, who may be a geologist, biologist, or archaeologist

➤ Camaraderie of the group

➤ Superb meals that you probably do not have to cook yourself

➤ Visiting areas you might not go to on your own

➤ The safety of hiking with a group

The popularity of these outings attests to their success. Who knows? With enough experience, you might become a trip leader yourself—what could be more fun than getting paid to go backpacking!

Conservation Organizations

There are several private organizations such as the Sierra Club that sponsor backpacking adventures. Like the treks sponsored by park associations, these can be expensive. However, they are popular because they provide people with opportunities they would not have if they were hiking alone.

International Hiking

Your hiking experiences do not have to be limited to the United States and Canada. Groups like the Sierra Club also sponsor backpacking trips on all continents except Antarctica. The arrangements are taken care of for you. Itineraries are planned ahead of time, accommodations are reserved (if the group is not camping), and all meals are decided upon. All you have to do is show up. In some cases, you do not even have to carry more than a day pack. Week-long trips in the British Isles, for example, may include staying at inns each night, and your gear being bussed each day to that night's destination.

Giving Back to Hiking

If you join one or more of the organizations that have been listed, your dues will probably help with trail maintenance and other projects that support hiking. At some point you may feel that you want to give back more than just your financial support; as important as that is, it's not the only way you can give support.

Trail Wisdom

Spend some time doing trail improvements. You will meet some great people doing so.

Service projects may include the construction of new trails or the maintenance or improvement of existing trails. Trails are like roads and sidewalks; once built, they do not last forever and require regular repair. By helping repair damage done by erosion, livestock, or careless hikers, you can feel you have contributed something worthwhile to an activity that you enjoy yourself. An added benefit is that trail crews are often known for having outstanding cooks. The meals themselves are reward enough!

Even if you do not feel physically capable of spending a week in the backcountry maintaining trails, there are other ways to volunteer. The national parks and national forests are always looking for volunteers to work at visitor centers, bookstores, and information booths.

The Internet

The organizations I have listed, and numerous more, have websites. Go on the Internet and look them up. You may find an organization close to home whose activities match your interests.

Conclusion

I hope you have found this book informative and interesting. If your hikes have been limited to trails close to home, I hope you feel motivated to explore new territory. In the words of that famous curmudgeon Edward Abbey, "May your trails be crooked, winding, lonesome, dangerous, leading to the most amazing view. May your mountains rise into and above the clouds."

Further Resources

Government Agencies

These sites provide information about activities, camping facilities, reservations, and contacts.

US National Park Service: www.nps.gov/index.htm

A pull-down menu allows you to search every state and territory for national parks, monuments, historic sites, recreation areas, and wilderness areas administered by NPS.

US Forest Service: www.fs.fed.us

A pull-down menu allows you to search every state for its national forests, grasslands, and wilderness areas administered by USFS.

Bureau of Land Management: www.blm.gov/wo/st/en.html

You can find information about national monuments recreation areas, and wilderness areas administered by BLM.

State Parks: www.stateparks.com/index.html

A pull-down menu allows you search every state for its state parks. Each state also has its own website for its state parks.

Canadian National Parks: www.pc.gc.ca/progs/np-pn/recherche-search_e.asp?p=1

Links are provided to websites for all national parks in Canada.

Canadian Provincial Parks:

Each province has its own website for its provincial parks which you can find by searching on search engines.

Non-governmental Organizations

American Hiking Society: www.americanhiking.org

The American Hiking Society works on behalf of America's trails and the hikers who use them.

Appalachian Trail Conservancy: www.appalachiantrail.org

The mission of the Appalachian Trail Conservancy is to preserve and manage the Appalachian Trail.

Appalachian Mountain Club: www.outdoors.org

The Appalachian Mountain Club promotes the protection, enjoyment, and understanding of the Appalachian region.

Pacific Crest Trail Association: www.pcta.org

The mission of the Pacific Crest Trail Association is to preserve and promote the Pacific Crest National Scenic Trail.

National Park Foundation: www.nationalparks.org

The National Park Foundation works to safeguard America's national parks and to inspire generations of national park visitors.

National Park Associations

Most national parks have nonprofit organizations that support programs and projects within their own park. Several of them sponsor outings. Examples include:

Yellowstone Association: www.yellowstoneassociation.org

Yosemite Conservancy: www.yosemiteconservancy.org

Grand Canyon Association: www.grandcanyon.org

Great Smoky Mountains Association: www.smokiesinformation.org

Everglades Association: www.evergladesassociation.org

Sierra Club: www.sierraclub.org

The Sierra Club is America's largest and most influential grassroots environmental organization. The Sierra Club sponsors numerous outings both at home and abroad.

INDEX

U

V

W

The Smart Guide Series

Making Smart People Smarter

THE **SMART** GUIDE TO

GREEN LIVING

The most complete guide to green living ever published

How green living benefits your health as well as the Earth's

How green living can save you lots of money

Why the green economy and job market is an attractive, new, lucrative frontier

Julie Kerr **Gines**

Available Titles

Smart Guide To Astronomy
Smart Guide To Bachelorette Parties
Smart Guide To Back and Nerve Pain
Smart Guide To Biology
Smart Guide To Bridge
Smart Guide To Chemistry
Smart Guide To Classical Music
Smart Guide To Deciphering A Wine Label
Smart Guide To eBay
Smart Guide To Fighting Infections
Smart Guide To Forensic Careers
Smart Guide To Forensic Science
Smart Guide To Freshwater Fishing
Smart Guide To Getting Published
Smart Guide To Golf
Smart Guide To Green Living
Smart Guide To Healthy Grilling
Smart Guide To High School Math
Smart Guide To Hiking and Backpacking
Smart Guide To Horses and Riding
Smart Guide To Life After Divorce
Smart Guide To Making A Fortune With Infomercials
Smart Guide To Managing Stress
Smart Guide To Medical Imaging Tests
Smart Guide To Nutrition
Smart Guide To Patents
Smart Guide To Practical Math
Smart Guide To Single Malt Scotch
Smart Guide To Starting Your Own Business
Smart Guide To The Perfect Job Interview
Smart Guide To The Solar System
Smart Guide To Understanding Your Cat
Smart Guide To US Visas
Smart Guide To Wedding Weekend Events
Smart Guide To Wine

THE SMART GUIDE TO

BACHELORETTE PARTIES

Planning your dream bachelorette party

Planning non-racy bashes, spa parties, dinners and Girls' Getaways

How to hire a hot male dancer

The most complete guide to bachelorette parties ever published

Sharon **Naylor**

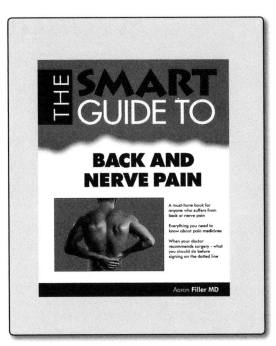

THE SMART GUIDE TO

BACK AND NERVE PAIN

A must-have book for anyone who suffers from back or nerve pain

Everything you need to know about pain medicines

When your doctor recommends surgery - what you should do before signing on the dotted line

Aaron **Filler MD**

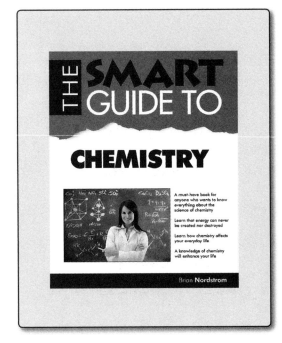

THE SMART GUIDE TO

CHEMISTRY

A must-have book for anyone who wants to know everything about the science of chemistry

Learn that energy can never be created nor destroyed

Learn how chemistry affects your everyday life

A knowledge of chemistry will enhance your life

Brian **Nordstrom**

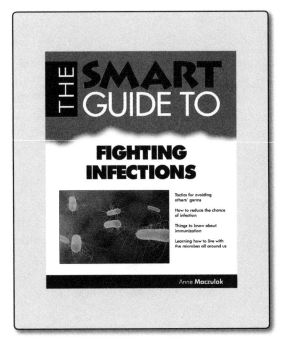

THE SMART GUIDE TO

FIGHTING INFECTIONS

Tactics for avoiding others' germs

How to reduce the chance of infection

Things to know about immunization

Learning how to live with the microbes all around us

Anne **Maczulak**

THE SMART GUIDE TO
BIOLOGY

A must-have book for anyone who wants learn the about world of living things

Understand the workings of plants and animals

Take the first step to understanding the biosphere

Anne **Maczulak**

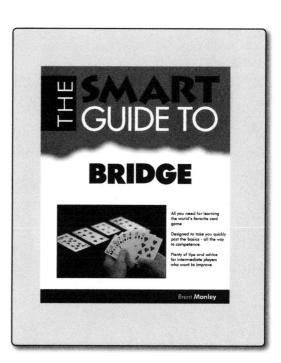

THE SMART GUIDE TO
BRIDGE

All you need for learning the world's favorite card game

Designed to take you quickly past the basics - all the way to competence.

Plenty of tips and advice for intermediate players who want to improve

Brent **Manley**

THE SMART GUIDE TO
FORENSIC CAREERS

A must-have book for anyone who wants to a career in forensic science

How to choose a forensic science degree program

What mistakes to avoid working in forensics

How to land that first forensic job

Max **Houck**

THE SMART GUIDE TO
FORENSIC SCIENCE

A must-have book for anyone who wants to fully understand forensic science

The science behind forensics completely explained

Learn how modern forensic sciences help solve cases

Max **Houck**

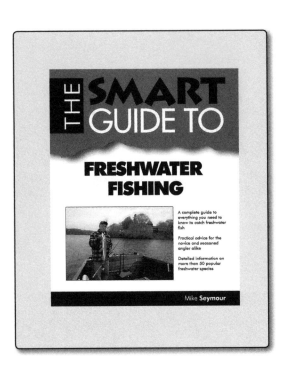

THE **SMART** GUIDE TO

FRESHWATER FISHING

A complete guide to everything you need to know to catch freshwater fish

Practical advice for the novice and seasoned angler alike

Detailed information on more than 50 popular freshwater species

Mike **Seymour**

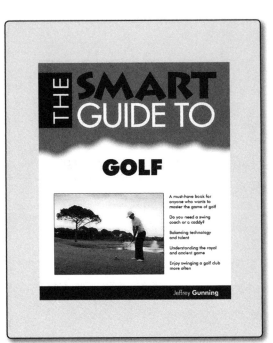

THE **SMART** GUIDE TO

GOLF

A must-have book for anyone who wants to master the game of golf

Do you need a swing coach or a caddy?

Balancing technology and talent

Understanding the royal and ancient game

Enjoy swinging a golf club more often

Jeffrey **Gunning**

THE **SMART** GUIDE TO

HIGH SCHOOL MATH

Know what questions your teacher is likely to ask on an exam

Study less - and get better grades

All the math you need to excel or "just get by" You decide what you need

Do as well as the nerds without having to become one

Jim **Stein**

THE **SMART** GUIDE TO

HIKING AND BACKPACKING

A must-have book for anyone who enjoys getting into the outdoors

Useful information for both beginning and experienced hikers and backpackers

Learn how to stay safe and healthy while hiking and backpacking

Brian **Nordstrom**

THE SMART GUIDE TO

GREEN LIVING

The most complete guide to green living ever published

How green living benefits your health as well as the Earth's

How green living can save you lots of money

Why the green economy and job market is an attractive, new, lucrative frontier

Julie Kerr **Gines**

THE SMART GUIDE TO

HEALTHY GRILLING

Low fat, low calorie grilling tips and techniques

Make succulent heart healthy burgers on your grill

Convert fish avoiders into seafood lovers

Grill fresh veggies so tasty even your kids will crave them

Barry **Fast**

THE SMART GUIDE TO

HORSES AND RIDING

Turn your dreams of riding a horse into reality

A complete resource for new horse owners

Communicating with and caring for horses

Skills and tips for every rider

Learn about horses, inside and out

Martha **Woodham**

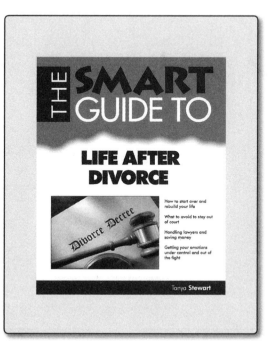

THE SMART GUIDE TO

LIFE AFTER DIVORCE

How to start over and rebuild your life

What to avoid to stay out of court

Handling lawyers and saving money

Getting your emotions under control and out of the fight

Tanya **Stewart**

THE SMART GUIDE TO

MAKING A FORTUNE WITH INFOMERCIALS

How to make a powerful infomercial for only $1,000

How to pick winning products and upsells

How to write a persuasive script

Everything you need to know to make money in the infomercial industry

Kevin **Harrington**

THE SMART GUIDE TO

MANAGING STRESS

Tame your worries and fears

Handle unreasonable people who stress you out

Reduce tension with loved ones and co-workers

Tips to beef up your resistance to stress

Bryan **Robinson**

THE SMART GUIDE TO

NUTRITION

Understanding the balanced diet

Learn the truth about sugar

Learn how to spot harmful fad diets

Managing salt intake and other nutrition pitfalls

How to select nutrient-rich foods

Anne **Maczulak**

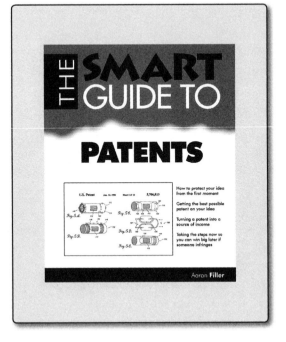

THE SMART GUIDE TO

PATENTS

How to protect your idea from the first moment

Getting the best possible patent on your idea

Turning a patent into a source of income

Taking the steps now so you can win big later if someone infringes

Aaron **Filler**

THE SMART GUIDE TO

MASTERING EBAY

A must-have book for anyone who wants to make money on eBay

Buying and selling on eBay like a pro

Building your own eBay store

Get a complete walkthrough of eBay

Nieves **Marcus**

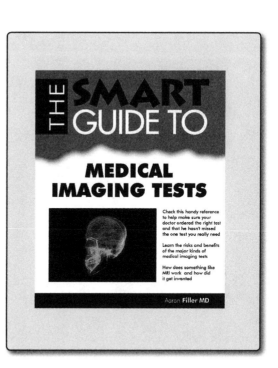

THE SMART GUIDE TO

MEDICAL IMAGING TESTS

Check this handy reference to help make sure your doctor ordered the right test and that he hasn't missed the one test you really need

Learn the risks and benefits of the major kinds of medical imaging tests

How does something like MRI work and how did it get invented

Aaron **Filler MD**

THE SMART GUIDE TO

PRACTICAL MATH

Answers to the problems you need to solve - in an easy-to-use format

Practical math problems for your home, your finances, your health, your business

Practical solutions that give you the fastest, cheapest, or easiest way to do a job

Jim **Stein**

THE SMART GUIDE TO

SINGLE MALT SCOTCH WHISKY

A must-have book for anyone who wants to know anything about single malt Scotch whisky

Information about all the distilleries and the whisky they make

Learn how to taste and appreciate single malt Scotch Whisky

Elizabeth Riley **Bell**

THE **SMART** GUIDE TO

STARTING YOUR OWN BUSINESS

A must-have book for anyone who wants to start their own business

Learn how to find startup and backup capital

Cheap marketing ideas and using publicity

First year problems and how to solve them

Barry **Thomsen**

THE **SMART** GUIDE TO

THE PERFECT JOB INTERVIEW

Get the job you want by crafting and directing the perfect interview

Learn novel ways to stand out from the competition

The absolutely best guide to creating the magic factor in an interview

Practice tips from a seasoned hiring manager

David **Holmes**

THE **SMART** GUIDE TO

UNDERSTANDING YOUR CAT

If only cats could talk, they'd tell us almost everything in this book

How to connect with your cat

Everything you need to know to make your cat feel at home in your home

Take a closer look at your lovable feline friend

Carolyn **Janik**

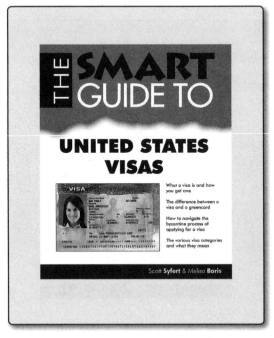

THE **SMART** GUIDE TO

UNITED STATES VISAS

What a visa is and how you get one

The difference between a visa and a greencard

How to navigate the byzantine process of applying for a visa

The various visa categories and what they mean

Scott **Syfert** & Melisa **Boris**

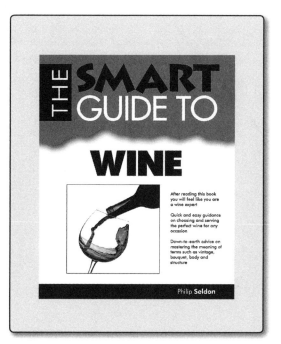

The Smart Guide Series

Making Smart People Smarter

Smart Guides are available at your local bookseller

or from the following Internet retailers

www.SmartGuidePublications.com

www.Amazon.com

www.BarnesandNoble.com

Smart Guides are popularly priced from $18.95

Smart Guides are also available in Kindle and Nook editions